SPECIAL EDUCATION DICTIONARY

747 Dresher Road, P.O. Box 980
Horsham, PA 19044-0980

"This publication is designed to provide accurate and
authoritative information in regard to the subject matter
covered. It is sold with the understanding that the publisher
is not engaged in rendering legal, accounting or other
professional services. If legal advice or other expert assistance is required, the services of a competent professional
person should be sought."

—From a Declaration of Principles jointly
adopted by a Committee of the American Bar
Association and a Committee of Publishers
and Associations.

Acknowledgments

Cognitive neuroscientist Barry Gordon, M.D., Ph.D., contributed many of the definitions of terms relating to the structure and operations of the brain, including those concerning our "higher mental functions." (You can look that term up here!) For almost three decades, he has personified my definition of genius.

My thanks to Sue Banerjee and the entire staff of the PRISE library at the Eastern Instructional Support Center in King of Prussia, Pennsylvania. They went beyond the call of the duty to accommodate me when I conducted my research there.

Susan Gorn
Editor

Introduction

The disciplines involved in the special education field are so varied, the body of knowledge so vast and ever-changing, that even the highly trained educator or lawyer occasionally confronts an unfamiliar word or term. This dictionary is for those times when a concise, easy-to-access explanation of a term is needed.

In our research to collect entries we took a portal-to-portal approach, beginning with terms concerning infants and toddlers with disabilities, continuing with terms related to meeting the educational needs of school-age children, and concluding with terms defining services and programs for adults with disabilities.

The entries themselves relate to a wide range of topics, including:

- childhood diseases or disabilities,

- words and phrases that are specially defined or have special meaning in laws about education or children with disabilities ("terms of art"),

- general legal terms that are relevant in special education law,

- screening tests and diagnostic instruments used to evaluate students with disabilities,

- assistive technology devices and modes of operation,

- instructional methods and related services for both mildly and severely disabled children,
- early intervention services for infants and toddlers with disabilities,
- discipline, behavior management and related issues for behaviorally disabled students,
- transition services and vocational education for older students, and
- neurological terms related to normal learning processes and disabilities.

To place the terms in context, we include brief explanations or illustrative comments for some of the more esoteric terms, particularly those legal terms that are both critical and, according to many, cryptic. In addition, the reader should be aware of the following conventions, which make the *Dictionary* more user-friendly. Main entries may consist of one word or several words combined to form a term; these entries appear in large-type boldface. Main entries are alphabetized letter-by-letter, with spaces between words and punctuation disregarded. Thus, **educationally deprived children** comes before **educational methodology,** and **secondary school** comes before **second priority children.** Within some definitions are words appearing in smaller-type boldface, indicating that these terms are themselves defined in the *Dictionary*. These cross-references are provided so the reader can easily identify unfamiliar words which can be looked up. For this reason, singular and plural variations of a main entry are bolded as cross-references. For example, there is a main entry for the term **learning disability**; within the definition for **Lab School,** the term **learning disabilities** is bolded as a cross-reference. Sometimes a boldface term is included in brackets. This signifies that the term, a variation of the preceding word(s), is defined in the *Dictionary*. Several terms are mentioned so frequently within definitions that we use their abbreviated form, and they do not appear in boldface as cross-references even though they are defined in the *Dictionary*. These terms are so integral to the field of special education that familiarity with them is essential to an understanding of many of the definitions. These terms (and their abbreviations) are: Diagnostic and Statistical Manual of Mental Disorders, 4th edition (DSM-IV); the Individuals with Disabilities Education Act (IDEA); Section 504 of the Rehabilitation Act of 1973 (Section 504); Part B of the IDEA (Part B); and Part H of the IDEA (Part H). The reader is encouraged to look at these definitions as a first step in using the *Dictionary*. Finally, at the beginning of main entries under each letter heading is a listing of acronyms and the terms they signify. The terms also are defined under the proper alphabetical listing as if the first word comprising the acronym were spelled out.

For the reader's convenience, several appendices include useful information condensed into an easy-to-read format. Appendix A is a complete list of every acronym in the *Dictionary* and the term it signifies. Appendix B outlines the organization of the U.S. Department of Education and some of its offices. Appendix C explains the United States appellate court system.

We reviewed many sources, both in print and on the internet, to compile this dictionary. Because this book is for those times when you just want to know what time it is, not how to make a clock, we do not include a bibliography. But three items merit special mention.

LRP Publication's *Individuals with Disabilities Education Law Report® (IDELR)* is the source of all the legal and administrative opinions and Department of Education policy letters and memorandum referenced here.

Legal Rights of Persons with Disabilities: An Analysis of Federal Law by Bonnie P. Tucker and Bruce A. Goldstein (LRP Publications) is a comprehensive treatise that is a good next step for further research about the legal terms you find here.

The Department of Education has many fine resources on line, all of which can be reached by starting with its home page at http://www.ed.gov.

A

AAC augmentative and alternative communication

AAMR American Association on Mental Retardation

ABA applied behavioral analysis

ABIC Adaptive Behavior Inventory for Children

ADA Americans with Disabilities Act

ADD attention deficit disorder

A-D/HD attention-deficit/hyperactivity disorder

ADHD attention deficit hyperactivity disorder

ADL activities of daily living

AIT auditory integration training

APE adaptive physical education

ASL American Sign Language

ability grouping In **regular education,** classroom placement according to a student's level of **academic achievement** or competence in a specific area, as determined by performance or **standardized test** scores. Also called tracking. As opposed to **heterogeneous grouping.**

abstract thinking Ability to understand concepts not specifically related to an object, person or occurrence and to apply those concepts in a variety of situations; **cognitive ability** required for **generalization.** As opposed to **concrete thinking.**

academic achievement
A student's level of performance in basic school subjects, measured either formally or informally.

academic inventory A test consisting of items arranged in order of increasing difficulty that accesses the academic level on which a student is functioning and serves as a basis for educational programming.

acalculia Inability to perform arithmetic calculations.

acceleration 1. In connection with problem behavior, an increase in the frequency with which a student performs a problem behavior. 2. In connection with educational programming for **gifted** students, programming that results in faster than usual educational progress.

accessible Generally, programs or buildings that are readily usable or equally convenient for students with physical, mental or sensory impairments.
Section 504 of the Rehabilitation Act of 1973 (29 U.S.C. § 794) establishes its accessibility requirement as: "No

otherwise **qualified individual with a disability** in the United States, . . . , shall, solely by reason of her or his disability, be excluded from participation in, be denied the benefits of, or be subjected to discrimination under any program or activity receiving **Federal financial assistance. . . .**"

access method In connection with **augmentative communication,** how an **individual with a disability** interfaces with the **augmentative communication device**; 2 primary methods: **direct selection** and **scanning,** with the choice of method based upon an analysis of the individual's cognitive, sensory and physical **skills** and **deficits.**

accommodation Generally, an adaptation or modification that enables a student with a disability to participate in educational programming, for example, complete school work or tests with greater ease and effectiveness, by enabling him or her to participate in the activity, to the extent possible, as if he or she were nondisabled. See also **reasonable accommodation.**

accommodation plan A written plan for a student receiving services under Section 504, analogous to an **individualized education program (IEP),** that is, individualized to meet the needs of a particular student and setting forth the components of the **free appropriate public education (FAPE)** to be provided with sufficient detail and specificity for planning purposes.

> While not technically required under Section 504, such a plan serves the best interest of both school districts and families, many commentators believe.

achievement on an individually administered standardized test substantially below that expected for a student of similar age, schooling and level of intelligence In connection with the diagnosis of a reading, writing or mathematics **learning disorder** under DSM-IV criteria, usually considered a discrepancy of more than 2 **standard deviations** between **achievement test** and **IQ scores,** using a variety of statistical approaches. See also **severe discrepancy between achievement and intellectual ability.**

achievement test A test that objectively measures educationally relevant skills or knowledge; a test that measures mastery of content in a subject matter area. As opposed to an **intelligence test.**

acoustic method A method of teaching deaf students to speak and understand speech by using sound vibrations produced by the voice to stimulate hearing and **tactile sense** perception.

acquired aphasia Disorder caused by focal lesion of the **central nervous system (CNS)** occurring in children who have already acquired some language skills. See also **developmental aphasia.**

acquisition In connection with learning, the learning of new information or a new skill.

acting-out behavior Inappropriate, usually destructive or aggressive behavior such as fighting or tantrums, that is considered more serious than minor misbehavior.

active listening In connection with teaching students with

3

disabilities, teacher use of animated gestures and responses to show interest in the student and motivate him or her to continue learning efforts.

activities of daily living (ADL)
Essential **self-care skills** needed to function independently in society, the most basic of which are feeding, toileting and dressing. Also called **independent living skills.**

adaptive behavior
Behavior that displays an **age-appropriate** level of self-sufficiency and social responsibility; **domains** of adaptive behavior include: (a) independent functioning, (b) physical development, (c) economic activity, (d) language development, (e) numbers and time, (f) vocational activity, (g) self-direction, (h) responsibility and (i) **socialization.**

Adaptive Behavior Inventory for Children (ABIC)
Consists of interviewing a child's primary caretaker with up to 242 questions in 6 **adaptive behavior scales** concerning the child's daily life activities across settings; scales include: (a) family, (b) peers, (c) community and (d) self-maintenance.

adaptive behavior scales
Assesses how well a child functions in non-intellectual skill areas, such as his or her **self-care skills** and social living skills; usually used in the assessment of children with **mental retardation.**

adaptive functioning
How effectively an individual copes with common life demands and meets **age-appropriate** personal independence standards.

adaptive physical education (APE)
1. Generally, developmental games, sports or similar activities designed for students whose disabilities prevent safe or successful participation in regular **physical education.** 2. A specially designed program of physical activities required when appropriate as **special education** under the IDEA (20 U.S.C. § 1401(a)(16)), which defines special education, in pertinent part, as "specially designed instruction . . . to meet the unique needs of a child with a disabil-

ity, including . . . instruction in physical education."

adaptive skill areas **Daily living skills** needed to function adequately in the community, consisting of: (a) communication, (b) **self-care skills,** (c) home living, (d) **social skills,** (e) leisure, (f) health and safety, (g) self-direction, (h) functional academics, (i) community use, and (j) work. See also **activities of daily living; leisure-time activities; special education.**

additional evidence The evidence, besides the administrative record, that either a trial court "shall hear . . . at the request of a party" in a **civil action** under 20 U.S.C. § 1415(e)(2) of the IDEA or that an **impartial review** officer "shall seek, if necessary" under 34 C.F.R. § 300.510. See also **administrative appeal; due process hearing.**

Although the language of the statute seems a congressional directive that a trial court admit all additional evidence moved for admission by the parties, case law has established the discretion of the court to deny admission of cumulative or irrelevant evidence or evidence that could have been introduced at the administrative proceeding but was not. See, e.g., *Town of Burlington v. Department of Education of Commonwealth of Massachusetts,* 1983-1984 EHLR 555:526 (1st Cir. 1984) and *Rheinstrom v. Lincolnwood Board of Education District 74,* 23 IDELR 1171 (7th Cir. 1995).

additional services **Related services** that traditionally have not been provided under Part B of the IDEA, such as **nutrition services** or **case management,** but are required under Part H. As distinguished from **overlap services.** See also **birth-mandate state.**

administrative appeal In connection with Part B, appeal of the decision of a local level due process hearing officer to a state level **impartial review** officer in a **two-tier administrative system.**

administrative hearing 1. Generally, an administrative proceeding in which a dispute is resolved and the rights and responsibilities of the parties to the proceeding are determined without resort to adjudication by a court; typically rules of evidence and other judicial for-

5

malities are relaxed, although witnesses testify under oath and the presiding officer can compel testimony. 2. In connection with the IDEA, see **due process hearing.**

administrative law judge (ALJ) Generally, the official who presides at an administrative hearing, such as a **due process hearing** officer.

administrative remedies 1. In connection with education generally, a school district's internal grievance system. 2. In connection with federal legislation concerning **children with disabilities**: for Part B of the IDEA, the due process hearing procedure is set out at 20 U.S.C. § 1415(b)(1)(e); for Section 504 at 34 C.F.R. § 104.36; and for Part H at 34 C.F.R. § 303.420.

adult As a matter of law, generally means an individual who is 18 years of age or older, as opposed to a **child.**

adult education Generally, programs that provide instruction to students 16 years or older who are not being served by the public high school and are not attending college; may include courses that prepare students for the high school Graduate Equivalency Degree (GED) examination, vocational programs and industrial arts; **post-school activities**, identified in connection with **transition services** under the IDEA.

adult services Governmental programs, such as Supplement Security Income (SSI) or those administered by state agencies, that provide services or benefits to eligible adults with disabilities; **post-school activities** identified in connection with **transition services** under the IDEA.

adversely affects educational performance The effect on the child that an impairment identified in IDEA regulations at 34 C.F.R. § 300.7(b)(1)-(13) must have in order to establish eligibility for **special education** and **related services** under Part B.

This term is not further defined in the regulations or authoritative case law, although the issue has been considered by the **Office for Civil Rights (OCR),** courts and administrative decisionmakers. Whatever the term does mean, a federal district court rightly points out that it should not be interpreted in a way that narrows the criteria for eligibility under the statute itself, which requires only that a student with a disability need special education. *Yankton School District v. Schramm,* 23 IDELR 42 (D.S.D. 1995).

Interpretation of this term has been an issue particularly in connection with speech impairments. In those cases, the issue has been whether the student's ability to make himself or herself understood is compromised sufficiently to deem his or her educational performance adversely affected. See, e.g., *Mary P. and Peter P. v. Illinois State Board of Education,* 23 IDELR 1064 (N.D. Ill. 1996), in which the student was IDEA-eligible even though he was performing at an **age-appropriate** academic level because his impairment was so severe as to inhibit his desire to communicate with others.

advocate See **lay advocate.**

affect An individual's outward manifestation of his or her emotional state. See also **labile.**

age appropriate In connection with **special education,** achievement consistent with a disabled student's developmental level and chronological age.

age-equivalent score A student's **raw score** or **standard score** for a test, expressed in the years and months of the chronological age of students for whom that grade is the average. Also called **mental age** or test age.

age norms Values representing typical or average performance of individuals with a specific chronological age on a test or in an activity.

age-out Lose entitlement to **special education** and **related services** under Part B of the IDEA as a result of reaching the maximum chronological age for eligibility, despite not having graduated high school. See also **age range; timeline for free appropriate public education.**

age range In connection with eligibility for Part B, set out at 20 U.S.C. § 1412(2)(B) and in some states' laws as starting at age of 3 and ending when the youth reaches age 22, unless he or she has graduated prior to attaining that age. See also **age-out; timeline for free appropriate public education.**

An exception is when a youth is entitled to **compensatory education** that extends his or her eligibility beyond the maximum age.

aggrieved party A party who has a right to bring a **civil action** under 20 U.S.C. § 1415(e)(2) because a final administrative **(due process hearing)** decision has been decided in the other party's favor, either in whole or in part.

Only parents, students and **local educational agencies (LEAs)** who are parties to due process decisions may be aggrieved parties. However, a party who has obtained a favorable hearing decision cannot file a civil action for enforcement. See e.g., *Robinson v. Pinderhughes,* 1986-1987 EHLR 558:239 (4th Cir. 1987). Neither can a **state educational agency (SEA),** even if the administrative decision required state-funded residential placement, nor a commercial insurance company if the decision results in responsibility for health related services.

agitographia In connection with **writing,** a disorder resulting in the omission of words or letters or the distortion of words.

agitolalia A disorder resulting in speech so fast it is nearly incoherent.

agnosia Inability to recognize familiar objects despite intact sensory reception.

alexia Inability to associate meaning with printed or written words.

alternate form reliability Assessed by administering 2 equivalent tests to the same group of test-takers. See also **reliability.**

alternative assessment Assessment by means other than by choice of response among restricted set of alternatives **[selection response tests],** such as multiple choice or true-false tests, instead requiring students to respond to more **open-ended questions** or to perform tasks.

alternative communication Communication through means other than an individual's own expressive skills, however enhanced; sometimes used to distinguish from **augmentative communication** and, in that context, more rarely needed or encountered.

alternative input interface Device or software that

provides an alternative means of controlling the cursor on the computer screen for those individuals with disabilities who cannot use or easily use a keyboard; includes systems based on control by gaze [**eyegaze input system**]; **mouthstick; headstick** or fist.

alternative school Generally, public school placement option that may be utilized for students who are not succeeding in the traditional school environment, but may benefit by modified **curriculum** or flexible programming.

Students with behavioral difficulties may benefit from instruction in alternative school programming for new and socially appropriate behavior, provided that, when the student is disabled, placement provides an appropriate education for the student in his or her **least restrictive environment (LRE)**.

ambu bag Portable **ventilator,** a device that artificially pumps air into the lungs of an individual incapable of spontaneous respiratory effort. See also **ambu bagging.**

ambu bagging Manual pumping of an air bag attached to a **tracheotomy tube** to artificially pump air into the lungs; performed as an alternate to ventilation in the case of **ventilator** maintenance or malfunction. See also **medically fragile; ventilator-dependent.**

ambulatory device Provides support when walking for an individual with a disability; includes **canes,** walking sticks or poles, **crutches** and walkers.

American Association on Mental Retardation (AAMR) Promulgates definition of **mental retardation** that is generally the same as the DSM-IV, but classifies impairment level in terms of patterns and intensity of needed supports: intermittent, limited, extensive and pervasive.

American Sign Language (ASL) A system of communication among deaf individuals based on movements of arms, hands and other body parts and facial expressions; a separate concept-based language that is not a gestural version of English or any word-based language; allows for communication of the full spectrum of intellectual, emotional and creative cognition. Also called Sign. See also **Deaf; sign language.**

Americans with Disabilities Act (ADA) Federal legislation enacted in 1990 to prohibit discrimination on the basis of disability in employment (Title I), public services (Title II) and public accommodations (Title III) that makes access to public facilities, employment and transportation services by persons with disabilities an entitlement; applies to **elementary schools** and **secondary schools;** codified at 42 U.S.C. §§ 12101-12213.

ancillary services In a generic sense, supplementary support or assistance; also sometimes used synonymously with the term **related services.** As distinguished from **auxiliary aids and services.** See also **supplementary aids and services.**

anechoic chamber A specially built room that has maximum sound absorption; best venue for testing hearing acuity, but not generally available. See also **hearing loss.**

anemia A blood disorder manifested as a deficiency of hemoglobin and a resultant loss of vitality; a student with anemia may be eligible for Part B services due to having an **"other health impairment"** under IDEA regulations at 34 C.F.R. § 300.7(b)(8). See also **sickle cell anemia.**

anencephalus A condition in which the brain of a fetus fails to develop and the brain is almost totally absent at birth.

anomia Difficulty finding the right word, even though the word is "known" to the speaker.

anorexia nervosa Mental **disorder** predominantly experienced by adolescent girls involving distorted body image, obsession with weight control, and restricting food intake or purging to reduce weight to below minimum normal weight range. As distinguished from bulimia, in which the individual maintains weight within a normal weight range.

In *Antkowiak v. Ambach,* 1985-86 EHLR 557:376 (W.D.N.Y. 1986), a young teenage girl with anorexia nervosa who required **residential treatment** was found educationally disabled under the IDEA, despite her IQ of 143 and earlier history of academic success.

anoxia Lack of oxygen to the brain resulting in brain damage.

antecedent In connection with **behavior management** and **behavior modification,** a stimulus that occurs prior to a behavior and sets the occasion for the behavior to occur.

any action or proceeding In connection with the award of **attorneys' fees** to a **prevailing party** under Part B (20 U.S.C. § 1415(e)(4)(B)), generally a **civil action** or administrative impartial **due process hearing.**

While the statutory language is unclear, court decisions have ruled that, in addition to a civil action, fees may be awarded in connection with statutorily required administrative impartial due process hearings or reviews. Some courts also have awarded attorneys' fees for time spent in **mediation** or settlement negotiations, or attendance at **IEP meetings.**

aphasia A **receptive language disorder** or, more commonly, **expressive language disorder** in children with normal intelligence and adequate sensory and motor skills; 2 basic types relate the onset to acquisition of language: **acquired aphasia** and **developmental aphasia.**

appellate court Generally, a court that reviews the evidence presented to a lower court and does not consider new evidence.

In the federal court system, Part B **civil actions** brought in federal district courts may be appealed to federal circuit courts of appeals and then to the U.S. Supreme Court. The circuit courts and the states that each encompass are as follows: First Circuit - Maine, New Hampshire, Massachusetts, Rhode Island and Puerto Rico; Second Circuit - New York, Vermont and Connecticut; Third Circuit - Pennsylvania, New Jersey, Delaware and Virgin Islands; Fourth Circuit - Maryland, West Virginia, Virginia, North Carolina and South Carolina; Fifth Circuit - Mississippi, Louisiana and Texas; Sixth Circuit - Michigan, Ohio, Kentucky and Tennessee; Seventh Circuit - Wisconsin, Illinois and Indiana; Eighth Circuit - Minnesota, Iowa, Missouri, Arkansas, North Dakota, South Dakota and Nebraska; Ninth Circuit - Montana, Idaho, Washington, Oregon, Nevada, Arizona, California, Alaska, Hawaii, Northern Mariana Island and Guam; Tenth Circuit - Wyoming, Colorado, Kansas, Oklahoma, New Mexico and Utah; Eleventh Circuit - Georgia, Al-

11

abama and Florida; D.C. Circuit - District of Columbia

applied behavioral analysis (ABA) A method of analyzing behavior into component parts to determine where a child (or an adult) fails to perform, and therefore permitting extra training to be applied to those specific parts; a method of using simple rewards and **reinforcers** to help train components of behavior. See also **discrete trial training.**

Applied behavioral analysis is the foundation of the **Lovaas program** for early intervention with autistic students.

appropriate In connection with education for **children with disabilities**: 1. The entitlement provided to children with disabilities under Part B of the IDEA at 20 U.S.C. § 1412(2)(B). 2. The entitlement provided to children with disabilities under Section 504 as described in Section 504 regulations at 34 C.F.R. § 104.33 (b)(1): "the provision of an appropriate education is the provision of regular or **special education** and related aids and services that. . .are designed to meet individual educational

needs of handicapped persons as adequately as the needs of nonhandicapped persons are met." See also **de minimus educational benefit; passing from grade to grade; potential maximizing standard.**

There is no statutory or regulatory definition of "appropriate" in connection with the IDEA because the contours of an appropriate education must be decided on a case-by-case basis, based on consideration of the unique needs of each individual eligible student. In *Board of Education of Hendrick Hudson Central School District v. Rowley,* 1981-82 EHLR 553:656, 670 (1982) the U.S. Supreme Court elucidated the following 2-part analysis for judicial evaluation of appropriateness:

"First, has the State complied with the procedures set forth in the [IDEA]? And second, is the **individualized educational program** developed through the [IDEA's] procedures reasonably calculated to enable the child to receive educational benefits? If this two-part analysis is met, the State has complied with the obligation imposed by Congress and the courts can require no more."

appropriate professional requirements in the State In connection with the personnel standards of the IDEA defined, as a term of art: 1. In connection with Part B in

regulations at 34 C.F.R. § 300.153(a)(1) as: "entry-level requirements that (i) are based on the highest requirements in the State appli-cable to the profession or discipline in which the person is providing **special education** and **related services;** and (ii) establish suitable qualifications for personnel providing special education and related services under this part to children and youth with disabilities who are served by State, local, and private agencies." 2. In connection with Part H in regulations at 34 C.F.R. § 303.361(a)(1) as: "entry-level requirements that (i) are based on the highest requirements in the State appli-cable to the profession or discipline in which a person is providing **early intervention services;** and (ii) establish suitable qualifications for personnel providing early intervention services under this part to eligible children and their families who are served by State, local and private agencies."

apraxia Inability to speak purposefully that is not the result of a motor impairment.

aromatics Aversive inter-vention involving the use of a noxious odor held under a child's nose immediately following an aggressive or injurious behavior.

arthritis Inflammation of the joints. See also **juvenile rheumatoid arthritis.**

articulation Using different movements of the jaws, lips, tongue and soft palate to make essential speech sounds.

articulation disorder A speech or language impairment resulting in the substitution of one sound for another or the omission or distortion of certain sounds; an inability to properly vocalize essential speech sounds.

Asperger's disorder 1. A neurological disorder involving severe and sustained impairments in social interaction and characterized by autistic behaviors such as literal thinking, excellent memory and social eccentricity; individuals with this disorder sometimes referred to as "high functioning" autistic individuals. Also referred to as Asperger's syn-

13

drome. 2. A neurological disorder the diagnostic criteria for which is defined in the DSM-IV as: "A. Qualitative impairment in social interaction, as manifested by at least two of the following: (1) marked **impairments** in the use of multiple nonverbal behaviors such as eye-to-eye gaze, facial expression, body postures and ability to regulate social interaction; (2) failure to develop peer relationships appropriate to developmental level; (3) a lack of spontaneous seeking to share enjoyment, interests, or achievements with other people (e.g., by a lack of showing, bringing, or pointing out objects of interest to other people); (4) lack of social or emotional reciprocity. B. Restricted repetitive and stereotyped patterns of behavior, interests and activities, as manifested by at least one of the following: (1) encompassing preoccupation with one or more stereotyped and restricted patterns of interest that is abnormal either in intensity or focus; (2) apparently inflexible adherence to specific, nonfunctional routines or rituals; (3) stereotyped and repetitive motor manner-isms (e.g., hand or finger flapping or twisting, or complex whole-body movements); (4) persistent preoccupation with parts of objects. C. The disturbance causes clinically significant impairments in social, occupational, or other important areas of functioning. D. There is no clinically significant delay in cognitive development or in the development of **age-appropriate** self-help skills, **adaptive behavior** (other than social interaction), and curiosity about the environment in childhood. F. Criteria are not met for another specific **Pervasive Developmental Disorder** or schizophrenia."

assessment 1. Broader than testing and typically includes gathering and integrating information to determine a student's current level of emotional, behavioral, academic and intellectual functioning, resulting educational needs and strategies for **remediation** to promote effective treatment; common assessment methods include **standardized tests, interviews, behavioral assessments, rating scales,** apperception tests and neurophysical tests. 2. In connection with Part H, defined, as a term of art, in Part H regulations at 34 C.F.R. § 303.322(b)(2) as: "the ongoing procedures used by appropriate qualified personnel throughout the period of a child's eligibility under this part to identify—(i) The child's unique needs; (ii) The family's strengths and needs related to development of the child; and (iii) The nature and extent of **early intervention services** that are needed by the child and the child's family to meet [their unique needs]." See also **evaluation.**

assessment of affective dimensions of behavior

In connection with clinical **neuropsychology,** assessment of emotional functioning and **social skills.**

assessment of cognitive processing

In connection with clinical neuropsychology, measurement of verbal and nonverbal level of functioning and sensorimotor functioning.

assisted ventilation

Mechanical device that allows an individual to inhale and exhale when that individual is unable to breathe in or out adequately. See also **medically fragile.**

Courts are divided on whether **nursing services** required to monitor and maintain a **ventilator-dependent** student are **related services** under the IDEA. See, e.g., *Neely v. Rutherford County School,* 23 IDELR 334 (6th Cir. 1994), in which the court held that the district was not required to provide either a nurse or a nursing assistant for a ventilator-dependent child who required **suctioning** of her breathing tube, monitoring of respiration and resuscitation when necessary.

assistive technology device

1. Generally speaking, a device used by individuals with disabilities to compensate for functional limitations and to increase autonomy and learning; used to support students with disabilities in 3 main areas: (a) communication aid for nonverbal individuals, (b) sensory aid, or (c) an aid to enable multiphysically disabled students to control their environment. 2. Defined, as a term of art, in the IDEA at 20 U.S.C. § 1401(a)(25) and in the **Developmental Disabilities Assistance and Bill of Rights Act of 1975** at 42 U.S.C. § 600(2) as: "any item, piece of equipment, or product system,

whether acquired commercially off the shelf, modified, or customized, that is used to increase, maintain, or improve the functional capabilities of individuals with disabilities." See also **assistive technology service.**

assistive technology service 1. Defined, as a term of art, in the IDEA at 20 U.S.C. § 1401(a)(26) as: "any service that directly assists a child with a disability in the selection, acquisition, or use of an **assistive technology device** [with such term including] (A) the evaluation of the needs of an individual with a disability, including a functional evaluation of the individual in the individual's customary environment; (B) purchasing, leasing or otherwise providing for the acquisition of assistive technology devices by individuals with disabilities; (C) selecting, designing, fitting, customizing, adapting, applying, maintaining, repairing, or replacing, of assistive technology devices; (D) coordinating and using other therapies, **interventions,** or services with assistive technology devices, such as those

associated with existing education and **rehabilitation** plans and programs; (E) training and technical assistance for professionals (including individuals providing education and rehabilitation services), employers, or other individuals who provide services to, employ, or are otherwise substantially involved in the major life functions of individuals with disabilities." 2. Defined, as a term of art, substantially similarly, in the **Developmental Disabilities Assistance and Bill of Rights Act of 1975** at 42 U.S.C. § 6001(3).

asthma Chronic respiratory condition marked by episodes of breathing difficulty; identified as a health problem that could be an "**other health impairment**" for purposes of IDEA eligibility in Part B regulations at 34 C.F.R. § 300.7(b)(8).

ataxia Type of **cerebral palsy** characterized by a lack of muscle coordination that results in loss of precision movements and balance. See also **athetosis; rigidity; spasticity.**

athetosis Type of **cerebral palsy** characterized by involuntary and purposeless movements of arms, legs, head and tongue, the last resulting in difficulty in producing understandable speech. See also **ataxia; rigidity; spasticity.**

at no cost Defined, as a term of art, in IDEA regulations at 34 C.F.R. § 300.17(b)(1) as meaning that: "all specially designed instruction is provided without charge, but does not preclude incidental fees that are normally charged to nondisabled students or their parents as part of the **regular education** program." See also **free.**

at risk Generally, a child or youth about whom one has a higher than usual expectation of future difficulties as a result of circumstances relating to his or her health status, disability or family or community situation; typical characteristics of a student who is at-risk for reasons other than disability may include being 1 or more grade levels behind in reading or mathematics achievement, chronic truancy, personal or familial drug or alcohol abuse, or low self-esteem.

at risk of having substantial developmental delays if early intervention services are not provided Condition of eligibility for **early intervention services** under Part H, at the state's option and as specifically defined by the state (20 U.S.C. § 1472(1)).

Note 2 to Part H regulations at 34 C.F.R. § 303.16 generally describes how a state may approach the category: "States may include well-known biological and other factors that can be identified during the neonatal period and that place infants 'at risk' for **developmental delay.** Commonly cited factors relating to infants include low birth weight, respiratory distress as a newborn, lack of oxygen, brain hemorrhage, and infection." See also **fetal alcohol syndrome (FAS).**

atrophy Wasting away or shrinkage of a body part, including muscle tissues, as a result of, among other things, inactivity.

attend In connection with learning, a student's ability to direct **perception** selectively and purposefully to some things, rather than others, in the environment.

17

attention deficit disorder (ADD) A **mental disorder,** the typical characteristics of which are: short attention span, distractive behavior, difficulty following directions, difficulty staying on task, and inability to focus behavior; frequently presents when the child attends school because it compromises many skills needed for academic success, including starting, following through with and completing tasks, moving from task to task and following directions; distinct from a **learning disability** and somewhat different from **attention deficit hyperactivity disorder (ADHD).** See also **attention-deficit/hyperactivity disorder (A-D/HD); other health impairment.**

> ADD/ADHD are not specific disabling conditions under the IDEA, although a student with either may be eligible as "other health impaired" by reason of the disability if the student's alertness or vitality is sufficiently compromised. In the majority of cases, though, students with ADD/ADHD do not meet IDEA criteria, but may come under the ambit of Section 504 if the disorder substantially interferes with a **major life activity,** such as learning.

attention deficit disorder, classroom and teaching modifications for Those identified as promoting success include: (a) shorter work periods, (b) small teacher to pupil ratio, (c) use of positive **reinforcers,** (d) frequent monitoring and checking of work, (e) clear directions and (f) behavioral interventions.

attention deficit hyperactivity disorder (ADHD) A **mental disorder,** the typical characteristics of which are short attention span; **distractibility; impulsivity; flight of ideas;** poor organizational skills, social immaturity, variable performance, inflexibility, mood swings, and poor **short-term memory,** as well as excessive activity, fidgetiness and difficulty staying seated; disorders that mimic ADHD include **conduct disorder, learning disability,** and manic-depression. See also **attention deficit disorder (ADD), attention-deficit/hyperactivity disorder (A-D/HD); other health impairment.**

attention-deficit/hyperactivity disorder (A-D/HD) A reclassification first appearing in the DSM-IV which combines previously separate diagnostic classifications for **attention deficit disorder (ADD)** and **attention deficit hyper-activity disorder (ADHD);** new classification characterizes the disorder in terms of criteria for inattention and/or hyperactivity-impulsivity and established subtypes that specify which characteristics predominate: "A. Either (1) or (2): (1) six (or more) of the following symptoms of inattention have persisted for at least 6 months to a degree that is maladaptive and inconsistent with developmental level: Inattention—(a) often fails to give close attention to details or makes careless mistakes in school work, work or other activities; (b) often has difficulty sustaining attention in tasks or play activities; (c) often does not seem to listen when spoken to directly; (d) often does not follow through on instructions and fails to finish schoolwork, chores or duties in the workplace (not due to odd or failure to understand instructions); (e) often has difficulty organizing tasks and activities; (f) often avoids, dislikes or is reluctant to engage in tasks that require sustained mental effort (such as schoolwork or homework); (g) often loses things necessary for tasks or activities (e.g., toys, school assignments, pencils, books, or tools); (h) is often easily distracted by extraneous stimuli; (i) is often forgetful in daily activities; (2) six (or more) of the following symptoms of hyperactivity-impulsivity have persisted for at least 6 months to a degree that is maladaptive and inconsistent . . . ; Hyperactivity—(a) often fidgets with hands or feet and squirms in seat; (b) often leaves seat in classroom or in other situations in which remaining seating is expected; (c) often runs about or climbs excessively in situations in which it is inappropriate (in adolescents . . . may be limited to subjective feelings of restlessness); (d) often has difficulty playing or engaging in leisure activities quietly; (e) is often 'on the go' or often acts as if 'driven by a motor'; (f) often talks excessively; Impulsivity—(g) often blurts out answers before questions have been completed; (h) often has difficulty waiting turn; (i) often interrupts or intrudes on others (e.g., butts into conversations or games). B.

19

Some hyperactive-impulsive or inattentive symptoms that caused impairment were present before age 7 years. C. Some impairment from the symptoms is present in two or more settings (e.g., at school . . . and at home). D. There must be clear evidence of clinically significant impairment in social, academic, or occupational functioning. E. The symptoms do not occur exclusively during the course of a **Pervasive Developmental Disorder,** Schizophrenia, or other Psychotic Disorder and are not better accounted for by another mental disorder."

A predominantly inattentive type disorder meets the criteria of A1, but not A2. A predominantly hyperactive-impulsive type meets the criteria of A2, but not A1. A combined type meets the criteria of both A1 and A2. There are no lab tests or other diagnostics besides the behavior observation approach of the DSM nor is it known what causes presentation of the behaviors. The disorder is much more frequent in males and prevalence is estimated to be 3-5% of all school-age children.

attorneys' fees 1. Available in Part B IDEA actions in accordance with 20 U.S.C. § 1415(e)(4)(B) which pro-
vides that: "[i]n any action or proceeding brought under [20 U.S.C. § 1415(e)], the court, in its discretion, may award reasonable attorneys' fees as part of the costs to the parents or guardian of a [disabled] child or youth who is a **prevailing party.**" 2. Available to prevailing parties in Section 504 actions other than the United States under 42 U.S.C. § 794(a)(2)(b) which provides that "[i]n any action or proceeding to enforce or charge a violation of a provision of [among other things, Section 504] the court, in its discretion, may allow the prevailing party, other than the United States, a reasonable attorneys' fee as part of the costs."

Attorneys' fees are not available under Part H according to *Letter to Kemmer,* 18 IDELR 624 (OSEP 1991). Reasoning from success with a similar strategy under other federal laws, it is possible that parents who join claims for relief under Section 504 or Section 1983 with their Part H claim may then seek fees under the other statutes after prevailing under Part H.

attribution theory How a child explains to himself or herself why he or she has experienced a failure; ability to continue efforts in the face of past failures relates, in part, to whether child blames self, others, or "fate."

atypical autism Developmental disorder that does not meet all the DSM-IV criteria for an **autistic disorder** because of, for example, late onset, subthreshold level of behaviors, or absence of the requisite number of behavioral criteria.

audiologist A licensed health care professional who diagnoses **hearing loss** and selects and fits hearing aids.

audiology 1. Generally, study of hearing and hearing disorders, including **assessment, habilitation** and **rehabilitation.** 2. A **related service** under Part B of the IDEA defined, as a term of art, in Part B regulations at 34 C.F.R. § 300.16(b)(1) as including: "(i) Identification of children with hearing loss; (ii) Determination of the range, nature, and degree of **hearing loss,** including referral for medical or other professional attention for the habilitation of hearing; (iii) Provision of habi-

litative activities, such as language habilitation, **auditory training,** speech reading (**lip reading**), hearing evaluation, and speech conservation; (iv) Creation and administration of programs for prevention of hearing loss; (v) Counseling and guidance of pupils, parents, and teachers regarding hearing loss; and (vi) Determination of the child's need for group and individual amplification, selection and fitting an appropriate aid, and evaluating the effectiveness of amplification." 3. An **early intervention service** under Part H of the IDEA defined, as a term of art, in Part H regulations at 34 C.F.R. § 303.12(d)(1) as including: "(i) identification of children with auditory impairment using at-risk criteria and appropriate audiologic screening techniques; (ii) determination of the range, nature and degree of hearing loss and communication functions, by use of audiological evaluation procedures; (iii) referral for medical or other services necessary for the habilitation or rehabilitation of children with auditory impairment; (iv) provision of auditory training, aural rehabilitation, speech

21

reading and listening device orientation and training and other services; (v) provision of services for prevention of hearing loss; and (vi) determination of the child's need for individual amplification, including selecting, fitting, and dispensing appropriate listening and vibrotactile devices, and evaluating the effectiveness of those devices."

audiometer An electronic calibrated instrument to measure **hearing loss,** expressed in terms of **decibels** or percentage of normal hearing sensitivity.

auditory closure Ability to decode a whole word upon hearing only part of it; inability to do so indicates **language disorder.** See also **cloze procedures.**

auditory decoding Ability to understand the meaning of spoken words and sounds.

auditory discrimination Ability to distinguish among sounds.

auditory integration training (AIT) An **intervention** used with individuals with **au-tism** to reduce perceived auditory impairments; involves a series of sessions in which the individual listens with headphones to music processed to eliminate high and low frequencies.

auditory-linguistic deficit **Reading disorder** involving difficulty linking written letters and words to their sounds; results in spelling and sequencing problems.

auditory processing Sensory processing skills involving rate of process, association of sounds and symbols, **auditory sequencing** and **auditory discrimination.**

auditory sequencing Ability to recall in detail and in the correct order what one has heard.

auditory training Training that enables a deaf individual to develop spoken language.

augmentative and alternative communication (AAC) Communication by means other than speech. See **augmentative communication.**

augmentative communication Communication through enhanced use of an individual's residual expressive communication skills, e.g., speaking skills, sometimes distinguished from **alternative communication,** involving no use of speech.

augmentative communication device Computerized communication devices with vocal output used by individuals who cannot communicate readily or at all through speech or writing, typically because of severe cognitive or physical impairments. See also **assistive technology device.**

augmentative communication system Used by individuals unable to communicate readily or at all through speech or writing, typically because of severe cognitive or physical impairments; types of systems include manual (gestures and signing), **communication board,** and **high-tech electronic communication aids** (such as **augmentative communication devices** or computer-generated synthesized speech).

aural Relating to spoken language and also including other words and sounds, organically or mechanically produced. See also **oral/aural method.**

authentic assessment See **performance assessment.** See also **alternative assessment.**

autism 1. A **pervasive developmental disorder** characterized by significant deficiencies in communication skills, social interaction and motor control; not the same as, but may be associated with, **mental retardation.** 2. Defined, as a term of art, in IDEA regulations at 34 C.F.R. § 300.7(b)(1) as: "a developmental disability significantly affecting verbal and nonverbal communication and social interaction, generally evident before age 3, that adversely affects a child's educational performance. Other characteristics often associated with autism are engagement in repetitive activities and **stereotypic behavior,** resistance to environmental change or change in daily routines, and unusual responses to sensory experiences." 3. Referred to in

23

the DSM-IV as **autistic disorder.**

autistic behaviors Behaviors associated with children with **autism,** although not every autistic child performs them all and children with other developmental disorders may also display, such as: (a) **self-stimulatory behaviors,** (b) avoidance of eye contact, (c) inattention to visual or auditory information coupled with unusual attention to other sensory information, (d) preoccupation with a particular object or the operation of an object without regard to function, (e) no speech or strange speech, such as **echolalia,** (f) inflexibility to the extent that a change in routine creates anxiety, (g) general low level of intellectual functioning with "islands" of normal or even supernormal functioning, sometimes referred to as **savant skills.**

autistic disorder A developmental disorder the diagnostic criteria for which is defined in the DSM-IV as: "A. A total of six (or more) items from (1), (2), and (3), with at least two from (1) and one each from (2)

and (3)—(1) qualitative impairment in social interaction, as manifested by at least two of the following: (a) marked impairments in the use of multiple nonverbal behaviors such as eye-to-eye gaze, facial expression, body posture, and gestures to regulate social interaction; (b) failure to develop peer relationships appropriate to developmental level; (c) a lack of spontaneous seeking to share enjoyment, interests or achievements with other people (e.g., by a lack of showing, bringing, or pointing out objects of interest to other people); (d) lack of social or emotional reciprocity . . . (2) qualitative impairments in communication as manifested by at least one of the following: (a) delay in, or total lack of, the development of spoken language (not accompanied by an attempt to compensate through alternative modes of communication such as gesture or mime); (b) in individuals with adequate speech, marked impairments in the ability to initiate or sustain a conversation with others; (c) stereotyped and repetitive use of language or idiosyncratic language; (d) lack of varied, spontaneous make-believe play or social imitative play appropriate to developmental level. (3) restricted repetitive and stereotyped patterns of behavior, interests and activities, as manifested by at least two of the following: (a) encompassing preoccupation with one or more stereotyped and restricted patterns of interest that is abnormal either in intensity or focus; (b) apparently inflexible adherence to specific, nonfunctional routines or rituals; (c) stereotyped and repetitive motor mannerisms (e.g., hand or finger flapping, or twisting, or complex whole-body movements); (d) persistent preoccupation with parts of objects. B. Delays or abnormal functioning in at least one of the following areas, with onset prior to age 3 years: (1) social interaction; (2) language used as social communication; (3) symbolic or imaginative play. C. The disturbance is not better accounted for by **Rett's Disorder** or **Childhood Disintegrative Disorder**." Used synonymously with **autism.**

automatic injunction A term sometimes used synonymously with **stay-put provision.** As distinguished from the judicial remedy of **injunction.**

automaticity Cognitive theory that, through practice, cognitive task performance once requiring active attention can be performed routinely or automatically.

automatism See **self-stimulatory behavior.**

autonomic hyperreflexia An uncontrolled visceral reaction to anxiety or a full bladder causing increases in blood pressure and heart rate and sweating.

Emergency catheterization [**clean intermittent catheterization**] capability in the event of autonomic hyperreflexia was ordered as a **school health service** for a 12-year-old student paralyzed and ventilator-dependent as a result of an auto accident in *Cedar Rapids Community School District,* 22 IDELR 278 (SEA IA 1994).

auxiliary aids and services Devices or services that enable individuals with hearing, vision or mobility impairments an equal opportunity to participate in, and enjoy the benefits of, programs or activities to the same extent as non-disabled individuals; obligation to provide is imposed upon recipients of **federal financial assistance** under Section 504 and **public agencies** and places of **public accommodation** under the **Americans with Disabilities Act.** As distinguished from **related services; supplementary aids and services.**

> Auxiliary aids and services useful for individuals with impaired vision include readers, Brailled materials, and telecommunications devices. Those useful for individuals with hearing impairments include **interpreters,** notetakers, and **TDDs.**

aversive intervention

Planned presentation of an **aversive stimuli** immediately after a child exhibits an undesirable behavior in order to stop that occurrence of the behavior and decrease the intensity or frequency of the same undesirable behavior in the future. Also called behavioral aversives.

> Use of such interventions is considered justified only after other, less restrictive techniques, have been unsuccessful.

aversive stimuli

Most common and controversial forms used in **aversive interventions** are, in approximate order of decreasing severity: electric shock (see **self-injurious behavior inhibiting system**), noxious liquids, slapping (see **corporal punishment**), and **physical restraint.**

B

BD behavior disordered

BLAT Blind Learning Aptitude Test

BTBC-R Boehm Test of Basic Concepts-Revised

back-chaining In connection with **basic skills** training, instructional method that breaks a task into temporal component parts and gradually requires the individual receiving instruction to finish a task from progressively earlier points in the task sequence. See also **chaining, forward-chaining.**

balanced reading approach Incorporates instruction in **phonics** to build **phonological awareness** with the reading-for-content and literature emphasis of the **whole language method**.

basal Highest level of a test on which all levels can be passed.

basal readers Generally on the elementary level, series of books used in classrooms to teach students to read; many commercially produced basal reading series; all typically use controlled vocabulary, content and word repetition as tools to control **readability level** and promote initial learning. See also **basal reading program.**

basal reading program Method of reading instruction based on use of **basal readers** and **phonics,** as opposed to **whole language method.**

baseline The beginning point for measurement, prior to

intervention or treatment, necessary to determine in order to measure effectiveness of the intervention or treatment. See also **behavior management.**

base rate Percentage of time or frequency with which a student performs a behavior within a certain amount of time. See also **behavior management; observational recording method; target behavior.**

basic achievement skills individual screener An individually administered **norm-referenced test** or **criterion-referenced test** in reading, mathematics and spelling used in diagnostic assessments prior to development of an **individualized education program (IEP)** or class placement.

basic floor of opportunity The entitlement of **children with disabilities** under the IDEA established by the U.S. Supreme Court in *Board of Education of Hendrick Hudson Central School District v. Rowley,* 1981-82 EHLR 553:656, 667 (1982). According to the Rowley court, consists of "access to specialized instruction and **related services** which are individually designed to provide educational benefit to the handicapped child." See also **de minimus educational benefit; potential maximizing standard.**

basic reading level As defined by the **National Assessment of Education Progress,** able to understand "uncomplicated narratives and high-interest informative texts."

basic skills Generally understood as the skills taught by explicit instruction in the first years of elementary schooling, includes learning the alphabet, how to sound out words, spelling, counting and arithmetic operations.

Battelle Developmental Inventory Standardized, individually administered assessment **battery** of key developmental skills in children up to age 8 in 5 **domains:** (a) **cognitive ability;** (b) communication skills; (c) interpersonal skills; (d) **psychomotor** skills; and (e) **self-care skills;** encompasses formal testing, interviews with adults and observation in a **natural environment.**

Battelle Developmental Inventory Screening Test

General **screening** tool used with children from birth to age 8 to assess developmental skills, monitor student progress and identify children with **developmental delays.**

battery In connection with educational evaluation, a group of tests.

Bayley Scales of Infant Development

Well-regarded **instrument** that assesses the development of infants between the ages of 2 months and 30 months with a Mental Development Index derived from a mental scale and a **psychomotor** index derived from a motor scale.

> Mental scale items concern shape discrimination, sustained attention, and purposeful manipulation of objects. Motor scale items concern such activities as walking, standing and sitting.

behavioral assessment

As defined by educators R.O. Nelson and S.C. Hayes: "the identification of meaningful response units and controlling variables (both current, environmental and organismic) for the purpose of understanding and altering . . . behavior."

behavioral checklist Class of assessment instruments used in evaluating students with a wide range of **behavioral disorders** for purposes of **diagnosis, intervention** and evaluation of the effectiveness of remedial programs.

behavioral disorder In connection with educational programming needs, school-related behavior problems such as disobedience and destructive or boisterous behaviors characterized by the immediate and disruptive impact they have on others.

behavioral intervention

Actions taken to extinguish, change or redirect undesirable behavior; 3 general types that vary in restrictiveness: (a) **positive reinforcement,** (b) **negative reinforcement,** and (c) **aversive intervention.**

behavioral rating scales

Written **instrument** that lists specific observable behaviors that, when filled out by parents, teachers or other professionals to indicate which the child performs, assess the severity of the child's emotional or behavior problems.

behavioral rigidity Difficulty in responding appropriately in new situations; characteristic of children with **autism.**

behavior disordered (BD) Terminology used in place of "seriously emotionally disturbed" in some state educational codes; usually indicates that a student is acting in inappropriate or disruptive ways that interfere with his or her own education or that of others and that are causally connected to a disability.

behaviorism Pedagogic theory that supports instruction by drilling and rote memorization.

behavior management Educational programming intended to change or control undesired behaviors; the goal is for a student to learn to include in his or her repertoire of behaviors appropriate responses to social situations and to use those new behaviors at appropriate times. See also **intervention; target behavior.**

behavior management plan Identifies potential unacceptable behaviors which may be caused by a student's disability and possible strategies for preventing and controlling them.

According to **the Office of Special Education Programs** (OSEP) (in *Letter to Huefner,* 23 IDELR 1072 (OSEP 1995)) Part B does not mandate the inclusion of a behavior management plan in the IEP of a student with a disability whose program has behavioral components. However, nothing in Part B precludes its inclusion, and it is considered good practice to include a behavior management plan in a student's IEP when behavioral problems have been apparent in the past or are anticipated in the future.

behavior modification Programming intended to modify or eliminate problem behavior(s) and to increase performance of desired behaviors. See also **behavior management; target behavior.**

Behavior modification techniques or methods include **shaping, modeling, prompting, chaining, and rein-**

forcement of incompatible behaviors.

behavior momentum

A **behavior modification** technique used to increase compliance by identifying a minimum of 3 requests with which the child has a high probability of compliance and making those requests immediately before making a request with which the child is less likely to comply.

behavior problems, evaluation of

Generally 3 methods of evaluation: (a) **adaptive behavior scales,** (b) **behavioral checklists** and (c) direct observation of behavior; wide variety of commercially produced norm-referenced adaptive behavior scales and behavioral checklists.

behavior therapy

Addresses the presenting problem behavior rather than its underlying causes; premised on the belief that **maladaptive behaviors,** being learned, can be modified through a learning process.

Bender Gestalt Test

Instrument that estimates maturation, **intelligence** and psychological disturbances by analysis of work samples of designs that a child copies.

Bender Visual Motor Gestalt Test for Children

Popular test of visual-motor perceptual skills in which a child is asked to copy 9 geometric designs; used to screen for **perceptual-motor disorder.**

beyond recognition

In connection with **inclusion** of **children with disabilities** in the **regular education** classroom, the characterization of the amount or quality of the change in the regular education **curriculum** that, if required, rules out the regular classroom as the **least restrictive environment (LRE)** for a child with a disability.

In *Daniel R.R. v. El Paso Independent School District,* 1988-89 EHLR 441:433 (5th Cir. 1989), the court elucidated analysis of curriculum modification as criteria for deciding whether the regular classroom was a student's LRE. In that case, and in the others that have adopted the same approach, the term "beyond recognition" is not precisely defined, rather it is a matter of case-by-case analysis.

31

bilingual education Programming designed to allow **limited-English proficient** students to concurrently learn English and master curriculum content; approaches differ in the extent to which content programming instruction is conducted in English and the amount of instructional time devoted to the instruction of English as a second language. See also **Bilingual Education Act.**

Bilingual Education Act Provides federal funds for the development of **bilingual education** programs for students whose primary language is not English; codified as Title VII of the **Elementary and Secondary Education Act** (20 U.S.C. § 6301 et seq.).

birth-mandate state A state that, prior to September 1, 1986, had a state law in effect guaranteeing a **free appropriate public education** to **children with disabilities** from birth through age two.

OSEP Policy Memorandum 90-14, 16 EHLR 708 (OSEP 1990), addressed the confusing issue of whether a birth-mandate state may assess a fee for provision of services under Part H that it had previously been providing **at no cost** to the parents under Part B. According to the **Office of Special Education Programs (OSEP),** the answer depends on whether the services are considered **overlap services** (no) or **additional services** (yes).

birth to age two, inclusive In connection with the age range for eligibility for **early intervention services** under Part H, defined in legislative history as "infants and toddlers from birth until they reach their third birthday."

Birth to Three Assessment and Intervention System: Checklist of Language and Learning Behavior Program designed to evaluate developmental skills; checklist component a criterion-referenced measure that involves observing and scoring 240 specific behaviors into 5 categories: (a) language comprehension, (b) language expression, (c) problem solving, (d) social personal behavior and (e) motor behaviors.

blind An individual who either has no vision or has, at most, light perception. As opposed to **legally blind.**

blindism Inappropriate term for **self-stimulatory behaviors.**

Blind Learning Aptitude Test (BLAT) Assesses the cognitive functioning of blind children and youth between the ages of 6 and 16 in a way that is similar to the **Raven Progressive Matrices** test, but is presented in a bas-relief form that is like **Braille,** except that it does not require the same degree of fine tactile discrimination.

Bliss method A non-oral means of communication typically used with a severely mentally disabled child or child with **cerebral palsy** that involves pointing to abstract symbols associated with actual experiences or words. See also **communication board.**

block scheduling 1. In connection with **itinerant services** such as **speech pathology,** programming in which the specialist spends a longer amount of time at 1 location and makes fewer moves in the course of 1 school year so that students may receive more in-tensive services. 2. In connection with **regular education,** division of at least part of daily schedule in larger than usual blocks of time (more than 60 minutes); advocates believe it permits flexibility for a diversity of instructional activities.

blood glucose monitoring Procedure used to determine the blood glucose level of a student with **diabetes** to adjust insulin dosage and nutritional intake and evaluate health status; may be a **school health service.**

Bloom's taxonomy Theory of how children learn that posits various levels of **cognition:** (in order of increasing cognitive complexity) knowledge, comprehension, analysis, synthesis and evaluation.

Boehm Test of Basic Concepts-Revised (BTBC-R) Standardized pictorial multiple-choice test for children in early primary grades that assesses mastery of such concepts as time and directionality.

bonus See **multiplier.**

borderline intellectual functioning Generally understood as an **IQ score** range slightly higher than 70 to 75, one of the criteria for **mental retardation** under the DSM-IV.

brace See **orthotics.**

Braille Tactile system for reading and writing with an official code or "alphabet" composed of Braille characters or **Braille cells** that consist of various patterns of raised dots that roughly correspond to alphabetic letters, punctuation marks and other symbols. Different types of Braille code include: **Grade I, Grade II, Grade III** and **Nemeth code;** when used with paper, produced by embossing, also processed by computers in Braille-ASCI form. See also **Braille writer; slate and stylus.**

Braille cell An arrangement of raised dots in a pattern of 2 across and 3 down (may be 4 down, although less common) with the arrangement and combination of dots within a cell signifying a particular letter, number or special character; cell size and spacing of dots within cells is always uniform.

Braille Display **Assistive technology device** that, in conjunction with a computer, converts text displayed on screen to a raised dot Braille text.

Braille printer **Assistive technology device** that, in conjunction with a computer, converts text in electronic form (ASCI) into raised printing on paper.

Braille writer A written communication device for the blind similar in concept to a typewriter and consisting of a metal frame, 7 keys (6 corresponding to the 6 dots in a **Braille cell**) plus a space bar and a platen, with knobs to insert and maneuver the paper.

brain injury "Insult to the brain" resulting in impairment of brain function; categorized types, depending on cause and extent of injury as acquired, closed, and mild.

acquired brain injury—not congenital

closed brain injury—resulting from impact of violent collision with a foreign object, typically causing diffuse tissue damage mild brain injury—traumatic brain injury resulting in temporary disruption of functioning, such as losing consciousness for 30 minutes or less.

brain stem Portion of brain that connects to the spinal cord and controls physiological survival functions such as breathing and cardiac functioning; when a child is born with only a brain stem, but no higher level brain material, he or she has **anencephalus** and **profound mental retardation.** See also **zero reject principle.**

Brekken-Drouin Developmental Spotcheck Screening device used to assess a preschool child's areas of developmental strengths and weakness and establish a **baseline** for educational planning.

Bruininks-Oresetsky Test of Motor Proficiency Individually administered test for children between the ages of 4 and 14 that measures **fine motor skills** and **gross motor skills.**

bruxism Nonfunctional grinding or gnashing of teeth, often associated with individuals with **mental retardation.**

Buckley Amendment 1974 amendment to the **Family Educational Rights and Privacy Act (FERPA)** that added the current definition of **education records** and established an administrative process for parents who wish to challenge and correct information in their child's education records that they claim is misleading, inaccurate or inappropriate.

burden of persuasion The duty of a party to a legal dispute to meet the applicable standard, or quantum, of proof; in a close—"tied"—case, the party with the burden of persuasion loses. See also **burden of production; burden of proof.**

burden of production The duty of a party to a legal dispute to be the first to introduce evidence to prove a disputed fact, such that if the party with the burden fails to satisfy its initial burden the other party wins without having to present its case. See also **burden of persuasion; burden of proof.**

Which party has the burden of production is a local matter, although some commentators believe that placing the burden on the **local educational agency (LEA)** in an admin-

35

istrative proceeding is appropriate regardless of who is assigned the burden of persuasion.

burden of proof Generically understood as the duty of one of the parties to a legal dispute to prove a fact or an issue in dispute such that the decisionmaker will rule in the party's favor; technically comprised of 2 separate components: the **burden of production** and the **burden of persuasion.**

Neither the IDEA statute nor regulations address who has the burden of proof in proceedings under the IDEA, making it largely a matter of state or local law. There is very little case law about which party has the burden of proof in administrative hearings; courts have followed several different approaches in allocating the burden in judicial proceedings under the IDEA. For example, in *Urban v. Jefferson County School District R-1,* 21 IDELR 985 (D. Colo. 1994), the court stated that the burden of proof varies depending on the adequacy of the IEP.

Bureau of Indian Affairs The agency within the United States Department of the Interior that operates schools at or near Indian reservations and provides supplementary educa-

tional services to Indian children attending public schools.

Under the IDEA (20 U.S.C. § 1411(f)) the Department of the Interior receives direct allocation of Part B funds to assist in the education of **children with disabilities** on reservations served by schools operated for Indian children by the Department of the Interior or receiving services provided under contract arrangements with an Indian tribe or organization.

button switch In connection with **assistive technology devices,** a **switch** that is positioned on top of a platform and is activated when the individual puts pressure on the button.

C

CAI computer-assisted instruction

CARS Childhood Autism Rating Scale

CFIDS Chronic Fatigue and Immune Dysfunction Syndrome

CFS Chronic Fatigue Syndrome

CIC clean intermittent catheterization

CMMS Columbia Mental Maturity Scale

CNS central nervous system

CP cerebral palsy

CPR cardiopulmonary resuscitation

CRT criterion-referenced test

Canadian elbow extension crutches Used by an individual with a disability who is able to walk with support, configured to provide support on both sides of the body while reducing stress on the underarm area. Also called forearm crutches.

cane Used by an individual with a **visual impairment** to enhance sensory awareness and by an individual with a physical disability for leg support.

cardiopulmonary resuscitation (CPR) Emergency procedures used when an individual has stopped breathing or whose heart has stopped. See also **Do Not Resuscitate order (DNR).**

Carl D. Perkins Vocational and Applied Tech-

nology Act Federal **grant** program under which students with disabilities must be granted equal access to federally funded **vocational education** programs and must be provided with **supplementary aids and services,** including curriculum modification, equipment modification, classroom modification, supportive personnel and instructional aids and devices; codified at 20 U.S.C. §§ 2301 et. seq.

Carnegie unit A standard of measurement used for secondary education that represents the completion of a course that meets 1 period per day for 1 year.

Generally, **special education** students should not be graduated simply because of completion of a specific amount of academic credits. For example, in *Mason City Community School District,* 21 IDELR 248 (SEA IA 1994), a hearing officer ruled that a policy that all students, including special educations students, who complete 40 credits (with each credit indicating successful completion of an academic course in **regular education,** special education, or regular education with **accommodations**) in at least 7 semesters must be graduated violated the IDEA because the decision to graduate was made without reference to the disabled stu-

dent's individual goals and objectives contained in his or her IEP.

carrel A study booth or cubicle that minimizes external distractions. See also **discipline.**

In *Honig v. Doe,* 1987-1988 EHLR 559:231 (1988), the U.S. Supreme Court identified study carrels as a "normal" disciplinary procedure, use of which in connection with students with disabilities does not implicate the **procedural safeguards** of the IDEA.

case conference See **IEP meeting.**

case management 1. Generally, services that help people arrange appropriate and available services and supports. 2. In connection with Part H of the IDEA, activities conducted by a **case manager** to assist a Part-H eligible child and his or her family to receive the rights, **procedural safeguards** and services available under the state's **early intervention program,** defined, as a term of art, in Part H regulations at 34 C.F.R. § 303.6(a)(1) as: "activities carried out by a case manager to assist and enable a child eligible under this part and the child's family to receive the rights, procedural safeguards, and services that are authorized to be provided under the State's early intervention program" that include the 7 specific case management activities set out in 34 C.F.R. § 303.6(b)(1)-(7). Distinguished from the early intervention service **case management services.**

case management services 1. Generally, services or activities for the arrangement, coordination and monitoring of services provided to meet the needs of individuals and families, including individual service plan development, counseling, securing and coordinating services; and assuring that the client's rights are protected. 2. An **early intervention service** under Part H defined in Part H regulations at 34 C.F.R. § 303.12(d)(2) as: "assistance and services provided by a **case manager** to a child eligible under this part and the child's family that are in addition to the functions and activities [to be provided to all Part H-eligible children and their families]."

case manager 1. Generally, the professional who orga-nizes and coordinates services and supports for the client being served. 2. The professional responsible under Part H for: (a) coordinating all services across agency lines and (b) serving as the single point of contact in helping parents to obtain the services and assistance they need, as specified in Part H regulations at 34 C.F.R. § 303.6(a)(2).

catchment area Geographic area served by a service provider or institution.

categorical approach See **labeling.**

catheter A narrow tube inserted into the body to introduce or remove fluid, for example, to empty the bladder; 2 types: external or indwelling (inserted into the bladder). See also **clean intermittent catheterization (CIC).**

caudal regression syndrome Birth defect that causes a child's legs to fold up under his or her body.

ceiling In connection with educational tests, the upper level or maximum degree of ability or achievement that can be measured, resulting in uniform scores for all students whose ability or achievement level exceeds the ceiling.

central line A **catheter** most frequently placed through the chest wall into the heart or a large central blood vessel for long-term intravenous administration of medications, fluids or nutrients.

central line care In connection with **central line,** includes ensuring that the dressing is intact and monitoring for and intervening in an emergency; may be a **school health service.**

central nervous system (CNS) The brain and spinal cord.

cerebellum A division of the brain, in the back part above the neck, that is responsible for integrating movements. See also **lobes of the brain.**

cerebral palsy (CP) Nonprogressive disease of the **central nervous system** that results in abnormal alterations in or limitations of voluntary movement, speech disorders or unintelligible speech, and **behavioral disorders;** children with cerebral palsy typically have normal **intelligence** but sensory or **emotional disorders** resulting from motor deficiencies; 5 types, classified according to particular way movement is affected: (a) **spasticity,** (b) **athetosis,** (c) **rigidity,** (d) **ataxia** and (e) mixed.

chaining A procedure in which desired behaviors are reinforced in sequence to enable the child to perform more complex behaviors. See also **backchaining; forward-chaining,**

challenging behaviors Generally refers to disruptive or antisocial conduct.

change in educational placement Under IDEA regulations at 34 C.F.R. § 300.504(a), one of the triggers for the requirement of prior written notice to parents imposed on school districts under the IDEA. Also termed change in placement. See also **significant change in placement.**
There is no comprehensive statutory or regulatory definition, but generally proposed modifications of the

program or services set out in a student's **individualized educational program (IEP)**, including a cessation of services for 10 or more days, is considered a change in educational placement. According to the Fifth Circuit Court of Appeals: "A change in placement occurs where there is a fundamental change in a basic element of the educational program." *Sherry A.D. v. Kirby,* 19 IDELR 339 (5th Cir. 1992). Conversely, a change in the location at which the educational program of a student with a disability is provided, without a concurrent change in the student's IEP, is generally not considered a change in educational placement. However, the **Office of Special Education Programs (OSEP)** has opined in policy letters (e.g., *Letter to Green,* 22 IDELR 639 (OSEP 1995)) that a change in location should be considered a change in educational placement, for purposes of triggering **procedural safeguards,** if it substantially or materially alters a student's program or his or her opportunities for interactions with nondisabled peers.

Chapter 1 Federal **grant** program authorized as part of Title I of the **Elementary and Secondary Education Act of 1965,** codified at 20 U.S.C. §§ 2701 et seq., under which **federal financial assistance** is provided for supplemental education services, such as instructional services, materials and equipment, designed to meet the special educational needs of **educationally deprived children,** as that term is defined in federal regulations.

While not usual in practice, as a matter of law a student with a disability receiving **special education** under the IDEA may also qualify for Chapter 1 services.

charter school Public school created by a formal agreement—charter—between an individual or group of individuals and a local school district, state or independent governing board; generally exempt from most state education regulations and local school district rules in exchange for agreeing to meet certain accountability requirements.

While charter schools are not exempt from the IDEA or Section 504 (or the **Americans with Disabilities Act (ADA)),** how these laws apply is now a matter of debate. Charter schools are public schools and no state has the authority to grant waivers of the IDEA or federal antidiscrimination statutes such as Section 504 to any public school. However, the extent of a charter school's obligations under these statutes turns, in part, on whether the school is considered an individual public school within the school district in which it is situated or a school district **local educational**

41

agency (LEA) itself. These definitional issues remain unsettled in many states.

Checklist of Birth to Three Assessment and Intervention System

Criterion-referenced [test] measure that observes, organizes and scores 240 behaviors in 5 categories: (a) language comprehension, (b) language expression, (c) problem solving, (d) social and personal behavior and (e) motor behaviors.

child As a matter of law, generally means an individual who has not attained age 18; as opposed to an **adult.**

Child Behavior Checklist

Checklist to be answered directly by a parent or in the course of an interview to assess the **social competence** or behavioral problems of a child from the ages of 2 to 16.

child development activities

Defined, as a term of art, in the federal **Developmental Disabilities Assistance and Bill of Rights Act of 1975** at 42 U.S.C. § 6001(4) as: "such priority area activities as will assist in the prevention, identi-

fication, and alleviation of **developmental disabilities** in children, including **early intervention services.**"

child find 1. In connection with Part B of the IDEA, the requirement set out in the statute at 20 U.S.C. § 1414(a)(1) that places an affirmative duty on **local educational agencies (LEAs)** and **intermediate educational units (IEUs)** to identify, locate and evaluate all **children with disabilities** within their jurisdictions. 2. In connection with Part H, the requirement set out in 20 U.S.C. § 1476(b)(5) that participating states establish a system to ensure that all infants and toddlers who are eligible for services are identified, located and evaluated and to determine which children are receiving **early intervention services** and which are not. 3. A requirement similar to that of the IDEA applying to school districts under Section 504 as set out in Section 504 regulations at 34 C.F.R. § 104.32.

The child find requirements of Part B of the IDEA are applicable to all children from birth through age 21, regardless of: the severity of the disability (*Letter to Anonymous,* 21

IDELR 65 (OSEP 1994)); whether enrolled in private or public schools (*Letter to Peters,* 19 IDELR 974 (OSERS 1993)) or an in-patient of a public or psychiatric hospital (*Letter to Lane,* 16 EHLR 959 (OSERS 1990)); or whether the parent has failed to request an evaluation (*Letter to Harris,* 1 ECLPR 123 (OSEP 1991)).

childhood autism Sometimes used synonymously with **autism.**

Childhood Autism Rating Scale (CARS) 15 scales that evaluate a child's functioning in all areas in terms of whether it is age appropriate, mildly abnormal, moderately abnormal or severely abnormal; scales include: (a) relationships with people, (b) imitation, (c) affect, (d) use of body, (e) relation to objects (not people), (f) adaptability to changes in the environment, (g) visual and auditory responsiveness and (h) anxiety reaction.

Childhood Disintegrative Disorder 1. Marked regression in multiple areas of functioning following a period of at least 2 years of apparently normal development, followed by onset of symptoms that mimic those of **autism.** 2. A developmental disorder the diagnostic criteria for which is defined in the DSM IV as: "A. Apparently normal development for at least the first 2 years after birth as manifested by the presence of age appropriate verbal and nonverbal communication, social relationships, play and adaptive behavior; B. Clinically significant loss of previously acquired skills (before age 10) in at least two of the following areas: (1) **expressive [language]** or **receptive language,** (2) **social skills** or **adaptive behavior,** (3) bowel or bladder control, (4) play, (5) motor skills; C. Abnormalities of functioning in at least two of the following areas: (1) qualitative impairment in social interaction (e.g., impairment in nonverbal behaviors, failure to develop peer relationships, lack of social or emotional reciprocity), (2) qualitative impairments in communication (e.g., delay or lack of the development of spoken language, inability to initiate or sustain a conversation, stereotyped and repetitive use of language, lack of verbal make-believe play), (3) restricted repetitive and ste-

43

reotyped patterns of behavior, interests and activities, including motor stereotypes and mannerisms; D. The disturbance is not better accounted for by another specific **Pervasive Development Disorder** or by **Schizophrenia.**" As distinguished from **autism; Rett's disorder.**

children with disabilities

A term of art identifying those children eligible to receive **special education** and **related services** under Part B of the IDEA; defined in the statute at 20 U.S.C. § 1401(a)(1) as: "(A) . . . children . . . with **mental retardation, hearing impairments** including **deafness,** speech or language impairments, **visual impairments** including blindness, **serious emotional disturbance, orthopedic impairments, autism, traumatic brain injury, other health impairments,** or **specific learning disabilities;** and who, by reason thereof, need **special education** and **related services;** (B). . . for children aged 3 to 5, inclusive, . . . children experiencing **developmental delays,** as defined by the State and as measured by

appropriate diagnostic instruments and procedures, in one or more of the following areas: physical development, cognitive development, communication development, social or emotional development, or adaptive development, and, who, by reason thereof, need special education and related services."

Essentially, to qualify for special education and related services under Part B of the IDEA, a child must be within the age range specified in the statute and satisfy both parts of the definition of a child with a disability. First, he or she must have 1 or more of the 13 categories of disabling conditions specified in the statute. Second, he or she must need both special education and related services as a result. **The Office of Special Education Program (OSEP)** has made it clear that the identification of the disabling conditions in the statute is exhaustive, not illustrative. See, e.g., *Letter to Fazio,* 21 IDELR 572 (OSEP 1994). However, the list of specific impairments included within the regulatory definitions at 34 C.F.R. § 300.7(b)(1)-(13) is not intended to be exhaustive.

child's teacher
In connection with personnel required to participate in the development of the **individualized education program (IEP)** for a child

with a disability, may include any of the individuals identified in IDEA regulations at Note 1 to 34 C.F.R. § 300.344, including, according to the circumstances, the child's **regular education** teacher or a teacher qualified to provide education in the type of program in which the child may be placed, or both.

child welfare services State or local governmental services generally directed toward protecting and promoting the welfare of all children, including assisting families in resolving problems that may result in neglect, abuse, exploitation or delinquency and assuring adequate care for children away from home in cases where removal from home is necessary. See also **protective services.**

chorea A nervous disorder characterized by spastic muscle twitching.

Chronic Fatigue and Immune Dysfunction Syndrome (CFIDS) See Chronic Fatigue Syndrome.

Chronic Fatigue Syndrome (CFS) A chronic disorder of unknown **etiology** that can be debilitating, with symptoms that can include persistent fatigue, sore throat, headaches, sinus congestion, muscle aches, sleep disruption, visual motor disturbances, poor attention span, memory deficits and swollen glands. Also referred to as Chronic Fatigue and Immune Dysfunction Syndrome (CFIDS). See **other health impairment.** According to the **Office of Special Education Programs (OSEP),** CFS (or CFIDS) may be a qualifying "other health impairment" under the IDEA if it results in the child having limited strength, vitality or alertness and needing **special education** as a result. *Letter to Fazio,* 21 IDELR 572 (OSEP 1994). In one instance, though, a hearing officer found that the **accommodations** made for a 16-year-old with CFS receiving a **regular education** program in her home did not constitute special education, thus making her ineligible for Part B related services. *West Highlands School District,* 24 IDELR 476 (SEA PA 1996).

chronic illnesses in children Most common are: **cystic fibrosis, diabetes, epilepsy, leukemia, juvenile rheumatoid arthritis, muscular dystrophy,** and **sickle cell anemia;** may result in eligibility under Part B on the basis of

45

having an **"other health impairment,"** provided the disability results in a need for **special education.**

chunking Cognitive strategies that enable individuals to process and mentally organize large amounts of information.

For example, in connection with **short-term memory,** a 7-digit phone number can be remembered more easily if the first 3 numbers are grouped together, with a pause before grouping the next 4.

circumstantiality **Thought disorder** characterized by speech with numerous digressions and unnecessary triviality. See also **clang associations; flight of ideas.**

civil action In connection with Part B, a judicial action that any party who is aggrieved (an **aggrieved party**) by the final decision of an **impartial hearing officer**, or the appeal of that decision by an impartial review officer in those states that have a **two-tier administrative system,** may bring in either a federal district court or a state court of competent jurisdiction (as designated by the state); authorized under 20 U.S.C. § 1415(e).

Civil Rights of Institutionalized Persons Act of 1980 (CRIPA) Federal legislation empowering the U.S. Attorney General to sue a state when state institutional conditions deprive residents of rights, privileges or immunities secured or protected by the U.S. Constitution or federal laws; codified at 42 U.S.C. § 1997.

clang associations A **thought disorder** similar to **flight of ideas,** except that the stimulus for the conversational shifts or digressions is similar-sounding words, rather than tenuous logical connections. See also **circumstantiality.**

class action A lawsuit in which one of the parties is a group of persons who have a common legal position and may sue or be sued as representatives of a class of similarly situated persons without needing to join every other such person; procedure available in federal court and in most state courts when the representatives fairly represent both the factual circumstances and legal position of the class, and the rights or responsibilities of all members of the class, named and unnamed, can be equitably and efficiently resolved in one proceeding.

Class actions have been used by **children with disabilities** alleging systemic violations of the IDEA. For example, in *Felix v. Waihee,* 21 IDELR 48 (D. Haw. 1994), a class of children with mental health disabilities eligible for IDEA services on that basis sued the state of Hawaii, claiming it had violated the IDEA because, among other things, it failed to provide a continuum of mental health services, programs and placements.

clean intermittent catheterization (CIC) A procedure that facilitates routine emptying of the bladder by the insertion of a **catheter** into the child; used for children with disabilities, such as **spina bifida,** that result in little bladder control. See also **medically fragile.**

In *Irving Independent School District v. Tatro,* 1983-84 EHLR 555:511 (1984) the U.S. Supreme Court ruled that CIC was a **related service** for an 8-year-old girl with spina bifida. The Court found that CIC is a **school health service** rather than an **excluded medical service** because it

is a simple procedure lasting only several minutes that needs to be performed only intermittently by a lay person who has received less than 1 hour of training. The Court left open whether services which deviate from this model in terms of complexity, intensity or training required also are considered school health services.

cleft palate Usually an opening in the roof of the mouth that causes malformations of the hard or soft palate or upper lip and resulting problems with **articulation;** usually treated by surgery and **speech pathology.**

clinical assessment interview An evaluation technique, used when children exhibit behavior problems, that differs from a regular conversation or a nonclinical interview because of formalized **protocols** for conducting.

clinical type appearance Typical physical appearance of individuals with a specific disability, such as **Down syndrome** or **cretinism.** See also **minor physical abnormalities.**

closed head injury Generally, **traumatic brain injury** in which the brain stays protected

47

by its covering, even though the skull may be fractured or the scalp may be lacerated and exposed. As distinguished from an **open head injury.**

When the injury results in impairments in one or more areas, such as **cognition;** language; **memory;** attention; reasoning; **abstract thinking;** judgment; problem-solving; sensory, perceptual and **motor abilities;** psychosocial behavior; physical functions; information processing; and speech, then the child may be eligible for IDEA services under eligibility requirements set out at 34 C.F.R. § 300.7(b)(12).

Cloze method Formula for estimating text difficulty and **readability level.**

cloze procedures Ability involved in use of semantic and syntactic clues to complete sentences; word prediction ability. See also **auditory closure.**

clubfoot Congenital abnormality in which the foot turns inward and downward at the ankle.

cochlear implant An electronic auditory device intended to give an individual age 2 or over who is **deaf** or has a **severe** hearing loss or profound hearing loss the sensation of sound; made up of external parts worn outside the body and internal parts implanted surgically. External parts include a microphone headset (encased in what looks like a behind-the-ear hearing aid case), external transmitter coil and a speech processor responsible for turning sound into electric current; internal parts include an internal receiver surgically implanted in the mastoid bone behind the ear and magnetically attracted through the skin to the external transmitter. Speech of cochlear implant wearers has been described as "Donald Duck talking underwater amidst popping bubbles."

As more younger children are receiving cochlear implants, recent disputes have addressed appropriate educational programming, including the Fifth Circuit Court of Appeals' decision in *Bonnie F. v. Calallen School District,* 2 ECLPR 98 (5th Cir. 1994). All agree that appropriate programming for children learning to communicate with the implant includes intensive 1-on-1 speech and language therapy and therapy to learn how to understand and process the auditory information.

cognition Thinking processes in the brain, both conscious and unconscious, as opposed to emotions and simpler reflex actions; involves mental activities such as paying attention, perceiving, learning, making decisions, problem solving, and memory.

cognitive ability "Involves reasoning and problem solving and is measured by most tests of general intelligence, particularly those with tasks involving reasoning, problem solving, concept formation, verbal and figural analogies, number series, and matrices." J. M. Sattler, Assessment of Children (3d Ed.) 1988), 52.

cognitive behavior modification therapy For **behavior modification,** premised on belief that students who are taught to recognize and change faulty cognitions, such as irrational beliefs or errors in logic, can eliminate the undesired behaviors that flow from those cognitions.

cognitive deficit An **impairment** in some aspect of cognition, any deviation from what was expected for or from that individual, even those that

may be related to genetics or developmental problems.

cognitive modeling Process of identifying basic assumptions and determining how they play out to produce the observed **cognitive abilities** or performance.

cognitive rehabilitation Process of trying to improve mental abilities by more or less specific retraining after a **deficit** has occurred. See also **Landau-Kleffner syndrome.**

Cognitive Skills Index score See **IQ score.**

cognitive style Specific pattern of approaches an individual uses to resolve a problem, for example, some people may back up and try to examine alternatives, while others may hope for an intuitive solution and begin to think about a problem only if their intuition seems to fail.

cohort In connection with educational testing or assessment, a group of students who are the same chronological age.

coincidental learning Takes place in the home or

community as the child goes about his or her daily activities; requires **social skills** and the ability to generalize [**generalization**]. See also **modeling.**

coin-click test A rough **screening** for hearing disorders in which the tester clicks 2 coins near the child's ear and continues clicking while walking away from the child to determine when the child stops hearing the clicks.

collaborative consultation **Prereferral intervention** involving school specialists, such as a **resource room teacher,** working directly with the referring teacher to plan, implement and evaluate instruction for a student who is having problems in the regular classroom.

collaborative learning Instructional method in which small groups of students with varying levels of skills or interests work together on a project.

Columbia Mental Maturity Scale (CMMS) **Standardized** test of reasoning ability for children between the ages of 3 and 9 that is useful in evaluating children with motor or **sensory impairments** or difficulty with **expressive language;** does not depend on reading, but rather involves making determinations about characteristics of objects, such as their shape, color or size.

coma State of unconsciousness so deep that the individual cannot be aroused and lacks any response to his or her environment.

It is unclear whether a child in a coma is eligible for services under the IDEA. In *Parks v. Pakovic,* 1984-85 EHLR 556:372 (7th Cir. 1985), the Seventh Circuit speculated that in the hypothetical case of a child in a coma, the child might be uneducable, and thus ineligible for IDEA benefits. However, the issue has yet to be confronted and resolved. See also **zero-reject principle.**

communication board A non-electronic **augmentative communication system;** a board with pictures or symbols that allows an individual who cannot speak or speak readily to communicate by pointing or gazing.

communication disorder When used in the broadest sense, a wide variety of disabilities affecting ability to use or benefit from meaningful symbolic communication in speech, language or hearing, including **articulation disorder, language disorder,** and **voice disorder.**

communication dissonance

When an individual understands far more receptively than he is able to communicate expressly. See also **expressive language; receptive language.**

community living activities

Defined, as a term of art, in the federal **Developmental Disabilities Assistance and Bill of Rights Act of 1975** at 42 U.S.C. § 6001(5) as: "such priority area activities as will assist individuals with **developmental disabilities** to obtain and receive the supports needed to live in their family home or at a home of their own with individuals of their choice and to develop supports in the community."

co-morbidity

Different diseases or disorders existing together.

For example, it is fairly common for a child to be diagnosed as having **attention deficit hyperactivity disorder (ADHD)** and a **conduct disorder.**

comparable benefits

In connection with the obligations of school districts to **private school students with disabilities,** the requirement set out in **Education Department General Administrative Regulations (EDGAR)** at 34 C.F.R. § 76.654 that such children receive benefits that are "comparable in quality, scope and opportunity for participation" to those children enrolled in public schools receive. See also **genuine opportunity for equitable participation.**

compensation strategies

Development of **skills** that are used to offset or make up for irremediable **deficits** in other skills, when those deficiencies interfere with satisfactory achievement of some task or attainment of some goal; an alternative to **remediation.**

compensatory damages

Pecuniary compensation, or sum of money, awarded by a court to an individual who has suffered a loss or injury as a result of the wrongful or negligent act of another; intended to restore the injured person to the position he or she would have been in, if the wrongful or negligent act had not occurred. See also **remedy.**

While the IDEA states broadly that courts "shall grant all appropriate relief" (20 U.S.C. § 1415(e)(2)), the consensus of courts that have addressed the issue is that the IDEA does not permit an award of compensatory damages, beyond **tuition reimbursement** and reimbursement of similar out-of-pocket costs, to students who have been denied **free apppropriate public education (FAPE).** Most federal courts have held that compensatory damages over and above these items are not available for violations of Section 504 or Section 1983 that are also violations of the IDEA, although the Third Circuit Court of Appeals in *W.B. v. Matula,* 23 IDELR 411 (3d Cir. 1995), held otherwise.

compensatory education 1. Generally, educational services above and beyond those normally due a student under his or her state's education law. 2. Not expressly identified as a **remedy** in the IDEA nor addressed by the U.S. Supreme Court, but acknowledged by most courts that have considered the issue to be an appropriate remedy when a stu-

dent has been denied **free appropriate public education (FAPE).** 3. May also be an available remedy under Section 504 according to official comments to Section 504 regulations at 34 C.F.R. Part 104, Appendix A.

competitive employment See **competitive work.**

competitive work Defined, as a term of art, in **Vocational Rehabilitation and Other Rehabilitation Services Act** regulations at 34 C.F.R. § 361.1(c)(2) as work that is performed weekly on a full-time or part-time basis, as determined in an **Individualized Written Rehabilitation Program** and for which compensation is paid in accordance with the provisions of the Fair Labor Standards Act (federal minimum wage law). Also called competitive employment.

complex motor tic Includes facial gestures and grooming behaviors; associated with **Tourette's disorder.** See also **simple motor tic.**

complex vocal tic Includes **echolalia** and **copralia;**

associated with **Tourette's disorder.** See also **simple vocal tic.**

compulsion Behavior performed in a ritualistic or repetitive fashion without rational purpose; typical compulsions include: washing and cleaning rituals, checking compulsions, repeating compulsions, symmetry compulsions (e.g., insisting that both sides of shoelace bow look exactly the same), or avoidance compulsions. See also **obsessive-compulsive disorder.**

compulsory school attendance laws In effect in nearly every state; particular age range can vary, but generally includes children ages 6 to 16.

computer-assisted instruction (CAI) Variety of instructional modes that are characterized by the ability of the student-user to vary from a fixed text by selecting the order in which he or she reviews material or to choose to skip or review supplemental material, depending on whether additional explanation is required. See also **hypertext.**

concrete thinking Literal comprehension of language, associated with an inability to generalize beyond specific object or circumstance being thought about or perceived; considered lower level of thinking, when compared to **abstract thinking.**

concurrent validity The extent to which the test results are similar to the results of other means of evaluation, such as a medical diagnosis. See also **validity.**

conduct disorder 1. Generally understood as chronic pattern of conduct in which the basic rights of others are violated or major age-appropriate social rules are flouted, as distinguished from voluntary rule-breaking by nondisabled students. 2. A disruptive behavioral disorder the diagnostic criteria for which is defined in the DSM-IV as: "A. A repetitive and persistent pattern of behavior in which the basic rights of others or major age-appropriate societal norms are violated, as manifested by the presence of three (or more) of the following criteria in the past

12 months, with at least one criterion present in the past 6 months: Aggression to People and Animals—(1) often bullies, threatens or intimidates others; (2) often initiates physical fights; (3) has used a weapon that can cause serious physical harm to others . . . ; (4) has been physically cruel to people; (5) has been physically cruel to animals; (6) has stolen while confronting a victim; (7) has forced someone into sexual activity. Destruction of Property—(8) has deliberately engaged in fire setting with the intention of causing serious damage; (9) has deliberately destroyed others' property (other than by fire setting). Deceitfulness or Theft—(10) has broken into someone else's house, building, etc.; (11) often lies to obtain goods or favors or to avoid obligations (i.e., 'cons' others); (12) has stolen items of nontrivial value without confronting a victim (e.g, shoplifting, but without breaking or entering, forgery). Serious Violations of Rules—(13) often stays out at night despite parental prohibitions, beginning before age 13 years; (14) has run away from home overnight at least twice while

living in the parental or parental surrogate home (or once without returning for a lengthy period); (15) is often truant from school, beginning before age 13 years; B. The disturbance in behavior causes clinically significant impairment in social, academic or occupational functioning; C. If the individual is age 18 years or older, criteria are not met for Antisocial Personality Disorder." See also **oppositional defiant disorder (ODD) seriously emotionally disturbed; socially maladjusted.**

DSM-IV establishes 2 subtypes and 3 severity levels (**mild conduct disorder, moderate conduct disorder** and **severe conduct disorder**). The disorder is more prevalent among males, and males more often meet criteria involving violence, while females more often meet the criteria involving sneaky, but nonviolent, behaviors.

DSM-IV classifications have no direct relationship with eligibility criteria under the IDEA. Decisionmakers on the judicial and administrative level have struggled with whether a student who has a conduct disorder is **seriously emotionally disturbed (SED)** (eligible for services), **socially maladjusted** (ineligible) on that basis, or whether the **diagnosis** is not dispositive one way or the other. Commentators believe best practice is to focus on whether the student meets the SED criteria as a legal matter, rather than focus on his or her DSM-IV diagnosis. Court cases that have addressed the eligibility of conduct-disordered students include *A.M. v. Independent School District,* 17 IDELR 950 (10th Cir. 1990). An administrative decision that well addresses the disjunction between DSM-IV classification and SED eligibility is *Henry County Board of Education,* 22 IDELR 761 (SEA AL 1995).

congenital central hypoventilation syndrome

Extremely rare disorder that results in breathing difficulties, including asthma; can be life-threatening if not properly managed.

Individuals with congenital central hypoventilation syndrome have extensive medical needs and require multiple medical technologies, procedures and equipment at all times to sustain life, including continuous oxygen supplementation, a **tracheotomy tube** and a machine for **suctioning** excess mucous from the lungs. Despite its rarity, the disorder figured in an authoritative court decision in 1995. In *Neely v. Rutherford County School District,* 23 IDELR 334 (6th Cir. 1995), the Sixth Circuit Court of Appeals held that a school district was not required to provide either a nurse or a nursing assistant for a 7-year-old child with congenital central hypoventilation syndrome

who required suctioning of her breathing tube, monitoring and resuscitation, if required, such services being **excluded medical services** rather than **school health services.** See also **medically fragile.**

consent

1. In connection with **procedural safeguards,** generally the approval of a parent for a recommendation for **evaluation,** programming or placement of child with a disability, or suspected of having a disability, that is made after being fully informed of all information reasonably pertinent to agreement to proceed as recommended. 2. Defined, as a term of art, in IDEA Part B and Part H regulations at 34 C.F.R. § 300.500(a)(1) and 34 C.F.R. § 303.401(a), respectively, as meaning that: "(1) The parent has been fully informed of all information relevant to the activity for which consent is sought, in his or her **native language,** or other **mode of communication;** (2) The Parent understands and agrees in writing to the carrying out of the activity for which his or her consent is sought, and the consent described that activity and lists the records (if any) that will be released and to whom;

and (3) The parent understands that the granting of consent is voluntary on the part of the parent and may be revoked at any time."

consent decree An agreement between parties to litigation acknowledged in court by the parties to be legally binding and enforceable.

consequences In connection with **behavior management** and **behavior modification,** the stimulus following a behavior that may result in an increase or decrease in that behavior in the future. See also **antecedent; reinforcer.**

construct validity The extent to which test questions measure the mental processes the test is intended to measure. See also **validity.**

consulting teacher A teacher who provides guidance and support about educating disabled students to other teachers rather than providing **direct services** to students.

content validity The extent to which test questions measure the student's knowledge of the

subject matter the student should have learned. See also **validity.**

contingency 1. In connection with **behavior modification,** the relationship between a behavior and subsequent events. 2. The action or event that follows the **target behavior.** See also **consequences.**

contingency contract In connection with **behavior modification,** a written agreement that states the **consequences,** or **reinforcers,** that will occur given the student's performance of specified appropriate behaviors and/or completion of academic tasks.

continuous schedule of reinforcement In connection with **behavior modification, positive reinforcement** technique in which each occurrence of a response is reinforced, often used to begin a teaching sequence or shape a new behavior.

continuum of alternative placements The range of placements in which a student with a disability may receive some or all of his or her **indi-**

vidualized education program (IEP); ranging from less restrictive to more restrictive: regular classroom, regular classroom with **resource room,** regular classroom with special class **(self-contained class),** full-time special class (self-contained class), **day school, residential treatment** facility; plus limited educational placements outside of school environment: **homebound instruction,** hospital, detention center. See also **least restrictive environment (LRE).**

contracture Shrinking or shortening of muscles resulting in loss of range of motion; often remediated by **physical therapy.**

control braces Used by an individual with an **orthopedic impairment** to direct purposeful movement and inhibit involuntary movement. As distinguished from **corrective braces.**

convergent thinking Purposeful analysis of information to build a single correct response to a question or solution to a problem. As distinguished from **divergent thinking.**

coordinated set of activities In connection with **transition services** under the IDEA, defined, as a term of art, in the IDEA at 20 U.S.C. § 1410(a)(17) as including "instruction, community experiences, the development of employment and other post-school adult living objectives, and, when appropriate, acquisition of **daily living skills** and functional **vocational evaluation.**"

coping strategies How an individual responds to stressors in his or her environment.

copraxia **Complex motor tic** consisting of making obscene gestures, often associated with **Tourette's disorder.** See also **simple motor tic.**

Cornelia de Lange syndrome A genetic disorder characterized by multiple severe impairments and chronic health problems.

corpolalia **A complex vocal tic** involving involuntary interspersing of obscenities in the course of speaking, often associated with **Tourette's disorder.** See also **simple vocal tic.**

    57

corporal punishment
Traditional method of disciplining students with the use of physical **punishment,** including paddling, caning and spanking.

Corporal punishment passed constitutional muster in the U.S. Supreme Court's decision in *Ingraham v. Wright,* 430 U.S. 651 (1977), although most states have outlawed it. In those states that permit corporal punishment under state law, when considering its use with students with disabilities, **IEPs** or **accommodation plans** should be reviewed to ensure that any administration of physical discipline is consistent with the educational needs of the student.

corrective braces
Used to support the body weight of individuals with **orthopedic impairments** to allow joint movement. As distinguished from **control braces.**

correlation
The extent to which the score on a test varies with the score on another test, when compared across individuals or within the same individual. See also **correlation coefficient.**

correlation coefficient
A numeric measure of the degree of **correlation** between variables ranging from +1.00 (certainty that presence of one variable indicates presence of second) to -1.00 (certainty that presence of one variable rules out presence of second) with a score of 0.00 indicating presence of one variable has no predictive value for presence of second.

cortical blindness
Blindness resulting from brain lesion in the **occipital lobe.**

counseling services
1. Generally, services or activities that apply therapeutic processes to personal, family or situational problems in order to bring about a positive resolution of the problem or improved individual or family functioning or circumstances. 2. As a term of art, a **related service** defined in IDEA regulations at 34 C.F.R. § 300.16(b)(2) as "services provided by qualified social workers, psychologists, guidance counselors, or other qualified personnel."

Courts and administrative decisionmakers have held that psychological counseling may be a related service if it is required to assist a child to benefit from **special education,** even if the counseling is not primarily for educational purposes. Thus, in resolving claims involving psychological counseling, courts often wrestle with whether the nexus between the need for the services and the resulting educational benefit is too tenuous to make the school district financially liable for their provision.

craniosacral therapy Manipulation of the bones of the skull, face and mouth reported to cause reductions in **self-injurious behavior** in children with autism.

creative and productive thinking Ability to make new connections between ideas that usually are not considered to be capable of being combined or synthesized to arrive at new meaning. See also **divergent thinking.**

creeper A mobility device on which an individual who cannot ambulate lies to propel himself or herself with his or her arms.

cretinism A type of **mental retardation** characterized by a **clinical type appearance,** characteristic vocal quality and torpor.

cri du chat syndrome Extremely rare chromosomal abnormality resulting in **severe mental retardation** or **profound mental retardation** and markedly delayed motor development.

One of the several judicial decisions in 1995 holding in favor of a more restrictive placement for a student with severe mental retardation was *Kari H. v. Franklin Special School District,* 23 IDELR 538 (M.D. Tenn. 1995). The court, ruling on the basis of the **Roncker portability test,** held that the **least restrictive environment (LRE)** for a 14-year-old girl with cri du chat syndrome was a **special education** classroom with partial **mainstreaming** for non-academic subjects. The previous year the student had a fully inclusive placement in a 4th grade class. While the parents believed placement in 5th grade was appropriate, the court held that the student's gains in her inclusive setting were marginal, far outweighed by the gains she could realize in a special education classroom with a smaller teacher-student ratio and peers with whom she could communicate.

criterion-referenced test (CRT) Measures a student's absolute level of mastery of a particular skill, often developed locally to reflect the content of the school district's **curriculum;** does not measure a student's level of mastery against that of other students. As opposed to **norm-referenced test.**

cross-tutoring Individualized instruction provided by an older child as an adjunct to classroom instruction. See also **peer tutoring.**

crutches Used by individuals with mobility impairments to allow ambulation by relieving body weight pressure; 4 basic kinds, with selection depending upon, among other things, the individual's arm strength and ability to put pressure on wrist or hands: (a) wooden auxiliary crutches, (b) metal auxiliary crutches, (c) platform, or forearm support, crutches and (d) **Canadian elbow extension crutches.**

cued speech A method to clarify communication with deaf individuals in which, while the deaf individual is reading lips, an **interpreter** is using hand signals near his or her mouth to supplement and clarify the **lip reading** by helping to distinguish between **homophenes.** See also **deaf education.**

cultural bias In connection with **standardized tests,** the contention that differences in test scores among various racial and ethnic groups are the result of inherent flaws in the ability of the **instruments** to take into account the environmental background and values of children who are members of discrete minorities; a contention that gained wide acceptance in the 1980s with regard to overrepresentation of African-Americans in **special education** programs on the basis of identification as mentally retarded. See also **racially or culturally discriminatory testing and evaluation materials.**

cumulative record The entire record of an individual child's educational experience over time that is kept by the schools he or she attends. See **education records.**

currently engaging in the illegal use of drugs In connection with individuals with disabilities excluded from eligibility under Section 504 or the **Americans with Disabilities Act (ADA),** defined by Section 504/ADA legislation at

29 U.S.C. § 706(8)(C)(ii) as *not* being the following: "[an individual who] has successfully completed a supervised drug rehabilitation program and is no longer engaging in the **illegal use of drugs,** or has otherwise been rehabilitated successfully and is no longer engaging in such use; or is participating in a supervised rehabilitation program and is no longer engaging in such use; or is erroneously regarded as engaging in such use."

Unlike its obligations under Section 504 or the ADA, a school district's obligations under the IDEA are unaffected by whether a student with a disability is currently engaging in the illegal use of drugs. *Letter to Uher,* 18 IDELR 1238 (OSEP 1992).

curriculum Broadly, content of program of instruction detailing what students should learn, when they should learn it and how they should be taught.

curriculum-based measurement Series of incremental assessments of what a student has learned. See also **short-term instructional objectives.**

curriculum for students with mild disabilities Generally, the **regular education** curriculum, but taught with modifications and provision of **accommodations.**

curriculum for students with severe disabilities Generally consists of **survival skills, functional curriculum** designed to optimize independence and ability to function responsibility in society.

curriculum in early childhood education Generally addresses developmental areas critical to later school success such as motor, cognitive, language, social and self-help skills.

cystic fibrosis Common hereditary childhood disease affecting most organs and body functions; generally does not affect intellectual functioning but is increasingly debilitating and may be an **"other health impairment"** under the IDEA.

D

DASI Developmental Activities Screening Inventory

DBRS Disruptive Behavior Rating Scale

DDST-R Denver Developmental Screening Test-Revised

DNR Do Not Resuscitate order

DPT diagnostic-prescriptive teaching

DRO differential reinforcement of other behaviors

DSM-IV Diagnostic and Statistical Manual of Mental Disorders, 4th ed.

DTVMI Developmental Test of Visual-Motor Integration

Daily Life Therapy Educational programming for children with **autism** founded by Higashi School in Tokyo, Japan and offered by the Higashi School in Boston, Massachusetts; both are **residential treatment** facilities, emphasizing the building of physical strength and the skills necessary for daily living.

> **Residential placement** is not the norm for students with autism. Two cases that discuss the circumstances, if any, under which a residential placement is appropriate for an autistic child are *Ash v. Lake Oswego School District No. 7J,* 18 IDELR 3 (D. Or. 1991) and *Rebecca S. v. Clarke County School District,* 22 IDELR 884 (M.D. Ga. 1995).

daily living skills Skills needed for personal self-care, on the lowest level include toileting, feeding and dressing. See also **functional curriculum; special education.**

dangerousness exception A proposed exception to the procedural requirements of the IDEA, particularly the **stay-put provision,** when **suspension** or **expulsion** of violent or dangerous students is at issue.

The U.S. Supreme Court declined to read such an exception into the IDEA in *Honig v. Doe,* 1987-88 EHLR 559:231 (1988). See also **Honig injunction.**

Daniel R.R. test Promulgated by the Fifth Circuit Court of Appeals in *Daniel R.R. v. State Board of Education,* 15 EHLR 441:433 (5th Cir. 1989), to determine compliance with the **least restrictive environment (LRE) mandate** of the IDEA: "First we ask whether education in the regular classroom, with the use of [**supplementary**] **aids and services,** can be achieved satisfactorily for a given child . . . If it cannot and the school intends to provide **special education** or to remove the child from **regular education,** we ask, second, whether the school has **mainstreamed** the child to the maximum extent appropriate." See also **Holland test; inclusion; Roncker portability test.**

day care services Services or activities for children (including infants, preschoolers and school-age children) in either a center or a home for a portion of the day, possibly including appropriate developmental activities for children, recreation, meals and snacks; generally subject to licensing and monitoring under state law. Also termed child care services.

Although day care is not considered an **early intervention service** under Part H, a **public agency** may be required to provide and fund needed early intervention services at a child care site if it is determined that a certain amount of interaction with peers makes participation in a day care center program a necessary element in the child's **individualized family service plan (IFSP).** *Letter to Dicker,* 22 IDELR 464 (OSEP 1995).

day school A school facility attended by **children with disabilities** whose needs cannot be met in a regular school but who spend the balance of their time out of the school setting in the community; on the **continuum of alternative placements,** more restrictive that a **self-contained class,** but less restrictive than **residential placement.** Also called special day school.

See also **least restrictive environment (LRE) mandate.**

day treatment In connection with mental health services for children and adolescents, a program lasting at least 4 hours a day that includes crisis intervention, **special education,** counseling, and parent training.

Deaf When capitalized, understood to mean an individual who communicates through **American Sign Language (ASL)** rather than signed or spoken English and who self-identifies as a member of the Deaf community and a participant in Deaf culture. See also **deaf education.**

deaf-blindness 1. From the educational perspective, a uniquely catastrophic disability due to the paramount importance both vision and hearing have in the learning process; 4 subgroups, based on whether congenitally or adventitiously deaf-blind or, if the losses did not occur at the same time, which came first. 2. Defined, as a term of art, in IDEA regulations at 34 C.F.R. § 300.7(b)(2) as: "concomitant hearing and visual impairments, the combination of which causes such severe communication and other developmental and educational problems that they cannot be accommodated in special education programs solely for children with deafness or children with blindness." 3. Defined substantially similarly for **Part C of the IDEA** in Part C regulations at 34 C.F.R. Part 307. See also **infants and toddlers with deaf-blindness.**

"Being deaf-blind is a disability in and of itself; it is not the sum total of deafness and blindness. . . . The concomitant nature of the dual losses can cause severe communication, social, emotional, behavioral, medical, educational, and vocational problems. It is the combination of sensory and related disabilities, more than the amount or type of hearing or vision loss that requires a person who is deaf-blind to be considered in a category by him- or herself." R. Rothstein & J. Everson, *Assistive Technology, A Resource for School, Work, and Community* (K. Flipp, K. Inge and J.M. Barcus, eds., 1995), 110.

deaf education 5 methods that relate to the chosen method of **alternative communication** in the absence of both hearing and speech: (a) **auditory training,** (b) **oral/aural [method],**

(c) oral/aural plus **cued speech** or other supportive modes of communications, (d) speech and **sign language,** and (e) visual only (gestural communication or sign language).

deafness 1. A **hearing loss** so extensive that one cannot understand speech, even with a hearing aid, usually considered a loss of 70 **decibels** or greater. 2. Defined, as a term of art, in IDEA regulations at 34 C.F.R. § 300.7(b)(2) as: "a **hearing impairment** so severe that the child is impaired in processing linguistic information through hearing, with or without amplification, that adversely affects a child's educational performance."

decibel (db) Unit for measuring sound volume. See also **hearing loss.**

decoding skills The **receptive language** skills that allow a child to understand and make use of auditory or visual information; in connection with **reading,** the ability to recognize words one has previously learned and discern the meanings of new words from sound or context.

dedicated device Augmentative communication device used for communication only; commercial **high-tech electronic communication aids** include the Canon Communicator, the AlphaTalker, and the Digivox.

deficit A lag in a student's skill or ability level, so that he or she is behind his or her age peers.

de minimus educational benefit In connection with whether a child with a disability is receiving an **appropriate** education, an educational benefit that is insufficient to constitute a **free appropriate public education (FAPE)** under the substantive standard set by the U.S. Supreme Court in *Board of Education of Hendrick Hudson Central School District v. Rowley,* 1981-1982 EHLR 553:656 (1982). See also **passing from grade to grade; potential maximizing standard.**

The term "de minimus educational benefit" was used most notably by the Third Circuit Court of Appeals in *Polk v. Central Susquehanna Intermediate Unit 16,* 1988-1989 EHLR 441:130, 142 (3d Cir. 1988), in which it stated that "[t]he *Rowley*

Court described the education that must be provided under the [IDEA] as 'meaningful.' The use of the term 'meaningful' indicates that the Court expected more than de minimus benefit." While most courts have agreed with the Third Circuit's formulation, the ongoing difficulty has been determining, on a case-by-case basis, whether a child is receiving a meaningful educational benefit or only a de minimus benefit. When students have severe cognitive disabilities or emotional disorders, this difficult issue is preceded by the equally thorny threshold issue of determining what constitutes an educational program for that child.

de novo hearing A hearing in which the court hears the matter as a court of original, not appellate, jurisdiction, in effect, trying a matter as if it had not been heard by a court before. See also **appellate court; independent decision based on a preponderance of the evidence; intermediate standard of review.**

Courts ruling on the standard of review in **civil actions** under the IDEA have differed on whether the statutory language at 20 U.S.C. § 1415(e)(2) requires de novo proceedings or a more deferential review of the decision of the **due process hearing.** For federal courts of appeals' decisions supporting de novo review, see, e.g., *Teague Indepen-*

dent School District v. Todd L., 20 IDELR 259 (5th Cir. 1993) and *G.D. v. Westmoreland School District,* 17 EHLR 751 (1st Cir. 1991).

Denver Developmental Screening Test-Revised (DDST-R) Screening instrument to identify infants and preschool children who may have serious **developmental delays** and should undergo further evaluation; has 105 items assessing 4 **domains** of infant and early childhood development: (a) personal-social skills, (b) **fine motor skills,** (c) language skills and (d) **gross motor skills.**

Denver Eye Screening Test Brief screening test used to detect problems in **visual acuity** in children ages 6 months to 6 years.

derived score Raw score that has been converted into a score for meaningful interpretation of a child's performance on a **norm-referenced test.**

destruction In connection with **education records,** defined, as a term of art, in 34 C.F.R. § 300.560 as: "physical destruction or removal of per-

67

sonal identifiers from information so that the information is no longer personally identifiable." See also **Family Educational Rights and Privacy Act (FERPA); personally identifiable information.**

destructive device A type of **firearm,** defined, as a term of art, in the federal crimes code at 18 U.S.C. § 921 as any explosive, such as a bomb or grenade, or any type of **weapon** that expels a projectile by use of an explosive or other propellant and has a bore of more than one-half inch in diameter.

Developmental Activities Screening Inventory (DASI) An informal **screening** measure for use with children between birth and age 5 to assess developmental skills and possible disabilities in 15 skill areas that include: imitation, sensory intactness, means-end relationships, causality, **memory,** seriation (arranging items in an orderly way) and sensorimotor organization.

developmental aphasia 1. A congenital **receptive language disorder** or, more commonly, **expressive language disorder** in children with normal **intelligence** and adequate sensory and motor skills which prevents acquisition of language. 2. Identified in IDEA regulations at 34 C.F.R. § 300.7(b)(10) as a **"specific learning disability."** See also **acquired aphasia.**

developmental approach Pedagogic theory that all children learn in the same basic way and in the same sequence, although at different rates.

developmental articulation disorder Now referred to as a **phonological disorder.**

developmental coordination disorder A developmental disorder the diagnostic criteria for which is defined in the DSM-IV as: "A. Performance in daily activities that require motor coordination is substantially below that expected given the person's chronological age and measured intelligence. This may be manifested by marked delays in achieving motor milestones (e.g., walking, crawling, sitting), dropping things, 'clumsiness,' poor performance in sports, or poor handwriting. B. The disturbance in Criterion A significantly interferes with academic achievement or **activities of daily living.** C. The disturbance is not due to a general medical condition (e.g., **cerebral palsy, hemiplegia,** or **muscular dystrophy**) and does not meet the criteria for a **Pervasive Developmental Disorder.** D. If **Mental Retardation** is present, the motor difficulties are in excess of those usually associated with it."

developmental delay 1. Generally, a delay in the areas of **cognition,** socialization, independent functioning, communication or motor skills resulting in a child having slower and more difficult skills **acquisition** than his or her typically developing age peers. 2. As a category for eligibility under either Part B (34 C.F.R. § 300.7(a)(2)) or Part H (34 C.F.R. § 303.316)), as defined by state law or regulation.

The IDEA empowers states to define a qualifying developmental delay by designating the levels of functioning that will determine eligibility. Wyoming, for example, defines a developmental delay as a 25% or more

delay in development compared to his or her age peers. Although determination of the level of functioning is thus left up to the states, insofar as Part H is concerned, federal regulations (at 34 C.F.R. § 303.16) require evaluators to consider all 5 of the specified developmental areas of functioning (cognitive development; physical development, including vision and hearing; language and speech development; psychosocial development; and self-help skills) and to deem children eligible when they fall below the designated level of functioning in any one or more of the areas. Part B similarly requires consideration of development in the areas of physical development, cognitive development, communication development, social or emotional development or adaptive development and eligibility for a child with a delay in any of those areas.

Developmental Disabilities Assistance and Bill of Rights Act of 1975 Provides federal aid to states to assist in providing comprehensive services to individuals with **developmental disabilities** to maximize independence; mandates provision of services in accordance with an **individual habilitation plan**; codified at 42 U.S.C. §§ 6000-6083.

developmental disability 1. Generic term for a substantial

69

continuing disability that starts in childhood and is not subject to **rehabilitation,** such as **mental retardation, cerebral palsy** and **autism.** 2. Defined, as a term of art, in the federal **Developmental Disabilities Assistance and Bill of Rights Act of 1975** at 42 U.S.C. § 6001(8) as "a severe, chronic disability of an individual 5 years of age or older that—(A) is attributable to a mental or physical impairment or combination of mental or physical impairments; (B) is manifested before the individual attains age 22; (C) is likely to continue indefinitely; (D) results in substantial function limitations in three of more of the following major life activities—(i) self-care; (ii) **receptive [language]** and **expressive language;** (iii) learning; (iv) mobility; (v) self-direction; (vi) capacity for independent living; and (vii) economic self-sufficiency; and (E) reflects the individual's need for a combination and sequence of special, interdisciplinary, or generic services, supports, or other assistance that is of life-long or extended duration and is individually planned and coordinated. . . ."

developmental dyslexia

Severe **reading disorder** which has no known **etiology** and is associated with individuals with high **intelligence.**

Developmental Inventory of Learned Skills Cri-

terion-referenced checklist for assessing the **learning styles** and strengths and weaknesses in basic learning areas of children from birth through age 8.

developmental model of intelligence Jean Piaget's

theory that a child's intellectual abilities develop in 4 stages as the child interacts with his or her environment; the stages are (a) sensorimotor period, (b) preoperational period, (c) concrete operations period and (d) formal operations period.

developmental reading

Reading to learn how to read; in the past, part of the **curriculum** for lower elementary grades only, but becoming part of curriculum for older students, particularly those with **learning disabilities** relating to **reading.** See also **basal reading program; phonics; whole language method.**

Developmental Screening Inventory, Revised

Uses direct observation of a child from birth to age 3 to determine if he or she is functioning at age level in the areas of **adaptive behavior, gross motor skills, fine motor skills,** language and personal-social interaction.

Developmental Test of Visual-Motor Integration (DTVMI)

Standardized individually administered test of **perceptual-motor [disorder]** ability for children between ages 4 and 13 in which the examinee is asked to copy up to 24 increasingly complex geometric designs.

diabetes

A metabolic disorder relating to a failure to secrete sufficient amounts of insulin or to properly absorb insulin; in more severe cases can result in water and electrolyte loss; may be an **"other health impairment"** under the IDEA and may entitle the student to **school heath services** under either the IDEA or Section 504. See also **blood glucose monitoring; insulin pump.**

diagnosed physical or mental condition that has a high probability of resulting in development delay

In connection with Part H, a condition that makes an **infant or toddler with a disability** eligible for **early intervention services;** more particularly described in Note 1 to Part H regulations at 34 C.F.R. § 303.16 as "conditions with known etiologies and developmental consequences, [examples of which] include **Down syndrome** and other chromosomal abnormalities, sensory impairments, including vision and hearing, inborn errors of metabolism, **microcephaly,** severe attachment disorders, including **failure to thrive, seizure disorders [seizure],** and **fetal alcohol syndrome."**

diagnosis

In connection with **special education** programming, taking information about a student that has been obtained from an **assessment** and classifying that information based on an accepted diagnostic system. See also **Diagnostic and Statistical Manual of Mental Disorders (DSM-IV).**

Diagnostic and Statistical Manual of Mental Disorders (DSM-IV)

The 4th revision of the statistical and clinical nomenclature system of the American Psychiatric Association, the fundamental system of medical **diagnosis** of **mental disorders** that is the standard in the medical community; categorical classification of mental disorders based on conformance of behavior observed by trained clinician to those behaviors identified as elements of a specific classification; diagnoses the presence of a disorder, not its **etiology.**

> The primary purpose of the DSM-IV is to provide a classification system of diagnostic categories to allow clinicians and other professionals the ability to diagnose, discuss and treat various disorders. It has no direct relationship with eligibility criteria under special education law.

Diagnostic Inventory for Screening Children

Diagnostic screening tool for children between birth and age 5 who are designated, but not diagnosed, as developmentally delayed to assess **skills** and identify where further **diagnosis** is needed; measures skills on 8 scales: (a) **fine motor** skills, (b) **gross motor skills,** (c) **receptive language,** (d) **expressive language,** (e) attention and **memory,** (f) auditory and **visual acuity,** (g) self-help skills and (h) **social skills.**

diagnostic-prescriptive teaching (DPT)

Individualized instruction designed to develop strengths and remediate weaknesses.

diagnostic test

An **instrument** to measure an individual student's strengths and weakness in a specific area and how his or her resulting educational needs can be met through regular instruction or **remediation.**

didactic method

Instructional method based on use of practical materials.

differential diagnosis

An evaluation to distinguish between similar disabilities.

differential reinforcement

A **behavior management** technique involving reinforcement of one class of one behavior, but not another, or reinforcement of the same behavior only when it is performed under one condition, but not another. See also **differential reinforcement of other behaviors (DRO); differential reinforcement of high rates.**

differential reinforcement of high rates A behavior **management** technique in which reinforcement is given for performing a behavior with increasing frequency.

differential reinforcement of other behaviors (DRO) A **behavior management** technique to decelerate a behavior in which behaviors other than the problem **target behavior** are systemically reinforced.

Differential Test of Conduct and Emotional Problems Screening instrument used to differentiate between students with conduct problems who may have a **serious emotional disturbance** and those who are not disabled but are behaving inappropriately nonetheless.

direct instruction Active teaching or explicit instruction which includes explaining to students exactly what they are expected to learn, demonstrating the steps needed to accomplish a task and providing opportunities for practice and feedback; suitable for large-group instruction, but does not easily accommodate **open-ended questions** or higher-order thinking. Also called traditional instruction.

Direct Instruction An instructional method for teaching students with **learning disabilities** to read based on **phonics** and involving an interactive, drill-based scripted method of teaching. See also **Orton-Gillingham method; Project Read.**

directionality An individual's ability to discern right from left, up from down and the like; inability to so discern in older children may be a **neurological soft sign.**

directory information Information in **education records** not generally protected from disclosure by the **Family Educational Rights and Privacy Act (FERPA);** defined, as a term of art, in FERPA regulations at 34 C.F.R. § 99.3 as "information contained in an education record of a student

73

which would not generally be considered harmful or an invasion of privacy if disclosed ... includ[ing], but not limited to, the student's name, address, telephone listing, date and place of birth, major field of study, participation in officially recognized activities and sports, weight and height of members of athletic teams, dates of attendance, degrees and awards received, and the most recent previous educational agency or institution attended." As distinguished from **personally identifiable information.**

In *A.P. v. North Tonawanda City School District Board of Education,* 18 IDELR 50 (W.D.N.Y. 1991), the district court for the Western District of New York held that under FERPA even directory information is to be kept confidential if a parent, after notice, has informed the **local education agency (LEA)** that such information should not be released without his or her consent.

direct selection Access method for **high-tech electronic communication aids** involving pointing at or otherwise selecting the desired information (e.g., touching "A" on a keyboard to have "A" appear on the screen) on the **augmentative communication aid.** See also **direct selection communicator.**

direct selection communicator Nonverbal communication device that allows the user to select a word card, phrase or object directly by using a body part, **headstick, mouthstick** or **eyegaze [input system]** light beam; includes manual and electronic communication, but not direct selection computer programs.

direct services In connection with a state's use and distribution of IDEA funds, defined, as a term of art, in IDEA regulations at 34 C.F.R. § 300.370(b)(1) as: "services provided to a child with a disability by the State directly, by contract, or through other arrangements." See also **support services.**

direct testing A basic way of getting assessment information in which a child with a disability has a specific opportunity to respond to a stimulus and demonstrate a behavior. See also **observational recording method.**

74

disability Limitation in performance resulting from a physiological (physical or mental) abnormality; as a matter of preferred terminology, an "individual with a disability" should be used, rather than a "disabled individual." May also be referred to as an **impairment**. See also **handicap**.

disciplinary actions and classroom interventions In connection with addressing critical behaviors in an **individualized education program (IEP),** may include: verbal reprimands and written warnings, **time-out,** study **carrels,** restriction of privileges, detention, physical restraint, **in-school suspension,** aversive techniques and alternative educational placement for disciplinary reasons, all to the extent imposition has no adverse effect on IEP goals and that they are not applied in a discriminatory manner. See also **behavior management plan.**

discipline A school's system designed to minimize disruption and promote positive social interaction; a broad category of techniques for **behav-**

ior management and control including **intervention** plans that encompass motivational techniques, such as **positive reinforcement, social skills** training, and development of problem-solving and decision-making skills, as well as **punishment.**

disclosure In connection with **education records,** regulated by the **Family Educational Rights and Privacy Act (FERPA)** and defined, as a term of art, in FERPA regulations at 34 C.F.R. § 99.3 as "access to or the release, transfer, or other communication of education records, or the **personally identifiable information** contained in these records . . . by any means, including oral, written, or electronic means."

discovery Generally, pretrial techniques with which one party to litigation obtains information about disputed issues from the other party in order to prepare for trial; under federal rules and the rules of those states who have adopted the same or similar systems, discovery techniques include deposition, written interrogatories, production of documents and compelled medical examinations.

The **"five-day rule"** of disclosure is the key discovery to which parties to a **due process hearing** are entitled under the IDEA. As a matter of practice, in simple appeals of administrative decisions the parties frequently forego additional discovery. Nonetheless, the general view is that they are entitled to take full advantage of the broad federal rules governing discovery or applicable state discovery provisions.

discrepancy formula In connection with determining if the difference between a student's achievement and potential is large enough to establish eligibility for **special education** on the basis of a **specific learning disability,** formula used to evaluate whether a child has a **"severe discrepancy between achievement and intellectual ability."**

IDEA regulations at 34 C.F.R. § 300.541(a)(2) do not specify which discrepancy formula(s) a state may, or must, use in evaluating specific learning disabilities, but it is accepted that use of a state-selected formula is generally permitted under federal law. According to the **Office of Special Education and Rehabilitative Services (OSERS),** a **multidisciplinary team** may use a formula to establish the existence of a severe

discrepancy between achievement and intellectual ability, as long as the team may override a purely mechanical application of the formula when appropriate. *Letter to Murphy,* EHLR 213:216 (OSERS 1989).

discrete trial training A method of breaking down functions into single steps which are rewarded on a trial-by-trial basis; also referred to as the **Lovaas program** in connection with use of the method with preschoolers with autism. See also **applied behavioral analysis (ABA).**

As an example of discrete trial training, the desired goal of having a child learn how to drink from a cup might be broken down into the following series of discrete steps: having the child learn to recognize the cup as containing something he or she wants; teaching the child to reach for the cup; teaching the child to pick up the cup; teaching the child to put down the cup. Each of these steps would be identified and trained separately and then gradually all chained together.

disorder of written expression 1. May present as particularly poor handwriting, copying ability, or inability to remember letter sequences in commonly written words. 2. A **learning disorder** the diagnostic criteria for which is defined in the DSM-IV as: "A. Writing skills, as measured by individually administered standardized tests . . . , is substantially below that expected given the person's chronological age, measured intelligence and **age-appropriate** education. B. The disturbance in Criterion A significantly interferes with academic achievement or **activities of daily living** that require writing skills. C. If a sensory deficit is present, the . . . difficulties are in excess of those usually associated with it." See also **learning disorder; writing; writing remediation.**

Disruptive Behavior Rating Scale (DBRS) 50-item inventory of behaviors associated with **attention-deficit hyperactivity disorders (ADHD), attention deficit disorder (ADD), oppositional defiant disorder (ODD)** and **conduct disorder (CO)** for which parents and teacher indicate, on a 4-point scale, how often the child engages in certain behaviors, the scale measures 4 factors: (a) **distractibility,** (b) oppositionality, (c) impulsive-hyperactivity and (d) antisocial behavior.

distractibility Generally, a child's attention to or interest in things other than what he or she should be concentrating on, responsiveness to irrelevant stimulation; high distractibility a characteristic of **attention-deficit hyperactivity disorder (ADHD)** or **attention deficit disorder (ADD).**

divergent thinking Formulation of new ideas on the basis of previously learned information; demonstrated by varied and insightful responses to **open-ended questions** or task assignments; colloquially put, "thinking outside the box"; related to, but subtly different from, **intelligence.** As opposed to **convergent thinking.**

diversity Commonly understood to refer to the demographic characteristics of American families that describe the characteristics of school students and the special needs they bring with them to school; different types of diversity include: racial or ethnic diversity; cultural diversity, including

77

primary language other than English at home; and economic diversity. See also **cultural bias; racially or culturally discriminatory testing and evaluation materials.**

domains In connection with **children with disabilities,** generally the functional areas in which a child's performance is assessed: physical, cognitive, social and emotional; by assessing a child's strengths and weaknesses in each domain, one can estimate the child's functional status.

> Instructional domains for children with severe disabilities are (a) domestic, including self-care; (b) leisure; (c) functioning in the community; and (d) vocational. Behavioral domains for children with mental retardation, developmental disabilities or other emotional disabilities are (a) independent functioning; (b) physical development; (c) economic activity; (d) language development; (e) numbers and time; (f) domestic activity; (g) vocational activity; (h) self-direction; (i) responsibility; and (j) socialization.

Doman-Delacato method Neurophysical approach to instruction of children with **cerebral palsy** or other physical disabilities relating to **brain in-**

jury in which the brain is stimulated through manipulated movements of the body. Also called patterning.

Do Not Resuscitate order (DNR) Indicates that life-sustaining measures, such as **cardiopulmonary resuscitation (CPR),** not be taken.

> An issue confronted by school districts is whether they must implement a parental request that life-sustaining measures not be taken for their severely disabled child with significant health or medical conditions. Although state law plays an important role in determining the appropriate course of action, the **Office for Civil Rights (OCR)** has indicated that a school district may adopt a policy that denies any request to withhold life-sustaining measures. *Lewiston (ME) Public Schools,* 21 IDELR 83 (OCR 1994).

Down syndrome A congenital condition consisting of an extra 21st chromosome and resulting in some degree of **mental retardation.**

> Children with Down syndrome often have the following physical characteristics, giving them the distinctive appearance associated with the condition: **epicanthal folds** over the eyes, eyes slightly slanted, somewhat smaller nose and ears, nasal bridge slightly depressed, and a single palmar crease, occasionally referred to

as **minor physical abnormalities.** See also **clinical type appearance.**

drugs In connection with individuals with disabilities excluded from eligibility under the ADA and Section 504 because they are **currently engaging in the illegal use of drugs,** defined, as a term of art, in 29 U.S.C. § 706(B)(4)(i) as: "controlled substance[s] as defined in schedules I through V of Section 202 of the Controlled Substances Act, 21 U.S.C. § 812."

Duchenne disease Childhood form of **muscular dystrophy** usually manifesting itself between ages 2 to 6 years.

One of the first published judicial opinions concerning a school district's obligations to provide **transition services** involved a 22-year-old man with Duchenne disease who used a wheelchair, had virtually no hand or motor function and required deep tracheal suctioning every 50 minutes and ventilator assistance 45 minutes per day. In that case, *Chuchran v. Walled Lake Consolidated Schools,* 20 IDELR 1035 (E.D. Mich. 1993), aff'd, 22 IDELR 450 (6th Cir. 1995), the court rejected the student's argument that the school district was required to continue to provide him with **transportation, nursing services, occupational therapy** and **physical therapy** while attending college as a remedy for failing to prepare a formal written **transition** plan.

due process hearing The process that either a parent or school district (or similar **public agency**) may initiate to resolve a disagreement about the identification, **evaluation,** educational placement, or provision of **free appropriate public education (FAPE)** for a child with a disability or suspected of being disabled under the IDEA, as established in the IDEA at 20 U.S.C. § 1415(b)(1)(e) and described as:

Identification—Whether or not a child has a disability under the IDEA and, if identified as having a disability, decisions about its nature or severity.

Evaluation—The type of assessment instruments used to determine the performance of the child, the appropriateness of the evaluation procedures used, parental agreement with the resulting evaluation and parental opportunity for an independent evaluation.

Educational placement—The type of school environment most appropriate to the child and which school or facility closest to the child's home provides the necessary resources and changes in placement, including changes as a result of **discipline** and,

79

when pertinent, a **manifestation determination.**

Provision of FAPE—**Special education** and **related services** designed to meet the child's unique needs.

due weight Terminology used by the U.S. Supreme Court in *Board of Education of Hendrick Hudson Central School District v. Rowley,* 1981-1982 EHLR 553:656, 670 (1982), when it ruled that the requirement that a court (trying a **civil action** under the IDEA) receive the records of the administrative proceedings "carries with it the implied requirement that due weight shall be given to those proceedings." See also **independent decision based on a preponderance of the evidence; intermediate standard of review.**

In the almost 2 decades since that U.S. Supreme Court decision, courts have puzzled over how to reconcile the Court's command to give due weight with the directive in the legislative history that a court make an "independent decision based on a preponderance of the evidence", leading to the often-posed question: How much weight is due weight? A related question, and a similar lack of consensus, has arisen when a state has adopted a **two-tier administrative system:** when the 2 administrative decisionmakers disagree, to whom should due weight be given?

dyscalculia **Specific learning disability** in mathematics, such that an individual's performance of some or all aspects of mathematical computation and reasoning is significantly below the performance expected of a student with his or her level of **intelligence** who has no sensory deficits, absent environmental or motivational influences.

dysfluency Hesitations or repetitions that disrupt normal speech, such as **stuttering.**

dysgraphia **Specific learning disability** in written language, such that an individual's performance of some or all aspects of written language skills or general adequacy of written communication is significantly below the performance expected of a student with his or her level of **intelligence** who has no sensory deficits, absent environmental or motivational influences; does not present as poor handwriting.

dyslexia 1. Receptive disorder in written language typically resulting in reading disabilities experienced by children of otherwise normal intellectual capacity who have received adequate instruction. 2. Identified in IDEA regulations at 34 C.F.R. § 300.7(b)(10) as a **"specific learning disability."**

A child with dyslexia may have difficulty pronouncing new words, distinguishing similarities and differences in words, discriminating differences in letter sounds, and applying what has been read to social or learning situations. Other problems may include reversing words and letters and incorrectly ordering words.

dysphasia Global deficit in oral and written language and reading marked by compromised ability to analyze words into **phonemes.**

dysphonia A **voice disorder** characterized by faulty resonance, phonation or pitch.

dyspraxia An inability to coordinate body movements.

dystonia A rare muscle disease of young children resulting in loss of **muscle tone** and usability.

E

EAHCA Education of All Handicapped Children Act

ED (also DOE) United States Department of Education

EDGAR Education Department General Administrative Regulations

EHA Education of the Handicapped Act

EMR educable mentally retarded

EPSDT Early and Periodic Screening, Diagnosis, and Treatment

ERIC Educational Resources and Information Center

ERIC/CASS ERIC Clearinghouse on Counseling and Student Services

ERIC/EC ERIC Clearinghouse on Disabilities and Gifted Education

ESD extended school day programming

ESEA Elementary and Secondary Education Act of 1965

ESL English as a second language

ESY extended school year programming

Early and Periodic Screening, Diagnosis, and Treatment (EPSDT)

Federally mandated component of the **Medical Assistance (Medicaid)** program that must be part of each state plan that, as specified in enabling legislation at 42 U.S.C. § 1396d(r)(5), is designed "to discover, as

83

early as possible, the ills that handicap our children" and to provide "continuing follow-up and treatment so that handicaps do not get neglected;" benefits for Medicaid-eligible children include **assessment,** diagnostic and treatment services. See **EPSDT Screening.**

early autism Name sometimes used as a synonym for **autism.**

Early Child Development Inventory Brief **screening** instrument used with children between the ages of 15 months and 3 years to identify potential developmental problems that may interfere with learning ability.

early childhood Age range generally considered to start at birth through age 2 years and end at ages 6 years through 8 years, although there is no one uniformly agreed range.

early childhood education Instruction or **intervention** that precedes traditional schooling to aid the educational success of children who have been identified as having a disability or being **at-risk.**

early identification and assessment of disabling conditions in children Defined, as a term of art, as a **related service** in IDEA regulations at 34 C.F.R. § 300.7(b)(3) as: "the implementation of a formal plan for identifying a disability as early as possible in a child's life," as distinguished from **child find** and **early intervention services** provided under Part H.

early infantile autism Term used synonymously with **autism** when discussing children; no longer generally used.

early intervention program Defined, as a term of art, in Part H regulations at 34 C.F.R. § 303.11 as: "the total effort in a State that is directed at meeting the needs of children eligible under this part and their families." See also **early intervention services.**

early intervention services 1. The specific types of services and supports which children eligible under Part H may receive. 2. Defined, as a term of art, in Part H legislation at 20 U.S.C. § 1472(2) as: "developmental services which—(A) are provided under public supervision; (B) are provided at no cost except where Federal or State law provides for a system of payments by families, including a schedule of sliding fees; (C) are designed to meet the developmental needs of an **infant or toddler with a disability** in any one or more of the following areas: (i) physical development, (ii) cognitive development, (iii) language and speech development, (iv) psychosocial development, or (v) self-help skills; (D) meet the standards of the State, including the requirements of this subchapter; (E) include—(i) **family training, counseling, and home visits,** (ii) **special instruction;** (iii) **speech pathology** and **audiology,** (iv) **occupational therapy;** (v) **physical therapy,** (vi) **psychological services,** (vii) **case management services,** (viii) **medical services for diagnostic or evaluation purposes,** (ix) early identification, screening, and assessment services, (x) **health services** necessary to enable the infant or toddler to benefit from the other early intervention services, and (xi)

social work services; (F) are provided by qualified personnel, including—(i) special educators, (ii) speech and language pathologists and audiologists, (iii) occupational therapists, (iv) physical therapists, (v) psychologists, (vi) social workers, (vii) nurses, and (viii) nutritionists; and (G) are provided in conformity with an **individualized family service plan** adopted in accordance with section 1477 of this title." 3. Defined, as a term of art, in the federal **Developmental Disabilities Assistance and Bill of Rights Act of 1975** at 42 U.S.C. § 6001(9) as "services provided to infants, young children and their families to—enhance the development of infants, toddlers and young children with disabilities and to minimize their potential for **developmental delay;** and enhance the capacity of families to meet the special needs of their infants, toddlers, and young children."

Eby Gifted Behavior Index

Collection of **instruments** that allows classroom teachers to observe and evaluate the extent to which students

85

exhibit the following behaviors: (a) perceptiveness, (b) independence, (c) goal orientation, (d) originality, (e) persistence, (f) productivity, (g) self-evaluation and (h) effective communication of ideas.

echolalia A **complex vocal tic** involving involuntary repetition of the words of others, associated with children with **severe mental retardation, autism** or **Tourette's disorder.**

echolation An auditory technique used by blind individuals involving perception of sound echoes with an **echolation device** to enhance mobility and anticipate and avoid obstacles. See also **mobility aids; mobility training.**

echolation device A device used by blind individuals to navigate by emitting high frequency sounds that bounce off objects, with the loudness of the sound indicating an object's size and the pitch indicating its distance. See also **electronic travel aid (ETA); mobility aids; mobility training.**

echopraxia Complex **motor tic** consisting of imitating the movements of others; associated with individuals with **Tourette's disorder.**

ecological   approach Changing the environment of a **behavior disordered** child as a way of modifying the child's behavior. See also **behavior management.**

ecological inventory Informal **instruments** used in the development of **age-appropriate** and functional programming for a student with a **severe disability.**

edible reinforcer Use of food as a reward for appropriate behavior; sometimes used with children with **autism.** See also **applied behavioral analysis; discrete trial training.**

educable mentally retarded (EMR) An educational category developed by some states to describe children with **mental retardation** that generally conforms to **mild mental retardation** under the classification of the DSM-IV.
     Most individuals classified as EMR have minimal sensorimotor deficits, are capable of minimum self-support, can achieve up to about the 6th-

grade level academically by late teens and can master vocational skills for **competitive work** (semi-skilled or unskilled).

educable mental retardation, educational programming for

Premised on experience rather than abstraction, showing the child how to cope in the environment and including good citizenship, basic **academic achievement,** vocational training, and home and personal lifestyle management.

educationally deprived children

In connection with children who are eligible for assistance under Title 1 of the **Elementary and Secondary Education Act (ESEA),** defined in Title 1 regulations at 34 C.F.R. § 200.6 as: "children whose educational attainment is below the level that is appropriate for children of their age" and generally involves children in institutions for neglected or delinquent children or children from low-income families.

educational methodology

Generally, choices in instructional methods or **curriculum** content.

Although questions of methodology have provoked fervid debate between school districts and the parents of **children with disabilities,** courts give school districts great leeway in selecting the appropriate methodology for educating students with special needs. All courts ruling in favor of school districts in cases concerning what is judged to be a dispute about educational methodology cite the U.S. Supreme Court's directive in *Board of Education of Hendrick Hudson Central School District v. Rowley,* 1981-82 EHLR 553:656 (1982): As long as the school district's choice of educational methodology is reasonably calculated to provide students with disabilities with educational benefit, that choice is entitled to court deference, even in the face of strong parental opposition. Methodology disputes have been a prominent part of the IDEA litigation landscape in connection with **deaf** students, **preschool** students with **autism,** and students with **learning disabilities.**

educational or vocational training

Generally, program for the **acquisition** of knowledge or skills to prepare an individual for gainful employment.

educational performance

In connection with Part B, what must be adversely affected to establish eligibility according to IDEA regulations at 34 C.F.R. § 300.7(b); undefined in

87

either the statute or regulations, but it is generally agreed to encompass more than **academic achievement.** See also **passing from grade to grade.**

According to the district court for the Northern District of Illinois, "'Educational performance' means more than a child's ability to meet academic criteria. It must also include reference to the child's development of communication skills, social skills, and personality, as the [IDEA] itself, requires." *Mary P. v. Illinois State Board of Education,* 23 IDELR 1064, 1068 (N.D. Ill. 1996).

Educational Resources and Information Center (ERIC)

A national information system supported by the **United States Department of Education** that provides information useful to educational programmers through 16 subject-specific clearinghouses, including: ERIC Clearinghouse on Adult, Career, and Vocational Education; **ERIC Clearinghouse on Assessment and Evaluation; ERIC Clearinghouse on Counseling and Student Services; ERIC Clearinghouse on Disabilities and Gifted Education;** ERIC Clearinghouse on Elementary and Early Childhood Education; ERIC Clearinghouse on Information and Technology; ERIC Clearinghouse on Languages and Linguistics; ERIC Clearinghouse on Rural Education and Small Schools; ERIC Clearinghouse on Science, Math and Environmental Education; ERIC Clearinghouse on Social Studies/Social Science Education; ERIC Clearinghouse on Teaching and Teacher Education; and ERIC Clearinghouse on Urban Education.

Education Department General Administrative Regulations (EDGAR)

Regulations promulgated by the **United States Department of Education** that concern various aspects the federal government's role in state and local educational systems; includes the following parts codified at 34 C.F.R. Part:

75 Direct Grant Programs

76 State-Administered Programs

77 Definitions that Apply to Department Regulations

79 Intergovernmental Review of Department of Education Programs and Activities

80 Uniform Administrative Requirements for Grants and Cooperative Agreements to State and Local Governments

81 General Education Provisions Act—Enforcement

86 Drug-Free Schools and Campuses.
See also **private school students with disabilities, EDGAR regulations concerning.**

Education for All Handicapped Children Act (EAHCA)

A former title of the federal law whose title was changed to the **Individuals with Disabilities Education Act (IDEA)** by federal legislation enacted in 1990; in addition, the entire language of the IDEA was changed to incorporate person-first language and use of the term "**disability**" instead of "**handicap**" (e.g., child with a disability).

Education of the Handicapped Act (EHA)

A former title of the federal law whose title was changed to the **Individuals with Disabilities Education Act (IDEA)** by federal legislation enacted in 1990; in addition, the entire language of the IDEA was changed to incorporate person-first language and use of the term "**disability**" instead of "**handicap**" (e.g., child with a disability).

education records

Defined, as a term of art, in the regulations implementing the **Family Educational Rights and Privacy Act (FERPA)** at 34 C.F.R. § 99.3 as: "those records that are: directly related to a student; and maintained by an educational agency or institution or by a party acting for the agency or institution" (but are not within the 5 exceptions set out in 34 C.F.R. § 99.3(b)(1)-(5)).

education sign system

See **sign language.**

effectively prevent

In connection with the parental right to make copies of **education records** under IDEA regulations at 34 C.F.R. § 300.562(b)(2), interpreted by the **Office of Special Education and Rehabilitative Services (OSERS)** in a policy letter as meaning that a parent resides too far from the school district to make inspection in person a reasonable option. *Letter to Kincaid,* EHLR 213:271 (OSERS 1989).

elective mutism

See **selective mutism.**

electronic speech clarifier

A speech aid that filters an individual's voice and out-

89

puts it mechanically to enhance its quality and intelligibility.

electronic travel aid (ETA) Helps blind individuals with **orientation** by sending out a signal that bounces back from objects in the path; several commercially sold models. See also **echolation device; mobility training.**

Elementary and Secondary Education Act of 1965 (ESEA) Federal law codified at 20 U.S.C. §§ 2701 et seq. that establishes various grants of federal assistance for education, including assistance for programs for **educationally deprived children** under Title 1 and development of **bilingual education** programs for students whose primary language is not English under Title VII. See also **Bilingual Education Act; limited-English proficient (LEP).**

elementary school Classification established by state law, generally composed of a span of grades not above grade 8 and may include **preschool** or kindergarten; a **day school** or residential school that provides elementary education, as determined under state law.

eligibility for special education and related services See **children with disabilities.**

emotional disorder In connection with educational programming needs, generally understood as a school-related emotional problem, such as withdrawal, depression, low self-esteem, excessive anxiety, and somatic complaints impacting interpersonal and social skills.

Educators and psychologists postulate that students with emotional disorders that do not result in disruptive behavior are "underdiagnosed" as being eligible for **special education** and **related services.**

employment outcome In connection with **vocational rehabilitation services,** defined, as a term of art, in the Rehabilitation Act of 1973 at 29 U.S.C. § 722(a)(4)(A) as: "entering or retaining full-time employment or, if appropriate, part-time **competitive [work]** in the integrated labor market (including satisfying the vocational outcome of **supported employment**)."

enclave Supported employment model involving groups of disabled adults trained and supervised by a third party public organization for employment with nondisabled workers in a private company or organization.

encoding 1. In connection with **augmentative communication systems,** an interfacing technique in which the **individual with a disability** activates a **switch** with a symbol in order to input more complex information, such as a preprogrammed sentence; most often used with students who have severe physical disabilities but intact **cognition** and memory. 2. Process of transferring information for transition from **short-term memory** to **long-term memory.**

enforced relaxation Type of manual restraint that also teaches the student to relax, used to restrain a student through physical means until he or she can control his or her behavior. See also **physical restraint.**

engaged time The amount of time a student attends to a task.

English as a second language (ESL) See **limited-English proficient (LEP).**

enrichment Educational programming for **gifted** or **talented** students in which the regular education **curriculum** is expanded to allow opportunities for more complex analysis and understanding. See also **acceleration; telescoping.**

entitlement program Generally a government program that guarantees each person identified as an intended beneficiary the right to receive the rights, **procedural safeguards,** and services that are authorized to be provided under the law.

Both Part B and Part H of the IDEA are entitlement programs, notwithstanding the fact that the states have some flexibility in determining the population of eligible children.

epicanthal fold Another term for **epicanthus.**

epicanthus A vertical fold of skin on either side of the nose extending over the skin on the inner sides of the eyes, giving the appearance of having slanted eyes; physical charac-

91

teristic associated with **Down syndrome.** See also **clinical type appearance; minor physical abnormalities.**

epilepsy Common neurological disease characterized by brief recurrent **seizures;** resulting loss of consciousness presents a safety hazard in a school environment. Also called a seizure disorder.

Overly broad restrictions on participation in school activities by students with epilepsy violates Section 504, notwithstanding the concern for safety that motivates the restrictions. For example, in *New Rochelle (NY) City School District,* 353:354 EHLR (OCR 1989), the **Office for Civil Rights (OCR)** found that the school district's guideline requiring students with epilepsy to be seizure-free for 1 year before being allowed to participate in swimming was not supported by adequate medical documentation and thus had the effect of denying otherwise qualified individuals with disabilities access to a program or activity.

episodic memory In one theoretical formulation, the memory for discrete facts and specific times. Also called semantic memory.

EPSDT screening Mandated **assessment** for Medic-

aid-eligible children that must include, at a minimum: (a) comprehensive health and developmental history in both the physical and mental health areas, (b) a comprehensive unclothed physical exam, (c) any immunizations required for the child's age and health history, (d) all laboratory tests (including blood testing for lead poisoning), (e) health education for both parents and child, (f) vision screen, (g) dental screen and (h) hearing screen.

equine therapy Horsemanship program for students with physical or psychological disabilities that may improve **muscle tone,** coordination, self-esteem and **social skills.**

Equine therapy could be reimbursable as a **related service,** provided no other item in the student's **individualized education program (IEP)** adequately provides the educational benefits the student derives from such activity. See, e.g., *East Windsor Board of Education,* 20 IDELR 1478 (SEA CT 1994).

ERIC Clearinghouse on Assessment and Evaluation Mission is to provide balanced information concerning educational assessment and resources to encourage responsible test use.

ERIC Clearinghouse on Counseling and Student Services (ERIC/CASS)

Scope includes school counseling, school social work, school psychology, mental health counseling, marriage and family counseling, and student development, as well as parent, student and teacher education in the human resources area.

ERIC Clearinghouse on Disabilities and Gifted Education (ERIC/EC)

Focuses on professional literature, information and resources relating to the education and development of persons of all ages who have disabilities or are gifted. See also **exceptional.**

Essential Tremor

A **neurological impairment** that presents as marked oscillations or tremor movements in an individual's fingers and hands, compromising one's ability to perform the **fine motor [skills]** movements entailed in holding and using writing implements.

Establishment Clause

The portion of the First Amendment to the U.S. Constitution that provides: "Congress shall make no law respecting an establishment of religion, or prohibiting the free exercise thereof. . . ." See also **excessive entanglement with religion.**

The Establishment Clause becomes an issue when a child with a disability attends a sectarian school. In *Zobrest v. Catalina Foothills School District,* 19 IDELR 921 (1981), the U.S. Supreme Court held that the Establishment Clause does not bar a school district from providing a sign language **interpreter** to a deaf student unilaterally placed by his parents at a parochial school. In so ruling, the Court left open the issue of whether a teacher or guidance counselor may be provided to a child with a disability, although it implied that such services could not be provided under the IDEA. Since *Zobrest,* the Second Circuit Court of Appeals has ruled that the First Amendment did not bar a school district from offering the services of a consultant teacher and a teacher's aide for support of core academic subjects to a 15-year-old student with **mental retardation** unilaterally placed by her parents at a parochial school. *Russman v. Sobel,* 24 IDELR 274 (2d Cir. 1996).

estoppel, collateral

Legal doctrine which prohibits the relitigation of claims in which the

    93

merits have been heard and a final judgment has been entered. See also **res judicata.**

estoppel, promissory

Legal doctrine which prevents a party to a lawsuit from asserting or denying a fact or set of facts in court when, by that party's previous conduct, the opponent in the litigation relied on the conduct in proceeding and would be at a disadvantage in the litigation if the opposing party were permitted to take an inconsistent position in the lawsuit; similar in concept to **waiver.** See also **estoppel, collateral.**

> Estoppel may be used in an IDEA action to, for example, bar an **LEA** from asserting the **statute of limitations** when it advises a parent to defer bringing an action. But the suitability of the estoppel doctrine when the issue is **free appropriate public education (FAPE)** as a substantive matter raises other concerns. As stated in the administrative decision in *Philadelphia School District,* 18 IDELR 846, 848 (SEA PA 1991): "[P]arent's counsel has cited no authority for the position that a child's FAPE should be determined by the doctrine of estoppel, rather than consideration of a child's disabilities and educational needs. We harbor serious doubts whether estoppel should be used in such a manner."

etiology Cause of disease or disability.

evaluation 1. Generally, an **assessment** conducted to determine eligibility and programming requirements for a child with a disability. 2. In connection with Part B of the IDEA, defined, as a term of art, in Part B regulations at 34 C.F.R. § 300.500(b) as: "procedures used in accordance with §§ 300.530-300.534 to determine whether a child has a disability and the nature and extent of the **special education** and **related services** that the child needs. The term means procedures used selectively with an individual child and does not include basic tests administered to or procedures used with all children in a school, grade or class." 3. In connection with Part H of the IDEA, defined, as a term of art, in Part H regulations at 34 C.F.R. § 303.322(b)(2) as: "the procedures used by appropriate qualified personnel to determine a child's initial and continuing eligibility under this part, consistent with the definition of 'infants and toddlers with handicaps' in S[ection] 303.16, including determining the status of the child in each of the developmental areas in paragraph (c)(3)(ii) of this section." As distinguished from **screening.**

event recording An observational recording method for the **systematic observation of behavior** in which a trained observer records all the instances of a specifically identified behavior; similar to **interval recording** except that the unit of measurement is the occurrence of the behavior rather than a specific fixed interval of time.

exceptional 1. In connection with children, a term used to indicate both students with disabilities and students who are considered **gifted** or **talented.** 2. Children whose mental, emotional, physical, social or sensory needs are sufficiently different from most of their chronological peers to require special services to benefit from education.

excess cost requirement Requirement in the IDEA (20 U.S.C. § 1414(a)(1)) designed to ensure that state and local agencies serving **children with disabilities** under Part B spend at least as much of other funds on their education as is spent, on average, for the children in that school district as a whole. See also **excess costs.**

excess costs In connection with Part B funding, those costs that are greater than the minimum average amount a school district or other **local educational agency** spends on children as a whole; defined, as a term of art, in the IDEA at 20 U.S.C. § 1401(a)(21) as: "those costs which are in excess of the average annual per student expenditure in a local educational agency during the preceding school year for an **elementary [school]** or **secondary school** student, as may be appropriate, and which shall be computed after deducting—(A) amounts received (i) under this subchapter, (ii) under chapter 1 of Title I of the Elementary and Secondary Education Act of 1965 . . . and (B) any State or local funds expended for programs that would qualify for assistance under such subchapter, chapter or title."

excessive entanglement with religion A circum-

95

stance that raises the bar of the **Establishment Clause** when providing federally funded educational services to students attending sectarian schools is at issue.

The U.S. Supreme Court held in *Aguilar v. Felton,* 473 U.S. 402 (1985), that public school employees could not provide remedial instruction to economically disadvantaged parochial school students pursuant to Title 1 of the **Elementary and Secondary Education Act** because that would result in excessive entanglement with religion. While the **Office of Special Education Programs (OSEP)** interprets the *Aguilar* case as applying only to Title 1 (*Letter to Orschel,* 16 EHLR 1368 (OSEP 1990)), some commentators believe such a distinction between ESEA or IDEA services is not meaningful.

excluded medical services Physician services for **children with disabilities** that are not necessary for the purposes of **diagnosis** and **evaluation**; by implication of Part B regulations at 34 C.F.R. § 300.16(b)(4) not **related services.**

Several courts have interpreted excluded medical services to be not only "physician services for other than diagnosis or evaluation" but other services performed by nonphysicians that are costly or complex, such as the range of services often required for a **ventilator-dependent** child to attend school. For example, the Sixth Circuit Court of Appeals decision in *Neely v. Rutherford County School,* 23 IDELR 334 (6th Cir. 1995), held that continuous care services needed to sustain life are excluded medical services, not related services for which the school district was responsible.

exclusionary clause In connection with **related services,** a clause contained in any health insurance policy that excludes insurance coverage for services or equipment that the insured is entitled to receive under federal law, such as the IDEA. See also **similar third party.**

According to the **Office of Special Education and Rehabilitative Services (OSERS),** prohibitions on exclusionary clauses are solely a matter of state law and not subject to regulation by the **United States Department of Education** under the IDEA. *Letter to Harmon,* EHLR 213:236 (OSERS 1989).

exhaustion of administrative remedies The doctrine set out in the IDEA at 20 U.S.C. § 1415(e)(2) that generally requires a litigant (a parent or school district) to pursue the statutory **administrative remedies** (i.e., follow the due process procedures) before seeking relief in court.

expanded keyboard A **keyboard for an individual with a disability** in which keys are larger and have more space between them, as well as other helpful features such as concavity.

expressive language An individual's written, oral or symbolic communication. See also **expressive language disorder; receptive language.**

expressive language disorder A language disorder the diagnostic criteria for which is defined in the DSM-IV as: "A. The scores obtained from standardized individually administered measures of individual expressive language development are substantially below those obtained from standardized measures of both nonverbal intellectual capacity and receptive language development. The disturbance may be manifest clinically by symptoms that include having a markedly limited vocabulary, making errors in tense, or having difficulty recalling words or

producing sentences with developmentally appropriate length or complexity; B. The difficulties with expressive language interfere with academic or occupational achievement or social communication; C. Criteria are not met for Mixed Receptive-Expressive Language Disorder or a **Pervasive Developmental Disorder;** D. If mental retardation, a speech-motor or sensory deficit, or environmental deprivation is present, the language difficulties are in excess of those usually associated with these problems."

expulsion Generally, a complete termination of educational services for an extended period of time; state laws generally specify grounds for which a school board may expel a student and set a legal and procedural framework for making the determination. As distinguished from **suspension.** See also **long-term suspension.**

expunge In connection with **education records, destruction** of inappropriate or incorrect records or entries.

Extended Merrill-Palmer Scale Individually administered test for children between the ages of 3 and 5 years that evaluates both what the test-taker thinks (thought content) and his or her thinking processes; contains 16 tasks measuring 4 Structure of Intellect dimensions (semantics, figural, production, and evaluation), the first 2 relating to thought content and the latter 2 to thought process; useful in assessing children with motor or language disabilities.

extended school day (ESD) programming

May be required under the IDEA as part of a comprehensive program of instruction and services offered to students with qualifying disabilities who require additional hours of a structured setting and consistent application of behavior-related programming.

ESD programming sometimes is used as an alternative to **residential placement** for students with **serious emotional disturbances** or **severe mental retardation.** Conversely, there may be students whose disabilities prohibit participation in a full day of programming and services. For these students, a shortened school day is not a denial of **free appropriate public education (FAPE).** See, e.g., *Christopher M. v.*

Corpus Christi Independent School District, 17 EHLR 990 (5th Cir. 1991).

extended school year (ESY) programming

Special education programming that extends beyond the 180 days of the traditional school year.

Under settled authoritative case law, school districts are required to provide ESY programming to IDEA-eligible students for whom it is appropriate, even if the school district does not ordinarily provide summer school or other educational services outside the regular school year. Generally a regression-recoupment analysis [**regression-recoupment problem**] must be performed to determine whether a student with a disability requires ESY programming to receive **free appropriate public education (FAPE).** In addition, at least one court—the Tenth Circuit in *Johnson v. Independent School District,* 17 EHLR 170 (10th Cir. 1990)—has identified a range of factors, in addition to regression-recoupment analysis, that may need to be considered when evaluating whether a student with a disability should receive ESY programming.

extended services

Ongoing support services provided under the **Vocational Rehabilitation and Other Rehabilitation Services Act** to those individuals with **severe disabilities** who require such services for support and maintenance in **supported employment** (29 U.S.C. § 706(27)).

extinction In connection with **behavior management,** a procedure to decrease undesired behaviors by withdrawing attention from a **target behavior** that used to be negatively reinforced, such as ignoring a tantrum, on the theory that the target behavior is maintained by attention and the withdrawal of attention will result in the child ceasing to perform that behavior.

extinction burst A dramatic increase or burst of performance of an inappropriate behavior that may occur before the behavior decreases when a behavior management technique involving **reinforcement of alternative behaviors** is used.

extracurricular activities Programs sponsored by a school district that are not part of the required **curriculum** but are instead offered to further the interests and abilities of students. See also **non-academic and extracurricular services and activities.**

eye coordination The ability of an individual to focus both eyes on the same object.

eyegaze input system A computer input method for individuals with motor disabilities who cannot use a keyboard that involves an interface to track the eye movements of the user as he or she looks at different squares on an on-screen keyboard and to accept the key if the gaze lasts longer than 2 seconds. See also **alternative input interface.**

FAE fetal alcohol effects

FAS fetal alcohol syndrome

FERPA Family Educational Rights and Privacy Act

FPCO Family Policy Compliance Office

FTE full-time equivalent

facilitated communication A technique used for certain nonverbal individuals, such as those with **autism,** in which the disabled individual's hand, wrist, elbow or shoulder is held by another as he or she spells out messages by pointing to or typing the appropriate letters on a keyboard or an alphabet display board.

The theory marshaled in support of this technique is that only the communications skills of the disabled individual are impaired, his or her cognitive ability and other receptive skills are substantially intact, thus the individual has information to impart. The validity of facilitated communication is an open issue in the educational field. Many agree with the Virginia review officer's opinion that it is "almost certainly bogus." *Loudoun County Public School,* 22 IDELR 833, 834 (SEA VA 1995).

fading **Behavior modification** technique involving the gradual elimination of stimulus that had been used as an **antecedent** for a desired **target behavior.**

failure to thrive When a child is not putting on the appropriate amount of weight or is not gaining weight appropriately (in terms of muscle, bone and tissue weight, as opposed to fluid weight).

family assessment In connection with Part H, an as-

101

sessment to determine the strengths and needs of the family as they relate to enhancing the development of the child.

family counseling Generally, counseling premised on the conviction that interlocking emotional problems within a family result in dysfunctional behavior by one or more of its members; may be a **related service** under Part B of the IDEA (34 C.F.R. § 300.16(b)(12)(ii)). As distinguished from **family therapy.**

> In connection with a student with a disability, the goal of family counseling is to create positive changes in the student by counseling family members to change their interactions with each other. While family counseling need not be essential for a student with a disability to benefit from **special education,** there must be a nexus between the counseling and the educational needs of the student. Thus, in *Board of Education of Portage Public Schools,* 23 IDELR 667 (SEA MI 1995), an administrative decisionmaker ruled that family counseling was a related service for a 14-year-old student because the parents' perceptions about their son's abilities and limitations and their resulting expectations for his educational performance were adversely affecting his ability to benefit from his educational programming.

Family Educational Rights and Privacy Act (FERPA) 1. Federal law protecting the privacy of students and parents by mandating that **personally identifiable information** about a student contained in **education records** generally must be kept confidential in the absence of written parental consent to their release and that school districts keep a record of all organizations to whom it releases education records; enacted as part of the **General Education Provisions Act (GEPA)** and codified at 20 U.S.C. § 1232. 2. Incorporated in the IDEA as the **Buckley Amendment,** which also gives parents and eligible students the right to access education records from any educational institution that receives funds from the **United States Department of Education.**

Family Policy Compliance Office (FPCO) The office within the **United States Department of Education** charged with enforcement of the **Buckley Amendment,** including investigating and resolving complaints of parents who believe their privacy rights have been violated.

family support services

Defined, as a term of art, in the federal **Developmental Disabilities Assistance and Bill of Rights Act of 1975** at 42 U.S.C. § 6001(11) as: "services, supports, and other assistance provided to families with members with developmental disabilities that are designed to—strengthen the family's role as primary caregiver; prevent inappropriate out-of-the-home placement and maintain family unity; and reunite families with members who have been placed out of the home, whenever possible. Such term includes **respite care, rehabilitation technology, personal assistance services,** parent training and counseling. . . ."

family therapy

A therapeutic method in which problems of individuals are treated in the context of interaction among members of a family unit.

> Family and marital therapy is one of the 4 recognized mental health disciplines, the others being psychiatry, psychology and social work. According to the **Office for Civil Rights (OCR),** family therapy is not the same as **family counseling** and is not considered a **related service.** *Township High School (IL) District #211,* EHLR 352:289 (OCR 1986). Nevertheless, published administrative decisions show that family therapy is occasionally provided or awarded as a related service, particularly when it is a part of the treatment regime of a facility in which the student has been placed for educational purposes.

family training, counseling and home visits

An **early intervention service** under Part H, defined at 34 C.F.R. § 303.12(d)(3) as: "services provided, as appropriate, by social workers, psychologists, and other qualified personnel to assist the family of a child eligible under this part in understanding the special needs of the child and enhancing the child's development."

federal financial assistance

In connection with Section 504 of the Rehabilitation Act of 1973 and federal education law generally, defined, as a term of art, in **ED-GAR regulations** at 34 C.F.R. § 77.1(b): "assistance provided by a Federal agency in the form of **grants,** contracts, cooperative agreements, loans, loan

103

guarantees, property, interest, subsidies, insurance, or direct appropriations, but does not include direct Federal cash assistance to individuals. It includes awards received directly from Federal agencies, or indirectly through other units of State and local governments." See also **recipient of federal financial assistance.**

fetal alcohol effects (FAE) Considered in some professional circles to be a cluster of abnormalities, including learning problems and behavioral problems, associated with a mother's consumption of alcohol during pregnancy. See also **fetal alcohol syndrome.**

fetal alcohol syndrome (FAS) Cluster of abnormalities that presents at birth or in infancy as low birth weight and **central nervous system (CNS)** impairments, such as **developmental delays** or **mental retardation,** in children whose mothers consumed relatively large amounts of alcohol during pregnancy; associated with **clinical type appearance** of short **palpebral fissures;** elongated, flattened midface; thin

upper lip; and underdeveloped **philtrum** between the upper lip and the nose.

field of vision The entire area one can see without shifting one's gaze; normal is considered 160 to 180 degrees on the horizontal plane and 120 degrees on the vertical plane.

figure-background disturbance An individual's inability to distinguish important from irrelevant aspects of one's environment.

fine motor skills Ability to use and manipulate the small muscle groups, primarily in the hands; involved in activities such as drawing and writing. As distinguished from **gross motor skills.**

Occupational therapy is a **related service** typically provided to **children with disabilities** who have **deficits** with their fine motor skills.

finger spelling Manual communication method in which 26 distinct hand configurations are used to form the letters of the alphabet, used mainly to supplement English-based sign languages. Distinguished from **American Sign**

Language (ASL), which is not English-based.

firearm Defined, as a term of art, in the federal crimes code at 18 U.S.C. § 921 as: "any weapon (including a starter gun) which will or is designed to or may readily be converted to expel a projectile by the action of the explosive; the frame or receiver of any such weapon; any firearm muffler or firearm silencer; or any **destructive device.** Such term does not include an antique firearm."

> The **Gun-Free Schools Act** and the **Jeffords Amendment** both adopt this definition to describe the **weapons** which, if brought into school, trigger their provisions. In so doing, these laws exclude knives. BB guns (also called pellet guns or air rifles), not having an explosive device, also appear to be outside the scope of the definition.

first priority children In connection with use of Part B funds by **state educational agencies (SEAs)** and **local educational agencies (LEAs),** defined, as a term of art, in Part B regulations at 34 C.F.R. § 300.320(a) as: "**children with disabilities** who—(1) are in an age group for which the State must make **FAPE** available under [34 C.F.R.] § 300.300 [of the Part B regulations]; and (2) are not receiving any education." See also **second priority children.**

fissure An opening or failure to close, as in, for example, a **cleft palate.**

"five-day rule" The **due process hearing** right set out in Part B regulations at 34 C.F.R. § 300.508(a)(3) that "prohibit[s] the introduction of any evidence at the hearing that has not been disclosed to [the opposing] party at least five days before the hearing."

> The purpose of the five-day rule is to give parties adequate time to prepare before the hearing and to prevent the introduction of "surprise" evidence that could give an unfair advantage to the party presenting it.

fixation ability Ability to accurately and smoothly visually track a moving object or a line of print; inability or **deficit** in ability termed a **visual tracking impairment.**

flaccid In connection with **muscle tone,** lacking normal degree of tension.

> Abnormal muscle tone is a distinguishing characteristic of **cerebral**

palsy and related problems. When muscle tone is too low it is too flaccid to fix posture. When it is too high, it interferes with mobility. In either case, **physical therapy** to normalize tonic reflex patterns may be a **related service.** For example, the multidisabled student in *Polk v. Central Susquehanna Intermediate Unit 16,* 1988-89 EHLR 441:130 (3d Cir. 1988), received **physical therapy** because he needed to learn to use his muscles properly in order to learn basic skills.

flight of ideas Rapid progression of thought characterized by shifting from one topic to the next with considerable digression from the beginning to the end of the expressed thought. See also **circumstantiality.**

The speaker's changing topics have some interconnection that others can discern, thus he or she has the appearance of lucidity. On the whole, though, the speaker's communication is not goal-oriented, but rather is susceptible to distraction.

floppy infant An infant who is droopy and does not seem to have the normal degree of **muscle tone** or resistance to movements; in the extreme such an infant acts like a rag doll, as compared to the normal infant who remains relatively stiff or at least firmly resistant to unwanted movements and can keep his or her head up.

fluency problem A speech impairment such as **stuttering.**

FM trainer A device that amplifies and transmits voices to earphones worn by an individual with a **hearing impairment** who is able to benefit from wearing a hearing aid.

fonator Device used by deaf individuals to convert spoken words into vibrations to supplement **lip reading** with tactile information. See also **cued speech.**

formal assessment Evaluation using standardized **norm-referenced test.** As distinguished from **informal assessment.**

form constancy Ability to recognize printed letters or other symbolic communication despite changes in appearance in color, size, background and the like.

forward-chaining In connection with basic skills training, the instructional method

that breaks a task into temporal component parts and gradually requires the individual receiving instruction to finish a task by starting with the first component of the task sequence and performing progressively more components in the task sequence. See also **back-chaining; chaining.**

foster care services Governmental provision of services or activities involving providing alternative family life experience for abused, neglected or dependent children; may involve placement of a child in a private individual or group home to take the place of the parental home usually for a temporary period; not synonymous with adoption. See also **foster parent; protective services.**

foster parent Generally an individual with whom a governmental unit places a child under its custody or control for care, usually on a temporary basis and in exchange for remuneration. See also **foster care services; parent; person acting as a parent of a child; surrogate parent.**

Part B regulations at 34 C.F.R. § 300.13 defining the term "parent" for purposes of the IDEA do not address the role of foster parents and neither require nor prohibit a state from recognizing a foster parent as a "parent." According to the **Office of Special Education Programs (OSEP),** states may permit foster parents to act as "parents" under the IDEA on a case-by-case basis based on the applicable state law concerning foster children, the length of the relationship and other pertinent factors. *Letter to Baker,* 20 IDELR 1169 (OSEP 1993).

four pillars of assessment Considered the necessary components for an informed **evaluation** of a child: (a) **norm-referenced tests,** (b) **interviews,** (c) **observations** and (d) **informal assessments.**

Fourteenth Amendment to the Constitution In connection with education, provides, in relevant part, that no State may deprive any person of life, liberty or property without due process of law. See also **minimum due process; Section 1983.**

While the U.S. Supreme Court has held that education is not a fundamental constitutional right (*Pyler v. Doe,* 457 U.S. 202 (1982)), its pronouncements in *Pyler* and other cases establish the importance it places on

107

education. Furthermore, in *Goss v. Lopez*, 419 U.S. 565 (1975), the Court held that, to the extent a state directs local authorities to provide free public education and establishes compulsory school attendance, the entitlement of school-age children to a public education creates a property interest which cannot be taken away without due process.

Fragile X syndrome Chromosomal abnormalities more frequently found in males and associated with **mental retardation, speech and language impairments** and behavioral dysfunctions; typical appearance of an individual with this condition includes a large head, large ears and elongated features. See also **clinical type appearance; minor physical abnormalities.**

free In connection with the right to a **free appropriate public education (FAPE)** under Section 504, defined, as a term of art, in Section 504 regulations at 34 C.F.R. § 104.33(c)(1) as: "the provision of educational and related services without cost to the handicapped person or to his or her parents or guardian, except for those fees that are imposed on non-handicapped persons or their parents or guardian." See also **at no cost; public expense; without charge.**

free appropriate public education (FAPE) 1. The entitlement of every child with a disability under both the IDEA and Section 504. 2. Defined, as a term of art, in the IDEA at 20 U.S.C. § 1401(a)(18) as: "**special education** and **related services** that—(A) have been provided at public expense, under public supervision and direction, and without charge; (B) meet the standards of the **State educational agency;** (C) include an **appropriate** preschool, elementary, or secondary school education in the State involved, and; (D) are provided in conformity with the **individualized education program** required under § 1414(a)(5) of this title." 3. Undefined in Section 504, although the concept of "appropriate" is given a regulatory definition. See also **special education, six basic principles of.**

There are 5 common characteristics of FAPE under both the IDEA and Section 504:

(1) FAPE is available to all children without regard to severity of disability **(zero reject principle).**
(2) FAPE is provided without cost to parents.
(3) FAPE consists of individualized programming and related services.
(4) FAPE provides an education that is appropriate, but not the best possible.
(5) FAPE is provided in the **least restrictive environment (LRE).**

frequency and intensity

In connection with **early intervention services** under Part H, descriptors of the services to be provided that must be included in the child's **Individualized Family Service Plan (IFSP);** defined, as a term of art, in Part H regulations at 34 C.F.R. § 303.344(d)(2)(i) as: "the number of days or sessions that a service will be provided, the length of time the service is provided at each session, and whether the service is provided on an individual or group basis."

Compare the above to the different requirement for **individualized education programs (IEPs)** under Part B. According to the **Office of Special Education Programs (OSEP),** school districts are not required to specify in the IEP the amount of services to be provided in terms of hours and minutes. However, when the na-

ture of the service lends itself to such description, precise daily allotments of services is preferred. *Letter to Copenhaver,* 21 IDELR 1183 (OSEP 1994).

frontal lobe
Front part of the brain involved in higher cognitive functions, such as planning and **abstract thinking.** See also **lobes of the brain.**

frustration tolerance
Ability to complete a task in the face of past failure or threat of failure.

full inclusion
Generally means integration of a student with a disability in **regular education** classrooms for 100% of his or her school day. See also **inclusion; integration and inclusion; mainstreaming.**

full scale IQ
Norm-referenced composite of **verbal scale** and **performance scale IQ** scores used to measure **intelligence,** in a global sense.

A significant disparity between an individual's performance and verbal IQ scores may be indicative of a **learning disability,** although it does not establish eligibility under the IDEA. See **severe discrepancy between achievement and intellectual ability.** Blending divergent scores can give a misleading assessment of performance. See **Wechsler Verbal-Performance Scale discrepancies.**

full-time equivalent (FTE)
Analysis of manpower needs on the basis of how many individuals working a customary full daily or weekly schedule are required to carry out the functions of that position or professional classification as a whole.

functional curriculum
Programming for **educable mentally retarded** students that emphasizes successful living in the community.

functional language
Communication skills used by an individual with a **severe disability** to make needs known.

functional literacy
The level of reading and communication ability one needs to live independently in the community, usually considered reading and communicating skills above the 4th-grade level.

functional reading
Educational program for students with mental disabilities that teaches basic "reading to survive" for vocational and daily living competence (traffic and restroom signs, for example). Also called survival reading.

functional skills
Generally considered skills for self-care, **social skills,** domestic maintenance (housekeeping), employment or vocational skills and recreation. Also called independent living skills.

functional skills training
Educational programming that instructs students with mental disabilities in the competencies needed for everyday living that most children learn incidentally from their environment or by **generalization.**

G

GED General Educational Development Test

GEPA General Education Provisions Act

Gastro Button A short tube that fits against the skin of the abdomen with a small plug that can be removed for feeding; used when a child with a disability is unable to ingest nutrition orally; less intrusive method of feeding than **gastrotomy tube feeding.**

gastrotomy tube feeding Provides liquid nutrients or medication through a tube extending through the abdomen to the stomach; used when a child with a disability is unable to ingest nutrition orally. Also called jejunostomy. See also **Gastro Button; nasogastric tube feeding; school health services.**

Gastrotomy tube feeding generally is considered to be in the class of health-related services, also including **clean intermittent catheterization, tracheotomy care,** changing of dressings or ostomy collection bags, that are **related services** under the IDEA and Section 504. See, e.g, *Letter to Del Polito,* EHLR 211:392 (OSEP 1986).

General Educational Development Test (GED) Test administered by the American Council on Education as the basis for awarding a high school equivalent certification.

General Education Provisions Act (GEPA) Federal legislation codified at 20 U.S.C. §§ 1221-1234 concerning the **United States Department of Education**'s administration of most programs within its authority.

generalization Ability to apply a skill or behavior learned in one setting to another setting or ability to apply a learned skill or behavior in similar situations.

Some **children with disabilities** are not able to easily or automatically transfer skills learned in the classroom to other environments, such as the home, under differing stimuli and differing distractions. Thus, such a child with a disability may have learned something in the classroom, yet not know it in any other environment. If no generalization of learning occurs, then a child with a disability will show no benefit from his or her education upon leaving school.

An issue that rises repeatedly in **special education** litigation concerning children with disabilities such as **autism** or **severe mental retardation** is whether a student who has not carried over into the home setting the behavioral gains made in the school environment has received an educational benefit from his or her program. Typically parents argue that without generalization of learned behavior across settings, there was no education. School districts, on the other hand, maintain that their responsibility to provide **free appropriate public education (FAPE)** does not extend into matters such as behavior at home, over which it has no control. Courts generally agree with the school districts, although this is by no means unanimous. Two well-reasoned judicial decisions that discuss the role of generalization in the provision of FAPE are *M.C. v. Central Regional School District,* 22 IDELR 1036 (D.N.J. 1995), *aff'd,* 23 IDELR 1181 (3d Cir. 1996) and *Rebecca S. v. Clarke County School District,* 22 IDELR 884 (M.D. Ga. 1995).

genius A colloquial, rather than scientific or educational, term generally understood as exceptionally high mental ability, with an **IQ score** of at least 150.

genuine opportunity for equitable participation In connection with the obligations of school districts to **private school students with disabilities,** what a **state educational agency (SEA)** and **local educational agency (LEA),** as a result of their receipt of **federal financial assistance,** are required to provide parentally placed private school children under **Education Department General Administrative Regulations (EDGAR)** at 34 C.F.R. § 76.651(a)(1). See also **comparable benefits; private school students with disabilities, EDGAR regulations concerning.**

The EDGAR regulations provide that, inter alia, benefits for private school students must be comparable to those provided to publicly enrolled students and those benefits must be determined after consultation with representatives of private school students. The **United States Department of Education** has interpreted the requirement to provide a genuine opportunity for equitable participation narrowly, stating that the "IDEA does not provide children [with disabilities] enrolled by their parents in private schools ... with an individual entitlement to receive **special education** and **related services.**" *Letter to Mentink,* 18 IDELR 276 (OSEP 1991). Under the Department of Education's interpretation, a school district can comply with the EDGAR regulations even if it elects to not serve every parentally placed child with a disability in its jurisdiction and/or to not provide the full range of Part B services to those children with disabilities it does choose to serve.

gifted A designation used in many states for exceptional children eligible for special educational programming on the basis of exceptionally outstanding intellectual ability, typically defined as having a score in a standardized **intelligence test** that is at least 2 **standard deviations** above the **mean** or an **IQ score** of a least 130, and 1 or more other traits or abilities, such as creativity. As distin-

guished from **talented.** See also **gifted and talented.**

gifted and learning disabled Students identified as exhibiting remarkable talents or strengths in some areas and disabling deficits in others; as a general matter historically grouped into 3 subcategories based on previous identification by the school: (a) identified **gifted** students with unidentified subtle **learning disabilities;** (b) unidentified students whose gifts and disabilities are both masked by average academic achievement; and (c) identified students with learning disabilities whose giftedness has not been identified.

gifted and talented 1. A designation used in some states for exceptional children eligible for special educational programming, typically defined as having unusually high intellectual ability, e.g., having an **IQ score** of a least 130 and one or more other traits or abilities, such as creativity, or having a high degree of ability in the creative or performing arts and, as a result, being capable of high performance. 2. Defined in Section 902 of the **Gifted and Talented Children's Education Act** as: "children and, whenever applicable, **youth,** who are identified at the **preschool, elementary [school],** or **secondary [school]** level as possessing demonstrated or potential abilities that give evidence of high performance capability in areas such as intellectual, creative, specific academic, or leadership ability, or in the performing and visual arts, and who by reason thereof, require services or activities not ordinarily provided by the school."

Gifted and Talented Children's Education Act

Title IX of the federal **Elementary and Secondary Education Act of 1965 (ESEA)** (codified at 20 U.S.C. §§ 2701 et seq.) that establishes **grants** of **federal financial assistance** for programs for gifted and talented children.

Goals 2000: Educate America Act

Federal legislation that provides **grants** to school districts that establish and meet challenging objectives for **academic achievement;** codified at 20 U.S.C. §§ 580 et seq.

grade equivalent score

Ranging from .01 to 12.9, a score that describes a student's test performance in terms of grade and month of the typical student who performs the same on the test.

For example, if a 6th-grader has a grade equivalent score of 8.2 on a test measuring performance on 6th-grade material, that means he or she has performed at the same level as the typical student of that grade (8.2) being tested on the same material. Grade equivalent scores are often misunderstood by parents or other non-educators, who misinterpret the above score to mean that the 6th-grade test-taker is capable of performing at an 8th-grade academic level or has been tested on 8th-grade-level material.

grade-level

1. Generally the level of classroom performance of a student who is learning material at about the same rate and quality as others in the same class. 2. When used in connection with a **standardized test**, scoring at the 50th **percentile rank,** meaning that about half the student's peers score higher and about half score lower.

Grade I Braille Introductory written tactile communication method for blind individuals in which every letter of every word is spelled out. See also **Braille cell; Grade II Braille; Grade III Braille.**

Grade II Braille Standard written tactile communication method for blind individuals in which about 300 contractions or abbreviations (combination of **Braille cells** to shorten word length) for common words are used as a shorthand to increase speed. See also **Braille cell; Grade I Braille; Grade III Braille.**

Grade III Braille Advanced written tactile communication method for blind individuals that uses a wide range of abbreviations and spacing conventions, making it similar to shorthand; vastly increases speed but may come at too high a cost in terms of complexity for most individuals. See also **Nemeth code.**

grammar In connection with **linguistic systems,** meaningful word order.

grant An award of financial assistance in the form of money or property. See also **federal financial assistance.**

grantee In connection with federal funding provided for education, the legal entity to which a **grant** of federal funding (for example, funds awarded under Part B of the IDEA) is awarded and which is accountable to the federal government for expenditure of the funds in accordance with the terms of the grant.

grapheme Visual shape of a letter of the alphabet.

graphesthesia Ability to recognize letters traced on one's skin; inability to do so is a **neurological soft sign.**

gross motor skills Ability to use and manipulate the large muscle groups involved in activities such as running and throwing; implicates body control, balance and coordination. As distinguished from **fine motor skills.**

group home Living arrangement to promote independence of disabled individuals

115

who cannot live at their family home; a residential environment within the community in which about 10 adults or adolescents with mental or physical disabilities who are elsewhere during the day live with appropriate amount of assistance and supervision; can be a permanent or transitional situation.

guardian In connection with children, a person not a parent who is appointed by a court as legally responsible for the child's care, management of his or her finances, or both.

> As made clear in Part B IDEA regulations at 34 C.F.R. § 300.13, a guardian is a **"parent"** for purposes of the IDEA. This is also the case for Part H, as specified in Part H regulations at 34 C.F.R. § 303.18.

guidance counselor School staff member whose activities involve counseling students and parents, consulting with other staff members on learning problems, evaluating the abilities of students, assisting students in personal and social development, providing referral assistance, and working with other staff members in planning and conducting guidance programs for students.

guinea pig effect In connection with direct **observation** as an **assessment** technique, a common change in a child's behavior because he or she is aware of and reacting to the observation. Also called reactivity. See also **halo effect.**

Gun-Free Schools Act
Federal legislation enacted in 1994 requiring school districts and similar **public agencies** to adopt a policy generally requiring the **expulsion** from school for a period of not less than 1 year of any student determined to have brought a **weapon** to school, although permitting exceptions to be made on a case-by-case basis for **children with disabilities;** codified at 20 U.S.C. § 3351.

> To implement the Gun-Free Schools Act consistently with the IDEA, as the law requires, school districts must proceed as directed by the **Office of Special Education Programs (OSEP)** in *OSEP Policy Memorandum 95-16,* 22 IDELR 531, 537 (OSEP 1995). Under that guidance, a student with a disability may be expelled only after a group of persons composed in accordance with the regulations governing composition of the **IEP team** or the **multidisciplinary team** determines whether or not a student's act of bringing of a fire-

arm into school was a manifestation of his or her disability. If so, the school official charged with administering the Gun-Free Schools Act is barred from expelling the student. If, on the other hand, the team determines that the behavior was not a manifestation of the student's disability, then the official may decide, "in the same manner as with nondisabled students in similar circumstances, whether or not to modify the expulsion requirement."

H

HCO hearing carry over services

HCPA Handicapped Children's Protection Act

H-NTLA Hiskey-Nebraska Test of Learning Aptitude

habilitation 1. Generally, the process of using various professional services to help individuals with disabilities maximize their vocational, social and mental abilities so they can live in the community as independently as possible, typically involved in connection with adults with **cerebral palsy, mental retardation** or **autism.** 2. In connection with many state laws providing assistance for individuals with **developmental disabilities,** a term of art referring to the education, training and care required to be provided to individuals eligible for services to help them reach their maximum development and the process by which such individuals are assisted in acquiring and maintaining life skills for coping more effectively with self-care, economic self-sufficiency and social interactions. As distinguished from **rehabilitation.**

habilitation plan A program designed for an individual receiving assistance under the **Developmental Disabilities Assistance and Bill of Rights Act of 1975** or similar state laws to assist eligible individuals in developing successful independent living skills; includes an assessment of the individual's strengths and weaknesses and a treatment plan. See also **individual habilitation plan (IHP).**

habilitation services, eligibility for Established under the federal **Developmental Disabilities Assistance and Bill of Rights Act of 1975,** at 42 U.S.C. § 6001(8), as an individual 5 years or older who has a severe chronic disability that is "attributable to a mental or physical impairment or combination of mental and physical impairments; manifested before age 22; likely to continue indefinitely; result[ing] in substantial functional limitations in 3 or more of the following areas of **major life activity:** self-care; receptive and expressive language; learning; mobility; self-direction; capacity for independent living and economic self-sufficiency; and reflect[ing] the person's need for a combination and sequence of special, interdisciplinary or general services, supports or other assistance that is of lifelong or extended duration and is individually planned and coordinated." As distinguished from **rehabilitative services.**

halo effect In connection with **systematic observation** of **behavior,** when the observer's general favorable impression of the child compromises his or her ability to observe and record behavior objectively. See also **guinea pig effect.**

Halstead-Reitan Neuropsychological Test Battery 14 tests, including tactual performance, aphasia screening test, speech sounds perception test and sensory imperception, to assess suspected brain damage; 2 versions, 1 designed for children between the ages of 5 and 8 years and the other for children between the ages of 9 and 14 years.

The test has a range of scores from 0 to 98. A score between 0 and 25 indicates no organic disability; a score of 26 and 40 indicates a mild disability; a score between 41 and 60 indicates a moderate disability; and a score between 61 and 90 indicates a severe disability.

hand-eye coordination The ability of an individual to combine and coordinate the function of one's eyes and hands to use one's hands for manipulative activities.

Successful performance of manipulative activities also requires adequate **fine motor skills.**

handicap Not a currently accepted synonym for "**disability**" or "**impairment.**"

Both the Rehabilitation Act of 1973 and the IDEA included the terms "handicap" and "handicapped" when originally enacted, with the terminology of the IDEA being updated in 1990 and the Rehabilitation Act in 1992.

handicapped Not a currently accepted descriptor for individuals who have disabilities.

Handicapped Children's Protection Act (HCPA) 1986 amendment to the IDEA permitting the award of **attorneys' fees** to a **prevailing party** under the IDEA and permitting **parents** to assert rights available under other applicable federal law in addition to the IDEA, providing the parent first complies with the IDEA's requirement for **exhaustion of administrative remedies;** codified at 20 U.S.C. § 1415(e)(4)(B)-(F).

handling How a child with a physical disability is picked up, carried, held and assisted.

handstick An **alternative input interface** for an individual who cannot use a keyboard but is able to grasp objects, allows the individual to push buttons with a stick.

hard of hearing Nonscientific term understood as meaning that one has a **hearing impairment** that usually makes it difficult, but not impossible, to understand speech (usually between 35-69 **decibels**).

harelip Congenital split or opening of the upper lip often associated with a **cleft palate.**

Head Start Federal program enacted in 1965 providing comprehensive health, educational, nutritional, social and other services to "economically disadvantaged" **preschool** children and their families to help better the chances for success in school; codified at 42 U.S.C. §§ 9831 et seq.

The Head Start legislation mandates enrollment opportunities for eligible **children with disabilities.** Under Part H (at 20 U.S.C. § 1476(b)(9)(B)) the Part H **lead agency** must identify and coordinate all available federal programs that provide **early intervention services,** including the Head Start program.

headstick An **alternative input interface** consisting of a pointer or extension device mounted to a headpiece, extending from the center of the forehead and angling downward for use as a **direct selection** device by an **individual with a disability** who is unable to use his or her hands to depress keys or make selections on a computer keyboard or **communication board.** Also called a headwand.

headwand See **headstick.**

health assessment In connection with **school health services,** the collection and analysis of information about the health situation of a student with a disability to determine his or her need for health-related supportive services.

health impairment Generally, a disease or other health condition that compromises functional ability or health.

health services An **early intervention service** defined, as a term of art, in Part H regulations at 34 C.F.R. § 303.13 as: "services necessary to enable a child to benefit from the other early intervention services under this part during the time that the child is receiving the other early intervention services [including] such services as **clean intermittent catheterization, tracheotomy care, tube feeding,** the changing of dressings or **ostomoy** collection bags, and other health services; and consultation by physicians with other service providers concerning the **special health care needs** of eligible children that will need to be addressed in the course of providing other early intervention services, [but not including] services that are surgical in nature (such as **cleft palate** surgery, surgery for **clubfoot,** or the **shunt**ing of **hydrocephalus**); or purely medical in nature (such as hospitalization for management of congenital heart ailments, or the prescribing of medicine or drugs for any purpose), devices necessary to control or treat a medical condition, or medical-health services (such as immunizations and regular 'well-baby' care) that are routinely recommended for all children."

hearing carry over (HCO) services In connection with

telecommunications for persons with hearing or speech impairments, a reduced form of **telecommunications relay services (TRS)** in which an individual with a speech disability is able to listen to the user on the other end and reply, with the help of a communications assistant who speaks the text as typed by that individual.

hearing impairment 1. Generally includes partial hearing resulting from **hearing loss** and **deafness.** 2. Defined, as a term of art, more restrictively in IDEA regulations at 34 C.F.R. § 300.7(b)(4) as: "an impairment in hearing, whether permanent or fluctuating, that adversely affects a child's educational performance, but that is not included under the definition of deafness in this section."

hearing loss 4 types, defined based on **etiology** as follows: (a) conductive hearing loss resulting from diseases or obstructions in the outer or middle ear; (b) sensorineural loss resulting from damage to the sensory hair cells in the inner ear; (c) mixed hearing loss resulting from damage to both the

inner and outer ear; (d) central hearing loss resulting from damage to the nerves or brain.

hearing officer See **impartial hearing officer.**

hearing vocabulary The range of words one understands when spoken, precedes **speaking vocabulary** in normal development.

Hebb's Theory The theory of neural organization upon which many instructional methodologies for children with **mental retardation** are based.

hemiplegia 1. Paralysis on one side of the body. 2. Form of spastic **cerebral palsy** affecting either the right or left side of one's body.

hemophilia A blood disease, usually hereditary, resulting in failure of the blood to clot normally; causes profuse bleeding and requires modifications in transportation, mobility and physical education.
Hemophilia may be an **"other health impairment"** for purposes of IDEA eligibility if the disease results in limited strength, vitality or alertness that adversely affects a child's educational performance (Part B regula-

tions at 34 C.F.R. § 300.7(b)(8)). Otherwise a student with hemophilia may be eligible for support under Section 504. The case of *Maurits v. Board of Education,* 1983-84 EHLR 555:364 (D. Md. 1983), shows how that determination makes a difference. In that case, the student with hemophilia was not IDEA-eligible because his educational performance was not adversely affected by his condition, although he did meet the eligibility criteria of Section 504. Thus, he was not entitled to receive **physical therapy** as a **related service** because he would benefit from his physical education program in the absence of such therapy. He was, however, entitled to receive a program of specialized physical education instruction under Section 504.

hepatitis An inflammation of the liver; of the several types the most common among children is infectious hepatitis.

Although school districts are legitimately concerned with controlling the spread of contagious diseases in the school environment, OCR has held Hepatitis B carriers are protected individuals with disabilities under Section 504 and unwarranted exclusion from school is a denial of **free appropriate public education (FAPE).** See, e.g., *Clare-Godwin (MI) Intermediate School District,* 16 EHLR 105 (OCR 1989).

heterogeneous grouping In **regular education,** placement of students of varying skill or ability levels in the same classroom, as opposed to **ability grouping.**

higher mental functions "Higher" abilities of the **central nervous system,** such as language, visual and spatial function, complex motor activities, reasoning and judgment. As opposed to **reflex activities.**

highest requirements in the State applicable to a specific profession or discipline In connection with the **personnel standards** of Part B and Part H of the IDEA (20 U.S.C. § 1413(a)(14) and 20 U.S.C. § 1476(b)(13), respectively), defined, as a term of art, in IDEA regulations at 34 C.F.R. § 300.153(a)(2) and 34 C.F.R. § 303.361(a)(2), respectively, as: "the highest entry level academic degree needed for any State approved or recognized certification, licensing, registration, or other comparable requirements that apply to that profession or discipline."

high school A **secondary school** offering the final years of school work necessary for graduation, usually includes grades 10, 11 and 12, but also may include grades 9, 10, 11 and 12.

high-tech electronic communication aids Many various commercially produced models for each of which the salient points are: **access method,** output method and **encoding** method.

high-technology device **Assistive technology device** that typically has electronic components and operates interactively with the user, such as an **augmentative communication device.**

Hiskey-Nebraska Test of Learning Aptitude (H-NTLA) Performance scale for children between the ages of 3 and 17 particularly useful for children who are deaf, bilingual or have mental retardation or speech and language disabilities because it can be administered without verbal instructions, test questions or responses; 12 subtests are: (a) bead patterns, (b) memory for color, (c) picture identification, (d) picture

association, (e) paper folding, (f) visual attention span, (g) block patterns, (h) completion of drawings, (i) memory for digits, (j) puzzle blocks, (k) picture analogies and (l) spatial reasoning.

hit rate In connection with **child find,** the percentage of children who have undergone **screening** who are found to be eligible for services after **evaluation.**

hoarseness When persistent, a **voice disorder.**

In *Mary P. and Peter P. v. Illinois State Board of Education,* 23 IDELR 1064 (N.D. Ill. 1996), a federal district court held that a 7-year-old whose voice abnormalities included hoarseness, squeakiness and fluctuations in pitch and low volume levels was eligible for **special education** under the IDEA on that basis and awarded 30 minutes of weekly speech therapy.

Hodgkin's disease A progressive enlargement of the spleen and lymph nodes that is fatal.

Holland test The test promulgated by the Ninth Circuit Court of Appeals in *Sacramento Unified School District*

125

v. Holland, 20 IDELR 812 (9th Cir. 1994), characterized as a hybrid of the **Roncker portability test** and **Daniel R.R. test** that uses a 4-factor balancing test to determine compliance with the **least restrictive environment (LRE) mandate** of the IDEA: (a) the educational benefits of full-time placement in a regular class; (b) the non-academic benefits of such placement; (c) the effect the disabled student has on the teacher and children in the regular class; and (d) the cost of **mainstreaming** the disabled student. See also **inclusion.**

> Rachel Holland was, at the time of the decision, an 11-year-old girl with moderate mental retardation and an IQ of 44. While the school district proposed placement in a **special education** class for academic subjects and a **regular education** class for non-academic activities such as art, music, lunch and recess, the court found the appropriate placement to be a full-time regular 2nd-grade classroom with some supplemental services, including an aide. One piece of evidence that the lower court found particularly supported the finding that placement benefited both Rachel and her nondisabled classmates: A class member walking by Rachel's desk nonchalantly turned her textbook right-side up.

home-based services

Services provided to children primarily in the child's home through intensive work with the child and his or her family; an approved service under **Head Start** and Part H under appropriate circumstances.

> Discrete trial training under the **Lovaas program** for preschoolers with **autism** is typically a home-based service.

homebound instruction

One of the most restrictive educational placements for children of school age, only appropriate when a disabled student's physical or mental condition makes placement with other students prohibitive; instruction provided by an **itinerant teacher.** As distinguished from **home schooling.** See also **continuum of alternative placements.**

> According to the **Office of Special Education Programs (OSEP),** the IDEA does not preclude other than homebound instruction for properly excluded students with disabilities. Rather, educational services may be provided in the student's home, in an alternative school or in another setting. *OSEP Memorandum 95-16,* 22 IDELR 531 (OSEP 1995).

home schooling Election
of parents to educate their chil-

dren at home; generally state laws establish standards for instruction by parents that permit relief from the otherwise applicable compulsory school attendance law.

The **United States Department of Education** interprets the IDEA as permitting home schooling of **children with disabilities** (*Letter to Farris*, EHLR 213:142 (ED 1988)), provided state law so allows. State law further determines whether home-schooled children with disabilities are considered **private school children with disabilities** entitled to services under § 300.403 of the IDEA regulations. *Letter to Anonymous*, 20 IDELR 177 (OSEP 1993). However, OCR has stated that home-schooled students are not entitled to Section 504 services. *Letter to Veir*, 20 IDELR 864 (OCR 1993).

homophenes Different **phonemes** that have the same visual appearance on the lips of the speaker, making it difficult for **lip reading** deaf individuals to understand what is being said. See also **cued speech.**

Honig decision Decision of the U.S. Supreme Court in *Honig v. Doe*, 1987-88 EHLR 559:231 (1988), holding that unilateral **expulsion** or **long-term suspension** of **children with disabilities** violates the IDEA because either action is a **change in educational placement** that cannot be instituted without compliance with the IDEA **procedural safeguards.**

Honig involved 2 different young men with disabilities who had been suspended long-term. One was a 17-year-old emotionally disturbed youth whose physical appearance, speech difficulties and poor grooming habits made him the butt of his classmates' ridicule. In one instance he responded to taunting with violence against students and property and was suspended without educational services for 39 days as a result. The other student was emotionally disturbed with a history of disruptive behavior, including stealing and sexual harassment. When, after already being warned, he made lewd comments to a female student, he was suspended indefinitely. In *Honig* the Court found the language of the IDEA unequivocally supported its ruling. "We think it clear . . . that Congress very much meant to strip schools of the unilateral authority they had traditionally employed to exclude disabled students, particularly emotionally disturbed students, from school." *Honig v. Doe*, 1987-88 EHLR 559:231, 239 (1988).

Honig injunction According to the U.S. Supreme Court in *Honig v. Doe*, 1987-88 EHLR 559:231, 239 (1988), the relief that a court is author-

127

ized to grant under the IDEA (20 U.S.C. § 1415(e)(2)) so as to remove a student with a disability who is dangerous from the school environment pending resolution of the **due process hearing** and appeal proceedings. As distinguished from an **automatic injunction** under the IDEA. See also **preliminary injunction.**

A school district seeking issuance of a *Honig* injunction must initiate a court proceeding to enable it to expel a student with a disability on the basis that the student presents a substantial danger to himself or herself or others. In such a proceeding the school district bears the **burden of production** and **burden of persuasion.** In *OSEP Policy Memorandum 95-16,* 22 IDELR 531 (1995), the **Office of Special Education Programs (OSEP)** explained the 2-part analysis a school district must use to meet its burden. First, the district must show that maintaining the student in his or her current placement is likely to result in either self-injury or injury to others. Second, the school district must demonstrate that it has made reasonable efforts to minimize the risk of injury. This second part was first elucidated in the Eighth Circuit Court of Appeal's opinion in *Light v. Parkway C-2 School District,* 21 IDELR 933 (8th Cir. 1994).

Hoover cane A long, thin cane used by blind individuals to safely navigate while moving on foot. Also called a long cane.

hospital school Provides educational services to children who need immediate provision of 24-hour medical and/or psychiatric care because of, among other things, self-destructive acts, prepsychotic and psychotic states, and medical health-related emergencies.

Huntington's chorea A hereditary, progressive degenerative disease of the **central nervous system** resulting in physical and communicative impairments and characterized by jerky, involuntary movements.

hydrocephalus Excess fluid in the cranial capacity creating pressure in the brain and an enlarged head; may be relieved by surgery or a **shunt,** but if untreated usually results in **mental retardation; shunt management** may be a **related service** under the IDEA.

hyperlexia Rare disorder on the continuum of **pervasive development disorders** in which poor reading comprehension and social deficits are coupled with a precocious ability to read.

The administrative decision in *Hampden-Wilbraham Regional School District,* 16 EHLR 534 (SEA MA 1990), describes a 17-year-old female student with hyperlexia as follows: "[The student] has strengths in the areas of rote learning, i.e., memory, acquisition of math facts, language and spelling facts, but has weaknesses in the areas of conceptualization, comprehension, analytical skills, sequencing and organization of language. She has difficulty sequencing ideas, making inferences, forming generalizations, drawing conclusions and expressing herself on an abstract or imaginative level. Further, she is weak in comprehending social cues and responding appropriately in social settings. She has behaviors which are unacceptable to others, i.e., she inappropriately touches others, walks too close, smiles and laughs at inappropriate times, and has a flat speaking voice. [Her] academic skills are **age appropriate** in her knowledge of math and language facts; her functional reading comprehension is approximately at the 6th grade level."

hypertext In connection with **computer-assisted instruction,** internal linkages within an electronic text that allow the student-user to select among alternative orders of review.

hypoactivity An **attention deficit disorder** marked by insufficient motor activity and an inability to focus and sustain attention, causing the student to present as lethargic, unmotivated and quiet.

hypoglycemia Physical disorder involving an abnormally low concentration of glucose in the blood, which may lead to symptoms such as headaches and irritability and, in the most dire instances, convulsions and **coma;** linked to ingestion of high amounts of sugar.

Section 504 services for children with hypoglycemia may include ongoing nutritional management and monitoring and emergency management planning.

I

IDEA Individuals with Disabilities Education Act

IEE independent educational evaluation

IEP individualized education program

IEU intermediate educational unit

IFSP individualized family service plan

IHP individual habilitation plan

ISO International Standard Organization

ISS in-school suspension

IWRP Individualized Written Rehabilitation Program

IEP Educational Diagnostic Inventories A device for use by teachers to screen and identify students with potential learning problems.

IEP meeting The forum in which parents and the school district jointly determine the disabled student's needs and develop a program that will provide him or her with an appropriate education; intended by Congress to make parents and school districts operate as equal participants in decisions regarding the disabled student's educational plan.

IEP meeting participants Must consist of at least the following: the child's **parent(s)** or **guardian(s),** the **child's teacher,** a representative of the **local educational agency (LEA)** or the **intermediate educational unit** who is qualified

131

to provide or supervise the specially designed educational program and, if the child has been evaluated for the first time, a member of the evaluation team or a person familiar with both the evaluation and the procedures used in the evaluation; may also include other individuals invited by either the parent(s) or the **public agency;** composition mandated by 20 U.S.C. § 1401(a)(20).

illegal use of drugs In connection with Section 504 and the ADA, defined, as a term of art, at 29 U.S.C. § 706(B)(4)(ii) as: "use of drugs, the possession or distribution of which is unlawful under the Controlled Substances Act . . . [but not including] use of a drug taken under supervision by a licensed health care professional." See also **currently engaging in the illegal use of drugs.**

immediate memory See **short-term memory.**

impairment As a matter of appropriate usage, generally used to mean a physiological abnormality or deficiency.

impartial due process hearing See **due process hearing.**

impartial hearing officer The individual appointed by the school district (or similar **public agency**) to conduct **due process hearings** under the IDEA; according to IDEA regulations at 34 C.F.R. § 300.507 the official may neither be employed by the public agency involved in educating the child nor have any other apparent conflict of interest with respect to the hearing.

impartial review State-level administrative review of **due process hearing** decisions permitted in those states that have a **two-tier administrative system** in which the losing party in a due process hearing conducted by a **local educational agency (LEA)** or **intermediate educational unit (IEU)** appeals the decision to an impartial review officer; authorized by IDEA legislation at 20 U.S.C. § 1415(e)(1).

impulsivity An approach to problem-solving associated with **attention deficit hyper-**

activity disorder (ADHD); responding abruptly without consideration of consequences or alternatives.

incidental learning Learning that is peripheral to the primary objectives of instruction; for example, **social skills** are usually incidentally learned in the regular classroom environment.

include In connection with interpretation of IDEA regulations for both Part B and Part H, defined as a term of art, at 34 C.F.R. § 300.9 and 34 C.F.R. § 303.15, respectively, as meaning "that the items named are not all of the possible items that are covered whether like or unlike the ones named."

The significance of defining "include" is particularly clear when considering how the eligibility category of **"orthopedic impairment"** is defined in 34 C.F.R. § 300.7(b)(7). The diseases, impairments or congenital anomalies specified in that definition are not exhaustive. On the other hand, the 13 disability categories listed in 34 C.F.R. § 300.7(a)(1) are.

inclusion Generally understood as the placement of a child with a disability with his or her chronological age peers in a **regular education** class; undefined in the IDEA itself or by the **United States Department of Education** (in *OSEP Memorandum 95-9*, 21 IDELR 1152 (OSEP 1995), OSEP refused to define); **mainstreaming** is a less preferred term. As distinguished from the **least restrictive environment (LRE) mandate** of the IDEA.

When a child with a disability is placed in a regular education classroom, he or she is expected to achieve at a level commensurate with his or her ability and IEP requirements, with the assistance of appropriate **special education** and **related services.** The child is not necessarily expected to keep pace with the nondisabled children in the class nor to achieve all the regular education requirements in order to be placed in the next grade level. Rather, he or she is expected to move on to the next grade level upon achieving success in the classroom, as measured against his or her own **individualized education program (IEP).**

independence Defined, as a term of art, in the federal **Developmental Disabilities Assistance and Bill of Rights Act of 1975** at 42 U.S.C. § 6001(13) as: "the extent to which individuals with **developmental disabilities** exert control and choice over their own lives." See also **integration and inclusion.**

independent core living services In connection with **independent living services** provided to individuals under the **Vocational Services and Other Rehabilitation Services Act,** defined, as a term of art, at 29 U.S.C. § 706(29) as: "(A) **information and referral services;** (B) independent living skills training; (C) peer counseling (including cross-disability peer counseling); and (D) individual and systems advocacy."

independent decision based on a preponderance of the evidence According to the U.S. Supreme Court in *Board of Education of Hendrick Hudson Central School District v. Rowley,* 1981-82 EHLR 553:656, 669 (1982), the type of decision Congress intended courts to make under the legislation at 20 U.S.C. § 1415(e)(2), authorizing judicial review of Part B administrative decisions. See also **due weight; intermediate standard of review.**

independent educational evaluation (IEE) 1. An **evaluation** of a child by a non-school district employee that parents may obtain as a right under the IDEA. 2. Defined, as a term of art, in IDEA regulations at 34 C.F.R. § 300.503(a)(3)(i) as: "an evaluation conducted by a qualified examiner who is not employed by the **public agency** responsible for the evaluation of the child in question."

Whenever parents obtain an IEE, the school district or other public agency must consider that evaluation when making any decision regarding provision of **free appropriate public education (FAPE).** The most significant practical issue, and one that has generated a fair bit of litigation at the administrative and judicial level, addresses who must bear the cost of obtaining the evaluation—the public agency or the parents. According to Part B regulations at 34 C.F.R. § 300.503(b): "[a] parent has the right to an independent educational evaluation at public expense if the parent disagrees with an evaluation obtained by the public agency. However, the public agency may initiate a **[due process] hearing** . . . to show that its evaluation is appropriate. If the final decision is that the evaluation is appropriate, the parent still has the right to an independent educational evaluation, but not at public expense."

independent living services

In connection with the **Vocational Services and Other Rehabilitation Services Act,** services provided to enable individuals with disabilities to live and work in the community as autonomously as possible, specified at 29 U.S.C. § 706(30) as including **independent core living services** and a myriad of other services specified at 29 U.S.C. § 706(B)(i)-(xxii).

independent living skills

See **functional skills.**

individual behavior plan

See **behavior management plan.**

individual habilitation plan (IHP)

A document similar to an **individualized education program (IEP)** required under the federal **Developmental Disabilities Assistance and Bill of Rights Act of 1975.** Under 42 U.S.C. § 6011(b) the IHP must be in writing and jointly developed by a representative of the program primarily responsible for delivery or coordination of the delivery of services to the individual for whom the plan is established, the individual himself or herself, and, when appropriate, the individual's parents or other representatives. The IHP must contain a statement of the long-term habilitation goals and the intermediate habilitation objectives, expressed in behavioral or other terms that provide a framework for measurement. The IHP further must describe how the objectives will be achieved and the barriers that might interfere with the achievement of such objectives. A program coordinator responsible for implementation of the plan must be identified and each agency which will deliver services must be identified.

individualized education program (IEP)

1. The cornerstone of the IDEA, a written document, ideally developed in a collaborative and cooperative effort between parents and school personnel, that describes the disabled child's abilities and needs and prescribes the placement and services designed to meet the child's unique needs. 2. Defined, as a term of art, in the IDEA at 20 U.S.C. § 1401(a)(20) as: "a written statement for each child with a disability developed in any meeting by a representative of the **local educational agency** or an **intermediate educational unit** who shall be qualified to provide, or supervise the provision of, **specially**

designed instruction to meet the unique needs of **children with disabilities,** the teacher, the **parents** or **guardian** of such child, and whenever appropriate, such child, which statement shall include—(A) a statement of the present levels of **educational performance** of such child, (B) a statement of annual goals, including **short-term instructional objectives,** (C) a statement of the specific educational services to be provided to such child, and the extent to which such child will be able to participate in regular educational programs, (D) a statement of the needed **transition services** for students beginning no later than age 16 and annually thereafter (and, when determined appropriate for the individual, beginning at age 14 or younger, including, when appropriate, a statement of the interagency responsibilities or **linkages** (or both) before the student leaves the school setting), (E) the projected date for initiation and anticipated duration of such services, and (F) appropriate objective criteria and evaluation procedures and schedules for determining, on at least an annual basis, whether

instructional objectives are being achieved."

individualized family service plan (IFSP) 1. A written plan for **early intervention services** to an **infant or toddler with a disability** and his or her family that must meet the procedural and substantive requirements set out in Part H legislation at 20 U.S.C. § 1477. 2. Defined, as a term of art, in Part H regulations at 34 C.F.R. § 303.340(b) as: "a written plan for providing early intervention services to a child eligible under this part and the child's family. The plan must—(1) Be developed jointly by the family and appropriate qualified personnel involved in the provision of early intervention services; (2) Be based on the multidisciplinary evaluation and assessment of the child, and the assessment of the child's family . . . ; and (3) Include services necessary to enhance the development of the child and the capacity of the family to meet the special needs of the child."

individualized instruction Instruction specifically

selected in contemplation of the specific educational strengths, weaknesses and objectives of a student with a disability; distinguished from 1-on-1 instruction, individualized instruction can take place in a group setting.

individualized progress plan The plan of instruction or **habilitation** mandated for individuals receiving services in accordance with the **Developmental Disabilities Assistance and Bill of Rights Act of 1975.** See also **individual habilitation plan.**

Individualized Written Rehabilitation Program (IWRP) A written plan similar in content to an **individualized education program (IEP)** required for all individuals entitled to **vocational rehabilitation services** under the **Vocational Rehabilitation and Other Rehabilitation Services Act.**

individual supported employment **Supported employment** model involving an **individual with a disability** who is employed alongside nondisabled workers and receives 1-on-1 job coaching until he or she becomes proficient at the job, at which time the job coaching services are gradually faded out, although the **job coach** continues to periodically follow up with the individual and his or her employer.

Individuals with Disabilities Education Act (IDEA) Federal legislation that requires states to provide all **children with disabilities** with a **free appropriate public education;** enacted in 1975 to address the failure of state education systems to meet the educational needs of children with disabilities; contains 8 subchapters (often referred to as Parts A-H); formerly known as the **Education of All Handicapped Children Act (EAHCA)** and codified at 29 U.S.C. §§ 1400 et seq.

individual vocational rehabilitation services Goods or services necessary to render an individual with a disability employable that must be provided to eligible individuals with disabilities under the **Vocational Rehabilitation and**

    137

Other Rehabilitation Services Act; codified at 29 U.S.C. § 723(a).

The law specifies that such services include, but are not limited to: "(1) an assessment for determining eligibility and vocational rehabilitation needs by qualified personnel, including, if appropriate, an assessment by personnel skilled in **rehabilitation technology**; (2) counseling, guidance, and work-related placement services for individuals with disabilities, including job search assistance, placement assistance, job retention services, personal assistance services, and follow up, follow-along, and specific postemployment services necessary to assist such individuals to maintain, regain, or advance in employment; (3) vocational and other training services for individuals with disabilities, which shall include personal and vocational adjustment, books and other training materials, and such services to the families of such individuals as are necessary to the adjustment or **rehabilitation** of such individuals, except that no training services in institutions of higher education shall be paid for with funds under this subchapter unless maximum efforts have been made to secure grant assistance, in whole or in part, from other sources to pay for such training; (4) physical and mental restoration services, including, but not limited to, (A) corrective surgery or therapeutic treatment necessary to correct or substantially modify a physical or mental condition which is stable or slowly progressive and constitutes a substantial impediment to employment, but is of such nature that such correction or modification may reasonably be expected to reduce or eliminate such impediment to employment within a reasonable length of time, (B) necessary hospitalization in connection with surgery or treatment, (C) prosthetic and orthotic devices, (D) eyeglasses and visual services as prescribed by qualified personnel, under State licensure laws, that are selected by the individual, (E) special services (including transplantation and dialysis), artificial kidneys, and supplies necessary for the treatment of individuals with end-stage renal disease, and (F) diagnosis and treatment for mental and emotional disorders by qualified personnel under State licensure laws; (5) maintenance for additional costs incurred while participating in rehabilitation; (6) **interpreter** services for individuals who are deaf, and reader services for those individuals determined to be blind after an examination by qualified personnel under State licensure laws; (7) recruitment and training services for individuals with disabilities to provide them with new employment opportunities in the fields of rehabilitation, health, welfare, public safety, and law enforcement, and other appropriate service employment; (8) rehabilitation teaching services and **orientation** and mobility services for individuals who are blind; (9) occupational licenses, tools, equipment, and initial stocks and supplies; (10) **transpor-**

tation in connection with the rendering of any vocational rehabilitation services; (11) telecommunications, sensory, and other technological aids and devices; (12) rehabilitation technology services; (13) referral and other services designed to assist individuals with disabilities in securing needed services from other agencies through agreements developed under § 721(a)(11) of this title, if such services are not available under this chapter; (14) **transition services** that promote or facilitate the accomplishment of long-term rehabilitation goals and intermediate rehabilitation objectives; (15) on-the-job, or other related **personal assistance services** provided while an individual with a disability is receiving services described in this section; and (16) **supported employment** services."

individual with a disability

Generally, the characterization used to describe an individual (including a child) who may be entitled to the protections of Section 504, the **Americans with Disabilities Act** (ADA), and the **Vocational Rehabilitation and Other Rehabilitation Services Act.** 2. In connection with Section 504 and the ADA defined, as a term of art, at 29 U.S.C. § 706(8)(B) as: "any person who (i) has a **physical or mental impairment** which substan-

tially limits one or more of such person's **major life activities,** (ii) has a record of such an impairment, or (iii) is regarded as having such an impairment" but not to the extent that the person is **currently engaging in the illegal use of drugs** (29 U.S.C. § 706(8)(C)(i)) or on the basis of homosexuality, bisexuality, transvestism or other sexual behavior disorders, compulsive gambling, kleptomania or pyromania. (3) In connection with the Vocational Rehabilitation and Other Rehabilitation Services Act, an individual whose disability (defined as above) is a "substantial impediment to employment" and who can benefit from receipt of the **vocational rehabilitation services** provided under the Act (29 U.S.C. § 706(8)(A)). See also **qualified individuals with disabilities.**

It is rare for the second (i.e., "record of") and third (i.e., "regarded as") prongs of the definition of an individual with a disability to be used in connection with elementary and secondary education students and they cannot be the basis upon which the requirement for **free appropriate public education (FAPE)** is triggered. *OCR Senior Staff Memo,* 19 IDELR 894 (1992).

individual with a severe disability Defined, as a term of art, for purposes of the **Vocational Rehabilitation and Other Rehabilitation Services Act** at 29 U.S.C. § (15)(A) as an individual with a disability "(i) who has a severe **physical or mental impairment** which seriously limits one or more functional capacities (such as mobility, communication, self-care, self-direction, interpersonal skills, work tolerance, or work skills) in terms of an **employment outcome**. . . and (iii) who has one or more physical or mental disabilities resulting from amputation, **arthritis, autism,** blindness, **brain injury,** cancer, **cerebral palsy, cystic fibrosis,** deafness, head injury, heart disease, **hemiplegia, hemophilia,** respiratory or pulmonary dysfunction, **mental retardation,** mental illness, multiple sclerosis, **muscular dystrophy,** musculo-skeletal disorders, neurological disorders (including stroke and **epilepsy**), paraplegia, and other spinal cord conditions, **sickle cell anemia, specific learning disability,** . . . or another disability or combination of disabilities, determined on the basis of an assessment for determining eligibility and vocational rehabilitation needs. . . to cause comparable functional limitations."

in effect In connection with the requirement that an **individualized education program (IEP)** be in effect before a student with a disability receives **special education** and **related services,** defined in Section 300.341 of the Notice of Interpretation (Appendix C) to Part 300 of the IDEA regulations as meaning that: "The IEP (1) has been developed properly (i.e., at a meeting(s) involving all of the **[IEP meeting] participants** specified in the Act [IDEA] (parent, teacher, agency representative, and, if appropriate, the child)); (2) is regarded by both parents and the agency as appropriate in terms of the child's needs, specified goals and objectives, and the services to be provided; and (3) will be implemented as written."

infants and toddlers with deaf-blindness Defined, as a term of art, in connection with services under Part C of the IDEA in Part C regulations at 34 C.F.R. Part 307 as: "individuals from birth through age 2 who are experiencing **developmental delays** in hearing and vision, have a diagnosed physical or mental condition that has a high probability of resulting in developmental delays in hearing and vision or at risk of having substantial developmental delays in hearing and visions if **early intervention services** are not provided."

infants and toddlers with disabilities

1. Children eligible for services under Part H. 2. Defined, as a term of art, in 20 U.S.C. § 1472(1) as: "individuals from **birth to age 2, inclusive,** who need **early intervention services** because they—(A) are experiencing **developmental delays,** as measured by appropriate diagnostic **instruments** and procedures in one or more of the following areas: cognitive development, physical development, language and speech development, psychosocial development, or **self-help** skills, or (B) have a **diagnosed physical or mental condition that has a high probability of resulting in de-**velopmental delay.** Such term may include, at a State's discretion, individuals from birth to age 2, inclusive, who are **at risk of having substantial developmental delays if early intervention services are not provided."**

informal assessment

Appraisal by other than standardized normed **instruments; alternative assessment** that may include anecdotal records, personality inventories, skill probe sheets, interviews and **observation.**

informal reading inventory

Non-norm-referenced reading materials used to assess a student's reading level and provide a basis for beginning reading instruction.

information and referral services

Services or activities designed to provide information about services provided by public or private services providers and a brief assessment of needs for the sole purpose of facilitating appropriate referrals.

information to be provided under Carl D. Perkins Vocational and Applied Technology Act

Specified under 20 U.S.C. § 2328(b)(1) as: "the opportunities available in vocational education programs; the requirements for eligibility for enrollment in such vocational programs; specific courses that are available; special services that are available; employment opportunities and placement."

informed consent

1. Generally, consent given after full disclosure of all the information a reasonable person would require to make an intelligent decision. 2. In connection with the IDEA, understood to mean parental consent that meets the requirements set out in Part B regulations at 34 C.F.R. § 300.500(a): "(1) The parent has been fully informed of all information relevant to the activity for which consent is sought, in his or her **native language** . . . (2) The parent understands and agrees in writing [to the carrying out of the activity] . . . (3) The parent understands that the granting of consent is

voluntary . . . and may be revoked at any time . . ."

in-home support

In connection with mental health services for children and adolescents, help provided in a family's home, including **parent counseling and training,** and working with family members to identify, find or provide other needed support; intended to avert the need for residential treatment. See also **wrap around services.**

injunction

An equitable **remedy** issued by a court forbidding a defendant from doing a wrongful act that injures the plaintiff or ordering a defendant to perform an act that benefits the plaintiff; an available remedy under the IDEA and Section 504. See also **preliminary injunction.**

An injunction is only appropriately issued when the plaintiff has no remedy at law, i.e., payment of **compensatory damages** is inadequate to remediate the injury the defendant's wrongful acts have caused plaintiff.

inpatient hospitalization

In connection with mental health services for children and adolescents, treatment in a hospital setting 24 hours a day; generally indicated when either short-term treatment is needed for a child who is in crisis and possibly a danger to himself or herself or others, or diagnosis or treatment in an outpatient facility is not appropriate.

Courts have differed about whether placement in a psychiatric hospital may ever be considered a **residential placement** for educational purposes. Because one category of IDEA eligibility is based on the student having a **serious emotional disturbance,** some courts have held that a psychiatric hospital placement may, in appropriate cases, be considered an educational placement, making the school district liable for the costs. See, e.g., *Babb v. Knox County School System,* 18 IDELR 1030 (6th Cir. 1992). Others have denied funding for treatment at a psychiatric hospital as a residential placement under the IDEA. The leading case taking this position is *Clovis Unified School District v. California Office of Administrative Hearings,* 16 EHLR 944 (9th Cir. 1990).

in-school suspension (ISS)
A disciplinary technique that involves excluding the student from the regular classroom and assigning him or her to a classroom that is some- ' at like a detention hall where students work and receive a minimum amount of privileges. See also **long-term suspension; suspension.**

ISS is considered a less restrictive alternative to sending a student home. In addition, it permits better supervision. Generally, in-school suspensions are considered neither an exclusion nor a **significant change in placement,** provided the student's program while in ISS is comparable in nature and quality to the program customarily provided to the student. Thus, imposition of an ISS generally does not trigger **procedural safeguards** under the IDEA or Section 504.

inservice teacher training
Special instruction provided by school districts to incumbent teachers, usually to supplement the collegiate educational curriculum, increase competencies or provide instruction in emerging pedagogic techniques or philosophy.

instrument
In connection with **assessment,** a particular test or method of evaluation. See also **four pillars of assessment.**

insulin pump
Small, battery-operated device worn on a belt or in a pocket to deliver a constant infusion of insulin through a **catheter** or needle,

generally used only by a child or young teenager with difficult-to-manage **diabetes.**

insult to the brain Generally refers to an occurrence of known brain damage, such as **brain injury** or infections of the **central nervous system;** as distinguished from **specific learning disability** or **minimal brain dysfunction,** where there is no history of a specific incident of brain damage.

integrated employment In connection with **transition services** under the IDEA, a **post-school activity** involving work settings in which individuals with disabilities interact on a regular basis in the performance of job duties with nondisabled employees or members of the public (34 C.F.R. § 361(c)(2)). Also called integrated work setting. As distinguished from **sheltered employment.** See also **competitive work; supported employment.**

integration and inclusion Defined, as a term of art, in the federal **Developmental Disabilities Assistance and Bill of Rights Act of 1975** at 42 U.S.C. § 6001(15) as: "the use by individuals with **developmental disabilities** of the same community resources that are used by and available to other citizens; living in homes close to community resources, with regular contact with citizens without disabilities in their communities; the full and active participation by individuals with developmental disabilities in the same community activities and types of employment as citizens without disabilities and utilization of the same community resources as citizens without disabilities, living, learning, working and enjoying life in regular contact with citizens without disabilities; and having friendships and relationships with individuals and families of their own choosing."

This defined term, along with the defined terms "**independence**" and "productivity," relate to and amplify the aspirations that infuse the law, as set out in Congress' statement of finding, purposes and policy: "[I]individuals with developmental disabilities, including those with the most severe developmental disabilities, are capable of achieving independence, productivity, and integration and inclusion into the community .... [I]individuals with developmental disabilities and their families have competencies, capabilities, and personal goals that should be recognized, supported, and encouraged. . . ."

intelligence 1. Globally, the mental ability to comprehend, adapt to and learn from one's environment; narrowly, the mental ability one displays by performance on **intelligence tests.** 2. As defined by David Wechsler, noted author of educational tests, "the aggregate or global capacity of the individual to act purposefully, to think rationally, and to deal effectively with his environment."

intelligence test (IQ test) **Norm-referenced test** designed to measure learning ability or intellectual capacity by measuring cognitive behaviors associated with mental ability, such as discrimination, **generalization,** vocabulary, comprehension, **abstract thinking** or reasoning, **memory** and sequencing; includes **Wechsler Intelligence Scales for Children-III (WISC-III), Stanford-Binet Intelligence Scale** or **Kaufman Assessment Battery for Children.**

Factors other than learning ability or intellectual capacity that may limit test performance include sociocultural background, primary language other than English or associated communication, motor or sensory disabilities. See also **racially or culturally discriminatory testing and evaluation materials.**

interagency agreement An agreement between the **state educational agency (SEA)** and other state and local agencies that is required under Part B and Part H of the IDEA (20 U.S.C. § 1413(a)(9) and 20 U.S.C. § 1476(b)(9)(F), respectively) and defines the responsibility of each for providing and funding **free appropriate education program (FAPE)** or **early intervention services,** as the case may be.

Part B does not regulate which **public agency** must provide FAPE. (The same is true under Part H.) That decision is within the discretion of the SEA. But, federal law requires interagency agreements specifying which public agency is responsible in order to address those instances in which multiple **local educational agencies (LEAs)** or other state agencies, such as, for example, the State Department of Mental Health and Mental Retardation, are implicated in the care and education of a child with a disability. This prevents "reverse" turf wars between or among public agencies. See,

145

e.g., the case of *Maine School Administrative District #3,* 22 IDELR 1083 (D. Me. 1995), in which the State Departments of Education and Mental Health and Mental Retardation both disclaimed responsibility for funding the **residential placement** of an 18-year-old student with severe autism and mental retardation.

interdisciplinary curriculum
Designed to integrate the methodology and terminology from more than one discipline to examine a central theme, issue or similar curriculum item.

interfacing technique
In connection with **high-technology devices,** the way in which a student with a disability operates the device; 3 main techniques: **direct selection, scanning,** and **encoding.**

interim alternative educational setting
The placement in which a school district or similar **public agency** may place a disabled student who possesses a **weapon** on school premises for a maximum of 45 days in accordance with the **Jeffords Amendment** to the IDEA (codified at 20 U.S.C. § 1415(e)(3)(B)).

interim IEP
Temporary placement of an IDEA-eligible child in a program before his or her **individualized education program (IEP)** is finalized. See also **preparatory individualized education program (IEP).**

Generally, an IEP must be in effect before **special education** and **related services** are provided to a child with a disability. Accordingly, interim IEPs usually will not meet the requirements of the IDEA. However, a Notice of Interpretation (Appendix C to Part 300 of the IDEA regulations) acknowledges 2 instances in which an interim IEP is permitted: when temporarily placing a child in a program as part of the evaluation process and when a student with a disability who is already receiving services moves into a new district, for the time period before his or her new evaluation is completed.

intermediate
In connection with **regular education** students, generally means students in grades 4 through 6 or ages 9 through 12 years. See also **middle school.**

intermediate educational unit (IEU)
1. Generally, an educational agency formed by a number of intrastate **local educational agencies (LEAs)** or school districts to pool re-

sources to provide **special education** services to students within those districts with **low-incidence disabilities** who cannot be served effectively or efficiently on an individual school district basis. 2. Defined, as a term of art, in the IDEA at 20 U.S.C. § 1401(a)(23) as: "any public authority, other than a local educational agency, which is under the general supervision of a **State educational agency,** which is established by State law for the purpose of providing free public education on a regional basis, and which provides special education and **related services** to **children with disabilities** within that State."

intermediate standard of review

Standard for judicial review of IDEA administrative decisions adopted by some federal appellate and district courts on the basis of their interpretation of the directive promulgated by the U.S. Supreme Court in *Board of Education of Hendrick Hudson Central School District v. Rowley,* 1981-82 EHLR 553:656 (1982), that courts should make **independent decisions based on a preponderance of the evidence.** See also **due weight.**

The intermediate standard was described by the First Circuit Court of Appeals in *Lenn v. Portland School Committee,* 20 IDELR 342, 345 (1st Cir. 1990), as follows: "[T]he law contemplates an intermediate standard of review on the trial-court level—a standard which, because it is characterized by independence of judgment, requires a more critical appraisal of the agency determination than clear-error review entails, but which, nevertheless, falls well short of complete **de novo [hearing]** review."

intermittent schedule of reinforcement

Positive reinforcement technique in which some, but not all, of the performances of a desired **target behavior** are reinforced, increasing the rate of performance and making the student's performance more stable and habitual. See also **interval schedule of reinforcement.**

internal consistency reliability

Assessed by dividing the test items into 2 equivalent tests and comparing scores. See also **alternate form reliability; reliability; test-retest reliability.**

International Standard Organization (ISO) standard

Measures **hearing loss** in terms of **decibels (db)** of loss:

20-40 db	slight hearing loss
40-55 db	mild hearing loss
55-70 db	marked hearing loss
70-90 db	severe hearing loss
90+ db	extreme hearing loss

interpreter

In connection with deaf individuals, an individual who facilitates communication between a deaf person and a speaking individual by translating spoken language to a manual language (**American Sign Language (ASL)** or otherwise) and vice-versa; ability to interpret effectively, accurately and impartially is essential.

In its first, and arguably most important, case interpreting the IDEA—*Board of Education of Hendrick Hudson Central School District v. Rowley,* 1981-82 EHLR 553:656 (1982)—the U.S. Supreme Court decided whether the school district was required to provide an in-class interpreter for 1st-grade Amy, a deaf student with minimal residual hearing and excellent **lip-reading** skills. It was not, because the IEP was reasonably calculated to provide educational benefit without the services of an interpreter. See also **passing from grade to grade.**

interval recording

An observational recording method for the **systematic observation of behavior** in which the trained observer records all the instances of a specifically identified behavior(s) during a specifically defined observation period.

interval schedule of reinforcement

Positive reinforcement technique in which a specified duration of time must pass and then the next performance of the desired behavior is reinforced. See also **intermittent schedule of reinforcement.**

intervention

Planned attempts to overcome a student's **deficit** or unproductive behavior and promote his or her welfare; conceptually 3 types of interventions: (a) preventive, (b) remedial [**remediation**], and (c) compensatory [**compensation strategies**].

interventions for distractibility

Generally 5 types: (a) medication, such as **Ritalin,** (b) **behavior management,** (c) **metacognitive [approach]** training, (d) environmental modifications to make the environment less stimulating, and (e) dietary regimen. See also **attention deficit hyperactivity disorder (ADHD); attention-deficit/ hyperactivity disorder (A-D/HD).**

interview Assessment technique in which the child's parents, teachers or other individuals who know the child convey information about him or her in their own words in response to **open-ended questions.**

inventory Questionnaire or checklist used to find out about a student's skills, abilities or the like in certain areas.

Inventory of Perceptual Skills
Screens students in **special education** programs from kindergarten through grade 12 to identify problem areas in resource center classrooms or to help with the development of **individualized education programs (IEPs).**

Inventory of Readiness Skills
Teacher-administered test used to make a diagnostic assessment of a child's mastery of fundamental skills before and after he or she participates in a formal program of instruction; suitable for the following populations: **preschool,** kindergarten, 1st grade, and children with **mental retardation** or **learning disabilities.**

IQ score
A test score intended to provide information about an individual's thinking abilities that may be derived from performance on a variety of standardized individually administered intelligence testing **instruments** now accepted and in use. Also called a cognitive skills index.

Scores for students are sometimes categorized as follows:

85-99	lower normal (intelligence)
100-114	upper normal (intelligence)
115-129	bright
130-144	**gifted**
145-159	highly gifted
160-above	profoundly gifted.

Ishihar colorplates
Materials used to test for color-blindness.

itinerant services
Resource services, such as **physical therapy,** offered at various locations. See also **block scheduling.**

149

itinerant teacher Teacher who provides services to students in out-of-school settings, such as homebound students. See also **homebound instruction.**

J

Jeffords Amendment Colloquial name for an amendment to the IDEA, made as part of the Improving America's Schools Act and effective October 20, 1994, under which a school district may, consistent with state law, place a student with a disability who has brought a **weapon** to school in an alternative educational setting for up to 45 calendar days even before determining whether the behavior was a manifestation of the student's disability; codified at 20 U.S.C. § 1415(e)(3)(B)(i). See also **Gun-Free Schools Act; manifestation determination.**

jejunostomy See **gastrotomy tube feeding.**

job coach An individual who supports and supervises an individual with a severe disability in supported employment** by accompanying the disabled individual to the work site for intensive on-site job skill training, observation and supervision.

joystick Manual device with a movable control lever that can be tilted in various directions to control a wheelchair, computer or other system.

J-tube See **gastrotomy tube feeding.**

judicial review, scope of In connection with a **civil action** under the IDEA, limited to only those issues that were raised during the **due process hearing,** as long as such issues could have been raised there. See also **additional evidence.**

juvenile court system A

separate court for juvenile offenders established as part of the criminal justice system in virtually every state; premised on adjudication for purposes of rehabilitation rather than punishment.

School districts may be entering uncertain territory when a student with a disability enters the juvenile court system. One question which lacks a definitive answer is whether a school district's initiation of juvenile proceedings against a student with a disability constitutes a change in placement, triggering the IDEA **procedural safeguards.** One federal appeals court, in *Morgan v. Chris L.,* 25 IDELR 227 (6th Cir. 1996), said it did, despite the school district's argument of undue interference with state juvenile justice law. Other recent court cases have considered the juvenile court's authority to order educational services or placement for a student identified as IDEA-eligible and, assuming it may, whether the school district remains financially liable. On that issue, the **Office of Special Education Programs (OSEP)** has stated that Part B does not limit the ability of state courts to hear cases involving students with disabilities—state law controls that. *Letter to Hayden,* 24 IDELR 387 (OSEP 1995).

juvenile delinquency Of-

fenses that violate a state's ju- venile code; generally 2 types: (a) conduct that is criminal no matter the age of the offender, such as robbery; and (b) conduct that is criminal only because it has been committed by a juvenile, such as truancy.

juvenile rheumatoid arthritis (JRA) A chronic form

of **arthritis** consisting of inflammation of the joints, resulting in stiffness and muscle pain; typically not an "**other health impairment**" under the IDEA, but may require program modifications, **supplementary aids and services,** and removal of architectural barriers under Section 504 for students with limited mobility or motor functioning.

K

K-ABC Kaufman Assessment Battery for Children

K-TEA Kaufman Test of Educational Achievement

Kabuki make-up syndrome Very rare genetic disorder resulting in **mental retardation;** characterized by unusual facial features that give the individual the appearance of wearing the make-up associated with that worn by actors in traditional Japanese theatrical presentations; many also have postural abnormalities.

Kanner's autism Sometimes used as an alternative name for **autism.**

Kaufman Assessment Battery for Children (K-ABC) Multi-subtest **battery** that measures **intelligence** and achievement in children ages 2 through 12, although not all subtests are used for all age groups; 4 scales include: (a) sequential processing scale, (b) simultaneous processing scale, (c) achievement scale, and (d) nonverbal achievement scale; generally not regarded as the primary instrument for assessing intelligence in children either with or without disabilities.

Kaufman Test of Educational Achievement (K-TEA) Individually administered **norm-referenced test** of **academic achievement** for children between the ages of 6 and 18 years; 5 subtests include: (a) reading decoding, (b) reading comprehension, (c) mathematics applications, (d) mathematics computation and (e) spelling.

keyboard for an individual with a disability

Special keyboards designed for computer user who is unable to use or use comfortably the regular keyboard as an input device, including **expanded keyboard, membrane keyboard** and **miniature keyboard.**

Keymath Diagnostic Arithmetic Test

Individually administered **norm-referenced test** useful in screening mathematics skills in children with **learning disabilities** or who are **educable mentally retarded** because it does not involve reading or writing; primarily used for children in grades 1 through 6; 14 subtests in the areas of content, operations and applications.

Kildonan School

A private day and residential school in New York state serving only students with **dyslexia;** instruction in reading is based on application of **Orton-Gillingham method** and concentrates on careful teaching of the sound-symbol relationship in a multi-sensory way. See also **Lab School, The.**

Several administrative and judicial decisions concern parents of students with dyslexia who seek publicly funded placement at Kildonan because their children have made miserable progress in public school. A 1996 case, in which a district court ordered the school district to fund a residential placement at the Kildonan School, concerned a 15-year-old student with severe dyslexia. Despite his failing every major academic subject in 7th grade, the district proposed promoting him to the 8th grade and continuing essentially the same **individualized education program (IEP).** *Evans v. Board of Education of Rheinbeck Central School District,* 24 IDELR 338 (S.D.N.Y. 1996).

kinesthesis

Sensation of movement arising from one's muscles, joints and inner ears.

kinesthetic method

In connection with reading, an instructional method in which alphabetic symbols are traced in clay, sand or the air; part of a **multisensory approach** to reading instruction.

kinesthetic sense

Self-awareness of movement resulting from the synthesis of tactile sensations with **motor**

activity; essential for **acquisition** of communication skills.

Kohn Problem Behavior Checklist
Rating scale assessing the presence or absence of behavior problems, such as defiance, in **preschool** or kindergarten children.

Kurzwell Reading machine
An **assistive technology device** that optically scans print and translates it into synthetic speech.

L

LACT Lindamood Auditory Conceptualization Test

LD learning disability

LEA local educational agency

LEP limited-English proficient

LNNB-C Luria-Nebraska Neurophysical Battery, Children's Revision

LOF Letter of Findings

LRE least restrictive environment

labeling Classifying or categorizing children on the basis of their disability, disfavored because of perceived misuse and stigmatizing effect.
While the IDEA, in effect, requires identification of disability for the purposes of **evaluation** and determining eligibility, the **Office of Special Education Programs (OSEP)** has stated that the IDEA does not require the use of labels for any purpose other than reporting data to OSEP. *Letter to Richards,* EHLR 211:440 (OSEP 1987). Further, any use by a state of labels that publicly identify a child as "being" a particular disability is contrary to the policy values sanctioned in the IDEA. *Letter to Stainback,* EHLR 211:389 (OSERS 1986).

labile Displaying inappropriate **affect** by exhibiting unstable emotional control with rapid shifts in mood and emotional overreactions.

Lab School, The An adjunct school of American University in Washington, D.C. solely for students with **learning disabilities.** See also **Kildonan School.**
Publicly funded placement at The Lab School has been litigated in sev-

eral judicial and administrative decisions. While the restrictiveness of such a placement is a significant issue, case law concerning the **least restrictive environment (LRE)** for a student with a learning disability is limited. However, in *Fort Zumwalt School District v. Missouri State Board of Education,* 24 IDELR 222 (E.D. Mo. 1996), a federal district court ruled that a private school limited to students with learning disabilities was the least restrictive environment for a 4th-grader who was not able to write a complete sentence prior to enrollment. Concerning the basic premise of **inclusion**—that self-esteem and other positive benefits flow from having students with disabilities interact with their nondisabled peers—the court held that in this case placement with only similarly disabled students was appropriate because it eliminated the student's feelings of being "different," raised his self-esteem and gave him an understanding of his disability.

laches An equitable doctrine under which a party's negligence in asserting a right or claim, taken together with a lapse of time or other circumstances, prejudices the opposing party so substantially that the first party is barred from asserting that right or claim.

Nonavailability of witnesses, memory failures or destruction of records could be the basis of a claim of laches. In *Murphy v. Timberlane Regional School District,* 19 IDELR 486 (D.N.H. 1993) a federal district court refused to dismiss a claim for **compensatory education** brought by a 24-year-old man on the basis of laches despite his almost 6-year delay in bringing the claim, holding that the school district failed to make a clear showing of how it was prejudiced by the delay.

Landau-Kleffner syndrome
A severe form of **communication disorder** characterized by **aphasia,** or loss of language skills; presents between the ages of 3 and 7 years in children who have otherwise had normal **expressive language** and **receptive language** development, but upon onset first lose receptive speech and then expressive speech; may be either gradual or sudden and may be accompanied by characteristics of **autism,** such as **perseverative behaviors** and poor eye contact.

In *River Forest School District No. 90 v. Illinois State Board of Education,* 24 IDELR 34 (N.D. Ill. 1996), the federal district court required the school district to fund out-patient **cognitive rehabilitation** services following corrective surgery and in-patient rehabilitation services for a 9-year-old boy diagnosed as having Landau-Kleffner syndrome. While the surgery and in-patient rehabilitation were **excluded medical services,** the court found the out-patient rehabilitation to be educational services because they focused on developing expressive and receptive language skills.

language delay Significant chronological delay in language acquisition characterized by delay in first sound productions, poor **articulation** and absence of **grammar,** occurring in children with normal **intelligence,** generally resolving itself by age 5. As distinguished from a **language disorder.**

language disorder Inability or decreased ability to use language for meaningful communication; 3 major subcategories of compromised functionality—**expressive language disorder, receptive language disorder,** and **deficits** in both; 3 types, in terms of **etiology:** (a) **specific language deficiencies associated with impairments of the central nervous system;** (b) **nonspecific deficiencies associated with impairments of the central nervous system;** and (c) speech or language deficiencies associated with motor or sensory deficits.

language, five components of The 5 different rule systems governing one's ability to communicate symbolically in a meaningful way: (a) **phonology,** (b) **morphology,** (c) **semantics,** (d) **syntax** and (e) **pragmatics.**

large print book Book with print size ranging from 18 to 24 points, may also have specially designed spacing between lines, special contrast between print and page, and glare-free paper quality to enhance ease of reading; an alternative to reading regular print with a magnifying glass for students with **low vision** offering a less restrictive **field of vision.**

laryngectomy speech amplifier Device that supplements lost or insufficient vocal tone.

larynx The bodily organ responsible for voice production, located in the **trachea** (windpipe).

lay advocate In connection with **special education,** a non-lawyer with special knowledge or training concerning the problems of **children with disabili-**

159

ties who represents parents and children in **due process hearings** and other nonjudicial proceedings seeking enforcement of a disabled student's educational rights. Also called parent advocate.

Neither the IDEA statute nor its legislative history state whether **attorneys' fees** are recoverable for representation by lay advocates at due process hearings or administrative reviews. Scant judicial authority suggests that attorneys' fees are not recoverable for the services of lay advocates who are the sole representatives of parents (e.g., *Arons v. New Jersey Board of Education,* 1987-88 EHLR 559:355 (3d Cir. 1988)), but may be recovered as an expense of counsel when the parents are represented by an attorney (e.g., *McCartney v. Herring Community Unit School District No. 4,* 20 IDELR 801 (S.D. Ill. 1993)).

lead agency State agency responsible for administration of funds provided under Part H of the IDEA for **early intervention services** and administration and oversight of the state's Part H program; analogous to the **state educational agency (SEA)** with regard to Part B.

lead poisoning Large amounts of lead in an individual's blood that may result in brain damage, **mental retardation,** liver and kidney damage, **developmental delays** and other physical and mental problems; identified as a health problem that could be an "**other health impairment**" for purposes of IDEA eligibility in Part B regulations at 34 C.F.R. § 300.7(b)(8).

Lead poisoning poses the greatest threat to children under age 6. Common sources of harmful exposure are found in the home, soil, water or other sources such as imported ceramics or pottery. Most houses and apartments built before 1978 used paint that contained lead. Children who chew on a lead painted windowsill or ingest lead paint chips are at high risk of lead poisoning.

learned helplessness In connection with students with **learning disabilities,** low self-esteem resulting from attributing one's history of academic failure to lack of competence and causing one to quit a task when it becomes difficult or to hesitate starting new tasks. See also **attribution theory.**

Learning and Behavior Problem Checklist Identifies specific student difficulties which interfere with success in classrooms; contains 193 of the most common learning and behavior problems exhibited by students, accompanied by corresponding **interventions.**

learning disability (LD) 1.
Generally speaking, a disability that results in a student being unable to achieve in a specific learning area on the same level as other students with the same or comparable mental ability **(intelligence)** and educational opportunities. 2. As defined by the National Joint Committee on Learning Disabilities: "a generic term for a heterogeneous group of disorders manifested by significant difficulties in the acquisition and use of listening, speaking, reading, writing, reasoning or mathematical abilities. These disorders are presumed to be due to **central nervous system** dysfunction. Even though a learning disability may occur concomitantly with other handicapping conditions (e.g., sensory impairment, **mental retardation,** social and emotional disturbance) or environmental influences (e.g., cultural differences, insufficient/ inappropriate instruction, psychogenic factors), it is not the direct result of those conditions or influences." Termed a **learning disorder** in the DSM-IV. See also **specific learning disability.**

learning disability, principles of remediation for
Prevalent in the field of special education: (a) **resource room,** (b) techniques and **interventions** in the regular classroom, (c) **peer tutoring,** (d) **applied behavioral analysis** to instruct and motivate students and (e) pharmaceuticals.

learning disability, regular classroom techniques for
Include: (a) present information in small manageable steps, (b) provide frequent feedback, (c) teach new materials in concrete ways, (d) provide outlines for lessons, (e) use graph paper to help with letter spacing in writing and number alignments in a calculation and (f) teach and encourage use of mnemonics.

learning disorder
1. As generally discussed in the DSM-IV, presents as academic functioning substantially below that expected given the student's chronological age, mea-

161

sured **intelligence** and **age-appropriate** education; diagnosed when **achievement on an individually administered standardized test is substantially below that expected for a student of similar age, schooling and level of intelligence** (in reading, mathematics, or written expression, as appropriate); often associated with or preceded by deficits in discrete processes involved in **cognition**—visual perception, linguistic processes, attention or **memory**—frequently found in connection with a diagnosis of **Fragile X syndrome, Fetal Alcohol Syndrome** or **lead poisoning.** 2. Although the DSM-IV does not address **etiology,** it identifies separate disorders on the basis of the specific area of difficulty: (a) **reading disorder,** (b) **mathematics disorder,** (c) **disorder of written expression** and (d) learning disorder, not otherwise specified.

learning modalities The 3 pathways through which students learn—visual, auditory and **kinesthetic [sense].** See also **multisensory approach.**

learning strategies Instructional methods used to help students acquire and remember content of instruction; generally includes: (a) stimulus response, (b) **chaining,** (c) verbal association, (d) discrimination, (e) concept and (f) problem-solving.

learning strategy approaches Instructional programming aimed at teaching students how to learn, rather than teaching a specific subject matter or content.

learning style The way in which a student attends to, processes and retains new information.

Two basic types of considerations go into determining the 2 aspects of a student's learning style: sensory (his or her preferred **learning modality**) and cognitive (e.g., sequential, literal, observational or experiental). Because the learning style of a child with a disability is considered to be unique, a learning style assessment is a required part of an **evaluation** for students with disabilities as an integral part of the **assessment** of the student's strengths and weaknesses. An appropriate **individualized education program (IEP)** must articulate the student's learning style and take it into account in program design, including **accommodations** and **learning strategies.**

The opinion in the due process hearing in *Brunswick School District,* 22

IDELR 1004 (SEA ME 1994), concerning an autistic child, illustrates the interrelation between assessment of learning style and design of special education programming: "[the student's] learning style is described as sequential, visual, associative, and literal. . . . Learning occurs in a highly structured environment breaking down into small steps each task and then linking concepts and systematically introducing variables, like a new location or person."

learning style interventions Modifications in teaching strategies to fit the **learning style** of students with disabilities; consistent with the **individualized instruction** mandate of the IDEA.

least restrictive environment (LRE) Generally, the appropriate placement for a child with a disability that most closely approximates where the child, if nondisabled, would be educated; not necessarily the **regular education** classroom and not synonymous with **inclusion** or **mainstreaming.**

least restrictive environment (LRE) mandate 1. The directive to segregate **children with disabilities** as seldom as possible set out in the IDEA at 20 U.S.C. § 1412(5)(B): "[T]o the maximum extent appropriate, children with disabilities, including children in public or private institutions or other care facilities, are educated with children who are not disabled and that special classes, separate schooling, or other removal of children with disabilities from the regular educational environment occurs only when the nature or severity of the disability is such that education and regular classes with the use of **supplementary aids and services** cannot be achieved satisfactorily. . . ." 2. The substantially similar requirement of Section 504 set out in Section 504 regulations at 34 C.F.R. § 104.34(a): "[An LEA] shall educate or shall provide for the education of, each qualified handicapped person in its jurisdiction with persons who are not handicapped to the maximum extent appropriate to the needs of the handicapped person. [An LEA] shall place a handicapped person in the regular educational environment operated by the [LEA] unless it is demonstrated by the [LEA] that the education of the person

163

in the regular environment with the use of supplementary aids and services cannot be achieved satisfactorily." See also **natural environment.**

A substantial amount of IDEA case law and published administrative decisions resolve disputes about the identification of the child's LRE. While the IDEA requires that each child's LRE be considered based on his or her unique circumstances, courts have developed and enunciated various generally applicable tests to be used in applying the LRE mandate to the determination of the legally correct placement for a particular child. Three federal circuit courts of appeal, in influential and often cited decisions, have crafted tests for applying the LRE mandate in connection with inclusion: the **Holland test** promulgated by the Ninth Circuit Court of Appeals in *Sacramento Unified School District v. Holland,* 20 IDELR 812 (9th Cir. 1994), the **Daniel R.R. test** promulgated by the Fifth Circuit Court of Appeals in *Daniel R.R. v. State Board of Education,* 15 EHLR 441:433 (5th Cir. 1989), and the **Roncker portability test** promulgated by the Sixth Circuit Court of Appeals in *Roncker v. Walter,* 1982-83 EHLR 554:381 (6th Cir. 1983).

legally blind Either central **visual acuity** of 20/200 or less in the better eye, as corrected, or visual acuity greater than 20/ 200 in the better eye, but a horizontal **field of vision** limited to no more than 20 degrees at the widest diameter.

leisure function Generally understood to mean assessment of constructive use of leisure time for enjoyment and enhancement of skills and opportunities to meet congenial people who share the same interests.

Assessment of leisure function is identified as a part of the related service of **recreation** in 34 C.F.R. § 300.16(b)(9)(i).

leisure-time activities In connection with **children with disabilities,** activities that enhance or build on academic or vocational activities that the individual enjoys; important because they may ameliorate or compensate for personal, social and academic limitations resulting from disability and, by allowing a child to choose among possible activities, give opportunities to exercise independence.

Leiter International Performance Scale Nonverbal test used to assess the **intelligence** of a child whose sensory or motor disabilities rule out administration of verbal tests of intelligence.

Lesch-Nyhan syndrome

Serious genetic disorder characterized by at least some degree of impairment in **cognition, spasticity** and renal disease; associated with intractible **self-injurious behavior.** See also **Self-Injurious Behavior Inhibiting System (SIBIS).**

Letter of Findings (LOF)

Document issued by the **Office for Civil Rights (OCR)** after it completes an investigation of a school or school district as a result of receipt of a complaint; when corrective action mandated, the school or school district is required to either comply with the LOF or challenge OCR in court.

leukemia Cancer of the white blood cells resulting in dysfunction of bone marrow, lymph nodes, kidney, liver, spleen, lungs and skin; acute type predominant in children treated so that remissions and longer survival are possible, although long-term prognosis re-

mains poor; identified as a health problem that could be an **"other health impairment"** for purposes of IDEA eligibility in Part B regulations at 34 C.F.R. § 300.7(b)(8).

level of intensity of needed supports

In connection with students with **mental retardation, American Association on Mental Retardation (AAMR)** classification system that replaces the categorization of mental retardation on the basis of IQ levels as either mild, moderate, severe, or profound, with the intensity of supports needed by the student in each of 4 functional dimensions (intellectual, psychological, physical health and environmental) as either intermittent, limited, extensive or pervasive.

limbic system

Brain system involved in regulation of emotions and formation of long-term memory.

limited-English proficient (LEP)

1. Students from language backgrounds other than English who need language assistance services in their own

165

language or in English in the schools. 2. Defined, as a term of art, in the **Bilingual Education Act** (20 U.S.C. § 1401) as a student who: "(1) meets one or more of the following conditions: (a) the student was born outside of the United States or whose native language is not English; (b) the student comes from an environment where a language other than English is dominant; or (c) the student is American Indian or Alaskan Native and comes from an environment where a language other than English has had a significant impact on his/her level of English language proficiency; and (2) has sufficient difficulty speaking, reading, writing, or understanding the English language to deny him or her the opportunity to learn successfully in English-only classrooms." See also **bilingual education.**

Lindamood Auditory Conceptualization Test (LACT) Individually administered test usually used to screen the ability of school-age children (kindergarten through 12th grade) to discriminate among speech sounds and iden-

tify the different speech sounds within words and sentences. See also **phonological awareness.**

Lindamood-Bell "Auditory Discrimination in Depth Program" An intensive program of 4 hours per day for 6 to 8 weeks for students with **reading disorders**; uses a teaching strategy merging the disciplines of linguistics and **speech pathology** to remediate reading problems; developed and taught by the privately owned and operated Lindamood-Bell Center in California.

The program's premise is that a student with a reading disorder must first develop phonemic awareness before he or she is able to develop reading and spelling skills commensurate with his potential. To develop phonemic awareness, the program provides direct and intensive stimulation to develop the student's ability to identify individual sounds and the order of sounds in words of 1 to 5 syllables. The program begins with teaching the student to respond to questions to facilitate the student's independent discovery of the motor actions required to produce sounds. Other instruction involves using a set of pictures of the mouth to show where sounds are made, engaging the student in activities with colored blocks that represent the sounds, and identifying sounds using letters in spelling and reading. (Description from opinion of the hearing officer in *Oak View Union School District,* 24 IDELR 183 (SEA CA 1995).)

linguistic capacity
The ability to construct language; generally not present in children with **autism, profound mental retardation** or developmental or congenital **aphasia,** who may instead use **augmentative communication systems** or devices to develop limited vocal communicative ability without the use of language.

linguistic systems
The components of language that contribute to the ability to use meaningful **expressive language** and **receptive language** for communication; includes **phonology, syntax, semantics** and **pragmatics.**

linkages
In connection with **transition services** under the IDEA, the responsibility of the school district to involve participating agencies in the transition process.

lip reading
Technique used by deaf or hearing-impaired individuals to comprehend spoken speech by perception of movement of the speaker's lips and facial muscles and other visual cues such as facial expression and context; not all hearing-impaired or deaf individuals can master the technique, and it has limitations even for those who can because of **homophenes**. Also known as speech reading.

lisp
Articulation disorder in which the improper expulsion of air results in speaking the sound "th" for "s" or "z."

literate
Usually considered having **functional reading** above the 4th-grade level.

lobes of the brain
Portions of the brain, each having specific functions and regulating specific human activity: (a) **frontal lobe,** (b) **parietal lobes,** (c) **temporal lobes,** (d) **occipital lobes** and (e) **cerebellum.**

local educational agency (LEA)
1. The public board of education or other public authority that exercises administrative control or direction over public **elementary schools**

167

and/or **secondary schools** in a public subdivision. 2. Defined, as a term of art, in the IDEA at 20 U.S.C. § 1401(a)(8) as: "a public board of education or other public authority legally constituted within a State for either administrative control or direction of, or to perform a service function for, public elementary or secondary schools in a city, county, township, school district, or other political subdivision of a State, or such combination of school districts or counties as are recognized in a State as an administrative agency for its public elementary or secondary schools. Such term also includes any other public institution or agency having administrative control and direction of a public elementary or secondary school." 3. Defined, as a term of art, in **Education Department General Administrative Regulations (EDGAR)** at 34 C.F.R. § 77.1(b), substantially similarly. See also **state educational agency (SEA).**

local-level nonsupplanting See **nonsupplanting.**

location In connection with **early intervention services**

under Part H, the description of where services are to be provided that must be included in the **Individualized Family Service Plan (IFSP)**; defined, as a term of art, in Part H regulations at 34 C.F.R. § 303.344(d)(2)(ii) as: ". . . where [subject to the Part H LRE requirement] a service is to be provided (e.g., in the child's home, early intervention centers, hospitals and clinics, or other settings, as appropriate to the age and needs of the individual child)."

locked-in syndrome A condition in which the individual is conscious and receptive skills are intact, but he or she is unable to move or speak because of a disconnection of the motor cells in the lower brain stem and spinal cells and the upper portions of the brain in which the controlling signals originate. As distinguished from a **persistent vegetative state** or **coma.**

lockstep Rigid system of annual across-the-board pupil promotion without retention; similar to **social promotion.**

locus of control The mechanism through which an individual determines his or her actions and controls his or her behavior.

lodestar amount In connection with the awarding of **attorneys' fees** under the IDEA, the prevailing hourly rate for an attorney in the community with the level of skill and experience of the attorney seeking fees, as determined by the court.

lodestar method In connection with the awarding of **attorneys' fees** under the IDEA, the **lodestar amount** multiplied by the reasonable number of hours expended by the attorney on the case, as determined by the court; 20 U.S.C. § 1415(e)(4)(C) states that fees must be based on "rates prevailing in the community in which the action or proceeding arose for the kind and quality of services furnished."

logopedics Study and treatment of speech defects.

longitudinal study Research in which the same subjects are followed over years in order to, e.g., determine long-term outcomes of educational interventions or programs.

long period of time In connection with establishing eligibility for Part B on the basis of a **serious emotional disturbance** under Part B, the durational requirement for the presentation of qualifying characteristics set out in regulations at 34 C.F.R. § 300.7(b)(9).

The term is undefined in the regulations, but a generally acceptable definition, according to the **Office of Special Education Programs (OSEP)**, is a range of time from 2 to 9 months, with the application of preliminary interventions and documentation of the degree of their effectiveness. *Letter to Anonymous,* EHLR 213:147 (OSEP 1989).

long-term memory Memory system that preserves information for more than a few seconds or minutes. Also termed permanent memory. See also **short-term memory.**

long-term suspension Generally, any suspension in excess of 10 school days.

In *Doe v. Honig,* 1987-1988 EHLR 559:231 (1988), the U.S. Supreme Court ruled that a suspension from school for more than 10 school days of a child with a disability (one eligible for programming under the IDEA) triggers **procedural safeguards.** In *Suspension of Handicapped Students-Deciding Whether Misbehavior Is Caused by a Child's Handicapping Condition* (OCR Memorandum Nov. 1989), the **Office for Civil Rights (OCR)** stated that the same protections available to students classified as disabled under the IDEA are generally available to students classified as disabled under Section 504.

lordosis Irregular curvature of the spine; preferred term for swayback.

Lovaas program Program for preschool-aged children with **autism,** variously referred to as treatment, therapy, or **educational methodology,** premised on **applied behavioral analysis (ABA).**

The Lovaas program typically consists of **discrete trial training** in a home setting in a 1-on-1 format for 35 to 40 hours per week. The training is provided by properly trained, although not necessarily degreed, professionals, with family members as active participants. The program's objective is successful integration with nondisabled children upon completion of the training (2 to 3 years). The Lovaas program is based on the research of Dr. O. Ivar Lovaas, a recognized expert in the use of ABA, and his team at the University of California at Los Angeles. In a 1987 study conducted by Dr. Lovaas, 47% of the autistic children in his study "recovered" with use of comprehensive therapy for 2 years, with recovery defined as needing no special support services or aids when placed in a regular 1st-grade classroom. While some researchers question the study, the possibility of a "cure" for autism is causing parents of children with autism to demand public funding of the Lovaas program, under either Part B or Part H, depending on the age of the child, in ever-increasing numbers. Due process brings mixed results. No decisionmaker has held that public agencies must always fund the Lovaas program under either Part B or Part H, although districts have been ordered to so fund or provide when they have not offered an alternative program held to be appropriate.

Lowe's syndrome Genetic disorder resulting in diseases or conditions such as impaired functioning of the brain, muscles, kidneys, bones and teeth and cataracts that cause **visual impairments** or blindness; affects only males.

low-incidence disability In connection with **special education,** a disability that affects relatively few of the total number of children with disabilities who are receiving special services; blindness, deafness and **mental retardation** are examples of low-incidence disabilities. See also **intermediate educational unit (IEU).**

low-technology device

Device that has no electronic components and functions more as a passive aid, such as a **crutch**. As distinguished from **high-technology device.**

low vision

Severe **visual impairment,** even after correction, that may be improved through the use of **low vision aids** and environmental modifications.

low vision aids

Optical aids that include: (a) magnifier stand for reading small print, (b) monocular telescope for seeing the blackboard, (c) light transmission devices such as absorptive lenses, filters and lens coatings to reduce glare, (d) reflection control devices such as visors and sideshields; linear magnification aids such as large print books and **assistive technology devices** to produce audio alternatives to visual materials.

low vision, educational programming for

Programming to instruct student how to maximize residual vision and use visual information to extract maximum useful information. See also **low vision aids.**

Luria-Nebraska Neuropsychological Battery, Children's Revision (LNNB-C)

Individually administered **battery** of **norm-referenced tests**; 149 items grouped in 11 scales to assess neuropsychological functioning in children between the ages of 8 and 12 years; scales are: (a) motor functions, (b) rhythm, (c) tactile functions, (d) visual functions, (e) **receptive language,** (f) **expressive language,** (g) writing, (h) reading, (i) arithmetic, (j) **memory** and (k) intellectual processing.

171

M

MA mental age

MCA McCarthy Scales of Children's Abilities

MCS multiple chemical sensitivity

MD muscular dystrophy

MDT multidisciplinary team

MMPI Minnesota Multiphasic Personality Inventory

magnet school School (or schools) established by a school district that offer different **curricula** or instructional models in order to attract students away from their home schools, e.g., a magnet school for art or science.

A magnet school can have admission requirements. Under law, the school must be open to all students in the district regardless of sex, race or disability, although some districts may have mandatory racial guidelines on enrollment in order to achieve **diversity.** According to the **Office for Civil Rights (OCR),** requiring students with disabilities to waive their rights to **special education** or **related services** in order to attend a magnet program violates Section 504. See, e.g., *Chattanooga (TN) Public School District,* 20 IDELR 999 (OCR 1993). Nevertheless, in *Milwaukee (WI) Public School,* EHLR 353:526 (OCR 1987), OCR acknowledged the existence, in some circumstances, of a justifiable limitation on participation of students with disabilities in magnet schools based on the difficulty of concurrently meeting the goals of the magnet school program and providing for individualized special education needs. The implication is that school districts are not required by Section 504 to alter the basic nature of a specialized program in order to provide some or more participation by students with disabilities.

mainstreaming Not a formal term, but common jargon

in the educational community typically accepted as meaning the placement of a child with a disability alongside nondisabled children in the **regular education** setting; less preferred term for **inclusion** or **full inclusion.**

A mainstreamed placement is not synonymous with **least restrictive environment,** although the **LRE mandate** of the IDEA is the legal support for mainstreaming as an educational philosophy. As explained by the Tenth Circuit Court of Appeals in its influential LRE decision, *Murray v. Montrose County School District RE-1J,* 22 IDELR 558, 564 n.10 (10th Cir. 1995): "The term 'mainstreaming' is also frequently used, often interchangeably, with the term LRE. In fact, they are different, 'Mainstreaming' means placing disabled children in regular classrooms, with non-disabled children. The IDEA does not require mainstreaming in all cases. . . . The term 'inclusion' is increasingly favored over the term 'mainstreaming' because 'mainstreaming connotes the shuttling of the disabled child in and out of the regular class without altering the class to accommodate the child [citation omitted].'"

maintenance   Student's ability to maintain performance of a skill after acquisition training is completed, but prior to and independent of **generalization** of that skill.

Maintenance ability is essential for students with disabilities who have difficulty with either **acquisition** or generalization.

maintenance of effort
Term commonly used to describe the **nonsupplanting** requirement found in Part B regulations at 34 C.F.R. § 300.230(b), which provides that to meet the nonsupplanting requirement of 20 U.S.C. § 141(a)(2)(B), in each fiscal year a school district must spend the same amount of state and local funds on **special education** as it did in the previous year, on either an aggregate or per capita basis.

IDEA regulations at 34 C.F.R. § 300.230(b) state that: "the total amount or average per capita amount of State and local school funds budgeted by the LEA for expenditures in the current fiscal year for the education of **children with disabilities** must be at least equal to the total amount of State and local school funds actually expended for the education of children with disabilities in the most recent fiscal year for which the information is available [with allowances made for decreases in enrollment of children with disabilities or unusually large expenditures for long-term projects]."

The maintenance of effort requirement is not found in the IDEA statute itself. Nevertheless, in *Washington v. United States Department of Education,* 905 F.2d 274 (9th Cir. 1990), the Ninth Circuit Court of Appeals ruled that the regulatory requirement was reasonable, approved by Congress and consistent with interpretation of similar statutes. The impact of the maintenance of effort mandate has been felt by states and local communities that have not been able to maintain previous levels of educational spending generally. For example, in *Letter to Fischer,* 18 IDELR 1033 (OSEP 1992), the **Office of Special Education Programs (OSEP)** stated that the requirement could not be waived for an economically depressed rural school district facing the prospect of across-the-board cuts in all educational spending.

major life activities 1. In connection with eligibility for the protections of Section 504, defined, as a term of art, in Section 504 regulations at 34 C.F.R. § 104.3(j)(2)(ii) as: "functions such as caring for one's self, performing manual tasks, walking, seeing, hearing, speaking, breathing, learning and working." 2. In connection with eligibility for benefits and services under state programs receiving support under the **Developmental Disabilities As-** sistance and Bill of Rights Act of 1975, includes self-care, **receptive language** and **expressive language,** learning, mobility, self-direction, capacity for independent living and economic self-sufficiency.

maladaptive behavior
Behavior that interferes with an individual's ability to function in society; maladaptive behavior **domains** generally include: (a) violent and destructive behavior, (b) antisocial behavior, (c) rebelliousness, (d) untrustworthiness, (e) withdrawal, (f) **stereotypic behaviors,** (g) odd mannerisms, (h) inappropriate social behavior and (i) self-abusive behavior.

maladaptive behavior, assessment of Generally 3 methods: (a) **behavioral checklists** completed by parents or teachers, (b) informal interviews with teachers, parents and peers, and (c) direct observation in different settings. See also **four pillars of assessment.**

maladaptive behavior, interventions for Vary with type of behavior, but gen-

175

erally include: (a) **behavior modification,** (b) special classrooms, (c) **behavior management plan,** (d) **cognitive behavior modification therapy,** (e) intensive **psychotherapy** and (f) pharmaceuticals.

manifestation determination In connection with the **discipline** of students with disabilities, a determination whether or not the misconduct at issue was either a manifestation of the disability or the result of an inappropriate placement. See also **nexus inquiry.**

> The **Office of Special Education Programs (OSEP)** interprets the U.S. Supreme Court's decision in *Honig v. Doe,* 1987-88 EHLR 559:231 (1988), as requiring a school to conduct a manifestation determination before it may consider a suspension of more than 10 school days **[long-term suspension].** Similarly, with respect to Section 504, the **Office for Civil Rights (OCR)** requires that before any **significant change in placement** is implemented, a student with a disability must be reevaluated.

manipulative A physical object used as a model in an instructional program.

> Coins can be a manipulative for math instruction.

mastery learning 1. Generally, an approach to **individualized instruction** in which students are allowed the time necessary to master a unit of the **curriculum** before proceeding to the next learning unit. 2. In connection with **special education** programming, breaking down a program of instruction into its smallest units and sequencing those units in hierarchical order from least difficult to most difficult or advanced, and teaching each unit to mastery before moving on the next unit; the instructional procedures implicit in the **individualized education program (IEP) mandate** of the IDEA. See also **individualized instruction; short-term instructional objectives.**

mathematics disorder A **learning disorder** the diagnostic criteria for which is defined in the DSM-IV as: "A. Mathematics ability, as measured by individually administered **standardized tests** . . . , is substantially below that expected given the person's chronological age, measured intelligence and **age-appropriate** education; B. The disturbance in Criterion A significantly interferes with **academic achievement** or **activities of daily living** that require mathematics skills; C. If a sensory **deficit** is present, the . . . difficulties are in excess of those usually associated with it."

McCarthy Scales of Children's Abilities (MCA)

Standardized, individually administered **instrument** that produces a score of a child's general level of **intelligence** as well as specific measures of verbal ability, nonverbal reasoning ability, **short-term memory** and coordination; consists of 6 scales: (a) verbal scale, (b) perceptual-performance scale, (c) quantitative scale, (d) memory scale, (e) motor scale and (f) general cognitive scale; useful in assessment of **learning disabilities** in younger children.

McGinnis Method

A method for instructing children with **learning disabilities** using sight, sound and **kinesthesis** and stressing attention, recall and retention. See also **multisensory approach; Project Read.**

mean With reference to test scores, the arithmetic average of the scores; the generally preferred **measure of central tendency;** other measures include **median** and **mode.**

measurement In connection with **behavioral assessment,** the assignment of numerical values to observed behaviors or actions; various measurement systems for which key factors in selection are **reliability** and **validity.** See also **scale.**

measure of central tendency

Describes the typical or average score in a population of test-takers, most commonly used are the **mean, mode** and **median.**

measure of dispersion

Describes the variability of a group of scores in a population of test-takers, most commonly used are: range, variance and **standard deviation.**

median With reference to test scores, the middle point or the 50th percentile; the **measure of central tendency** most apt when most scores are either at the high end or low end of the range. See also **mean; mode.**

mediation An informal process in which parents and school districts resolve differences about the identification, programming or placement for a student with a disability without conducting a **due process hearing.**

Mediation is an intervening step that may be used prior to conducting a formal due process hearing. Although mediation may be a less costly and divisive way to resolve disputes concerning identification, evaluation, educational placement or the provision of a **free appropriate public education (FAPE),** neither the IDEA nor its regulations require it. While the **United States Department of Education** encourages states to use mediation as an alternative dispute mechanism, states cannot require parents to submit to mediation. See, e.g., *Letter to Decker,* 19 IDELR 279 (OSERS 1989).

Medical Assistance (Medicaid) Joint federal-state program authorized under Title XIX of the Social Security Act designed to provide medical assistance to individuals whose income and resources are insufficient to meet the costs of necessary care and services;

codified as a matter of federal law at 42 U.S.C. § 1396-1396s.

Each state operates its own Medicaid program under a state plan that, within limits imposed by the federal government, allows states to establish their own eligibility criteria and range of covered services. The limit most pertinent to serving **children with disabilities** is contained in Part B regulations at 34 C.F.R. § 300.601, which makes it clear that states may not reduce assistance available to children with disabilities by eliminating coverage of services that are also part of a **free appropriate public education (FAPE)** and, in the absence of other available funding, would be the responsibility of the school district.

medically fragile 1. Generally, requiring intensive and prolonged health care as a result of a catastrophic medical event or congenital condition. 2. In connection with **special education,** having extreme medical needs that require specific procedures be provided or available during the day in order for the student to attend school, thus complicating provision of a program designed to meet educational needs; sometimes also referred to as **technologically-dependent.** See also **excluded medical services; school health services.**

The administrative decision in *Cedar Rapids Community School District,* 22 IDELR 278 (SEA IA 1994), concerned a 12-year-old student identified as medically fragile. He was paralyzed from the neck down and depended on use of a ventilator for life support [**ventilator-dependent**]. For the student to attend school during the day he needed catheterization [**catheter**], **suctioning** of his **tracheotomy tube,** monitoring of his ventilator, **ambu bagging,** and assistance with eating, drinking and **positioning.**

medical model An educational approach that focuses on the underlying cause of the overt behavior or observed problem that **adversely affects the educational performance** of a student with a disability. See also **etiology.**

The medical model is most clearly applicable when the student has a physical impairment. Because it is static and does not take into account the role of psychoeducational intervention, its use in connection with students who have mild mental disabilities has been subject to criticism.

medical services In connection with **special education,** the limited range of physician services that must be provided as a **related service;** defined, as a term of art, in IDEA regulations at 34 C.F.R. § 300.7(b)(4) as "services provided by a licensed physician to determine a child's medically related disability that results in the child's need for special education and related services." See also **excluded medical services; school health services.**

medical services for diagnostic or evaluation purposes An **early intervention service** defined, as a term of art, in Part H regulations at 34 C.F.R. § 303.12(d)(5) as: "services provided by a licensed physician to determine a child's developmental status and need for early intervention services."

membrane   keyboard Keyboard with flat, touch-sensitive surface rather than keys, with size, place and characters on the surface modifiable; **alternative input interface** for individuals with disabilities who lack the **fine motor skills** to manipulate a standard keyboard. See also **keyboard for an individual with a disability.**

memory Process of storing, processing and retrieving information.

179

memory disorder A deficiency in the storage or retrieval of information resulting from either **brain injury** or neurological disease.

meningitis Inflammation or infection of the membranes surrounding the brain and spinal cord.

Children recovering from meningitis may have residual mental functioning impairments.

mental age (MA) A calculation to identify a student's mental ability in terms of the average chronological age of other students who have the same score on a mental ability test.

If a child's score is the same as the mean score of children of a certain chronological age, then that chronological age is the child's mental age. Mental age computation is disfavored as a measurement because it is vulnerable to misinterpretation. For example, no useful comparisons can be made between the mental ability of 2 students with the same mental age when one student is chronologically older than his or her mental age and the other younger.

mental disorder 1. Very generally, a disease or condition that presents as disruption in thought processes, behavior, emotions or perceptions and that impacts one's relations with others or ability to achieve in educational, vocational, personal, social or **leisure-time activities.** 2. A disorder the diagnostic criteria for which is defined in the DSM-IV as: "a clinically significant behavioral or psychological syndrome or pattern that occurs in an individual and is associated with present distress, ... disability ... or significantly increased risk of suffering, death, pain, disability, or an important loss of freedom."

mental retardation 1. As defined by the **American Association on Mental Retardation (AAMR),** an individual is considered to have mental retardation if: (a) the intellectual functioning level (**IQ score**) is below 70 to 75; (b) there are significant limitations in 2 or more **adaptive skill areas** (students with IQs under 50 have serious limitations in functioning); and (c) these conditions present themselves during childhood. 2. A disorder the diagnostic criteria for which is defined in the DSM-IV as: "A. Significantly subaverage intellectual functioning: an IQ of approximately 70 or below on an individually administered IQ test (for infants, a clinical judgment of significantly subaverage intellectual functioning); B. Concurrent **deficits** or impairments in present adaptive functioning (i.e., the person's effectiveness in meeting the standards expected for his or her age by his or her cultural group) in at least two of the following areas: communication, self-care, home living, social/interpersonal skills, use of community resources, self-direction, functional academic skills, work, leisure, health and safety; C. The onset is before age 18 years, and categorized as mild, moderate, severe or profound, based upon the severity of intellectual impairment (IQ score). 3. 1 of the 13 disabilities for eligibility under the IDEA, defined, as a term of art, in 34 C.F.R. § 300.7(b)(6) as: "significantly subaverage general intellectual functioning concurrently with deficits in adaptive behavior and manifested during the developmental period that adversely affects a child's educational performance."

mental status examination The part of the psychiatric, general medical, or **neurologic assessment** that specifically examines an individual's level of consciousness, language, ability to perceive through sight, to have higher motor movements (such as reaching), and to have **memory** and other **higher mental functions.**

mentorship Educational programming for **gifted** students in which a member of the school system, or the community generally, agrees to serve as a counselor and guide for a student's independent efforts in the mentor's area of expertise.

metacognitive approach Instructional approach encouraging a student to become aware of his or her own thinking processes and to use that awareness to self-regulate his or her own **academic achievement** by facilitating use of his or her **cognitive abilities** and preferred **learning styles**.

methodology See **educational methodology.**

181

Metropolitan Achievement Tests Assessment **instrument,** available in 14 levels from kindergarten through grade 12, assessing student achievement in: **reading,** mathematics, language, science, social studies and critical thinking skills; also measures content mastery in areas such as vocabulary, mathematical concepts and problem solving, composing and editing.

microcephaly The condition in which the brain is markedly smaller than normal, typically due to genetic developmental defects or in-utero infections, such as those caused by viruses. See also **anencephalus.**

middle school School usually comprising grades 7, 8 and 9.

mild conduct disorder A **conduct disorder** diagnosed on the basis of meeting the minimum number of DSM-IV diagnostic criteria for a conduct disorder, with none of those criteria involving harming others. See also **moderate conduct disorder; severe conduct disorder.**

mild disability Imprecise term generally understood to include students with **mild mental retardation, learning disabilities** or emotional disturbances who spend the larger part of the school day in the regular classroom. See also **severe disability.**

mild hearing loss Difficulty hearing faint sounds.

mild mental retardation In connection with terminology of the DSM-IV, generally associated with individuals with **mental retardation** whose **IQ scores** are in the 50-55 to 70 range; substantially similar to the criteria for those considered **educable mentally retarded** under some state educational codes.

mild spasticity Type of **cerebral palsy** characterized by awkward gait and lack of balance. As distinguished from **moderate spasticity.**

milieu therapy Method for teaching language and social skills to children with autism or other children whose disabilities impair communicative or **social skills.**

miniature keyboard Standard keys on a smaller surface for those with limited arm movement or use of only one hand. See also **keyboard for an individual with a disability.**

minimal brain dysfunction 1. Generally, a once common term in medical or scientific literature describing an occurrence of impaired attention and **memory** and resulting learning problems without a known **insult to the brain.** 2. Identified in IDEA regulations at 34 C.F.R. § 300.7(b)(10) as a "**specific learning disability,**" but not further defined.

> The inquirer in *Letter to Latham,* 21 IDELR 1179, 1183 (OSEP 1994), argued that medical literature supports defining a minimal brain dysfunction as what we now more commonly refer to as **attention deficit disorder (ADD)** or **attention deficit hyperactivity disorder (ADHD).** Accordingly, the inquirer advocated the explicit identification of those 2 disorders as specific learning disabilities for purposes of establishing IDEA-eligibility. The **Office of Special Education Programs (OSEP)** declined, responding that "[t]he Department [of Education] does not believe that the clarification you are seeking will either alter the eligibility of, or enhance services and programs for, children with ADD who need **special education** and **related services.**"

minimum average amount spent on children as a whole In connection with Part B funding, the amount computed on the basis of the formula set out in IDEA regulations at 34 C.F.R. § 300.184.

minimum due process In connection with disciplinary action, the constitutional requirement established by the U.S. Supreme Court in *Goss v. Lopez,* 419 U.S. 565 (1975), requiring schools to give students some kind of notice and some kind of hearing before imposing **suspensions** of up to 10 school days. See also **short-term suspension.**

> The minimum due process requirements are, of course, far less rigorous than the **procedural safeguards** triggered by a proposed suspension of a student with a disability for more than 10 school days. Schools may nonetheless choose to establish an intermediate level of due process for short-term suspensions of students with disabilities that exceeds the *Goss v. Lopez* standard. For example, the school district in *Parents of Student W. v. Puyallup School District No. 3,* 21 IDELR 723 (9th Cir. 1994),

183

established suspension guidelines under which each short-term suspension triggered a **manifestation determination** and a consideration of any cumulative effect of the suspensions on the student's educational program.

Minnesota Multiphasic Personality Inventory (MMPI) Assessment instrument for major psychological characteristics used to disclose the extent, if any, of a child's social and personal maladjustment, including disabling psychological dysfunction; widely used clinical method of testing for hostility and potential for aggression.

minor physical abnormalities Collectively, the physical features associated with the unique physical appearance of children with mental disabilities such as **Down syndrome.** See also **clinical type appearance.**

mirror reading A **learning disability** in which words are seen in reverse and read from right to left.

misconduct In connection with school **discipline,** generally understood to be student behavior that is unacceptable to school officials but does not violate criminal statutes, including absenteeism, tardiness, bullying and inappropriate language.

mixed dominance An inconsistent use of one's right or left hand found among students with **learning disabilities** more frequently than one would expect as a matter of statistical probability.

mixed receptive-expressive language disorder A **language disorder** the diagnostic criteria for which is defined in the DSM-IV as: "A. The scores obtained from a **battery** of standardized individually administered measures of both **receptive [language]** and **expressive language** development are substantially below those obtained from standardized measures of nonverbal intellectual capacity. Symptoms include those for **Expressive Language Disorder** as well as difficulty understanding words, sentences, or specific types of words, such as spatial terms; B. The difficulties with expressive language and receptive language interfere with academic or occupational achievement or social communication; C. Criteria are not met for a **Pervasive Developmental Disorder;** D. If mental retardation, a speech-motor or sensory deficit, or environmental deprivation is present, the language difficulties are in excess of those usually associated with these problems."

mobile work crew **Supported employment** model in which an employment group of 4 to 6 adults with disabilities and a crew supervisor work together at various job sites to perform functions such as janitorial work.

mobility aids Devices such as **canes,** service animals and electronic devices that help blind individuals orient themselves in their physical location and move about safely. See also **echolation device.**

mobility instruction Integration of specific **daily living skills** into the educational program of a child with a moderate or severe mental disability to assist him or her to navigate safely in the community. As distinguished from **mobility training.**

mobility specialist A professional with formal training evidenced by a bachelor's or master's degree who provides **mobility training,** including **orientation,** to blind individuals.

mobility training Techniques to help blind individuals move safely and independently within the community, including **orientation** and using a **cane.** As distinguished from **mobility instruction.** See also **orientation.**

In its *Policy Guidance on Educating Blind and Visually Impaired Students,* 23 IDELR 377 (OSEP 1995), the **Office of Special Education Programs (OSEP)** opined that educational programming for blind and visually impaired students should address their unique needs, including orientation and mobility.

modality A specific **physical therapy** treatment, such as hot packs or whirlpool baths.

mode With reference to test scores, the **measure of central tendency** that indicates the score occurring most frequently. See also **mean; median.**

modeling Imitation by a child of desired behaviors performed by peers or teachers, even in the absence of either **positive reinforcement** for so performing or **negative reinforcement** for performing behavior inconsistent with the desired behavior.

When considering inclusion of students with **mental retardation** in **regular education** classrooms, courts have made it clear that academic progress is not the only consideration. The possible development of social and communication skills, as well as improved self-esteem, through peer association and role modeling, have all been identified as benefits of **inclusion.** See, e.g., *Oberti v. Board of Education of Borough of Clementon School District,* 19 IDELR 908 (3d Cir. 1992) and *Daniel R.R. v. State Board of Education,* 1988-89 EHLR 441:433 (5th Cir. 1989).

mode of communication As defined in Note (2) to Part B regulations at 34 C.F.R. § 300.12 defining **native language,** in connection with an individual who is deaf, blind or has no written language, how that individual normally communicates, such as **sign language, Braille,** or oral communication.

moderate conduct disorder A **conduct disorder** diagnosed on the basis of meeting more than the minimum number of criteria required for a **mild conduct disorder** or meeting those criteria that involve harm to others, but not meeting criteria either as numerous or as harmful as those that meet the diagnostic criteria for a **severe conduct disorder.**

moderate hearing loss Involves retention of residual hearing but probably requires a hearing aid.

moderate mental retardation Terminology of DSM-IV generally associated with individuals with **mental retardation** whose **IQ scores** are in the 35-40 to 50-55 range; substantially similar to the criteria for those considered **trainable mentally retarded** under some state educational codes.

moderate spasticity Type of **cerebral palsy** in which one's legs rotate inward and flex at the knees, resulting in a scissoring gait. As distinguished from **mild spasticity.**

monitoring and compliance Office of Special Education Programs ongoing assessment of system effectiveness to ensure that **state educational agencies (SEAs)** meet their responsibility under the IDEA (20 U.S.C. § 1412(6)) to ensure that all the requirements of Part B are carried out.

In *OSEP Memorandum 95-13,* 22 IDELR 414 (OSEP 1995), OSEP explained its monitoring procedures and identified the specific IDEA requirements that are emphasized in its compliance reviews.

monoplegia Rare form of **spasticity** affecting 3 limbs. See also **cerebral palsy.**

Montessori Method Instructional method, usually for **preschool** and **elementary school** children, based on **individualized instruction,** extensive sensory and motor training, and reading and writing instruction starting at an early age.

moot With regard to a **civil action,** a finding by a court that if it were to enter a decision or judgment in the case, it would have no practical legal effect upon the parties or circumstances as they exist at that time or are likely to exist in the future; results in dismissal.

Article III of the U.S. Constitution and the constitutions of the states limit the jurisdiction of courts to actual ongoing cases or controversies. This requirement extends throughout the pendency of the action, not just at the time the case is filed. If no controversy exists, the case is rendered moot unless a party can show likely involvement in the same controversy at a later date if there is no current resolution—the "capable of repetition, yet evading review" exception to the mootness doctrine. While the sheer passage of time involved in litigating an IDEA claim may change the exact nature of the student's educational needs, a student's claim is not rendered moot as long as there is a retrospective remedy, such as **compensatory education** or **tuition reimbursement.** However, in *Randolph Union High School District No. 2 v. Bayard,* 23 IDELR 312 (D. Vt. 1995), the court dismissed as moot a claim for attorneys' fees filed by the parents of a student who committed suicide prior to the issuance of the hearing officer's decision, ruling that, despite the hearing officer's subsequent favorable decision, the attorneys' fees claim could not save the claim from being dismissed as moot.

morpheme The smallest unit of meaningful language. See also **phoneme.**

morphology Rules of language governing **morphemes.**

motion detection switch In connection with **assistive technology devices,** a sensor switch that is activated by small, controlled muscle movements, such as blinking one's eyes.

motor activity Movement of body muscles.

motor learning For students with sensorimotor disabilities, programming to master **fine motor skills** and **gross motor skills** required for daily living; helps students with such disabilities use their cognitive skills to learn movements that nondisabled students are able to learn automatically and perform habitually without **cognition.**

mouthstick An **alternative input interface** held in the mouth by individuals unable to use their hands to depress keys on a computer keyboard or make selections on a communication device.

multidisciplinary In connection with **early interven-**tion services for **infants and toddlers with disabilities,** defined, a term of art, in Part H regulations at 34 C.F.R. § 303.17 as: "the involvement of two or more disciplines or professions in the provision of integrated and coordinated services, and including **evaluation** and **assessment** activities ... and development of the IFSP [**individualized family service plan**]."

multidisciplinary team (MDT) 1. Generally, a functioning unit of individuals with varied professional training that coordinates services for a child with a disability, also called an interdisciplinary team. 2. The group of persons who conduct the **evaluation** and determine the placement of a child with a disability under the IDEA and Section 504.

The composition of the MDT is identified in IDEA regulations at 34 C.F.R. § 300.532(e) as "a group of persons, including at least one teacher or other specialist with knowledge in the suspected area of disability."

When the child is being evaluated for a suspected **specific learning disability (SLD),** the MDT must include the specific individuals further identified at 34 C.F.R. § 300.540.

According to the **Office of Special Education Programs (OSEP),** with the exception of the requirements in 34 C.F.R. § 300.540 concerning SLDs, there are no further federal standards for determining the composition of the MDT. The **state educational agency (SEA)** is responsible for establishing qualifications for team members. *Letter to Cohen,* EHLR 213:105 (OSERS 1987).

Section 504 regulations at 34 C.F.R. § 104.35(c) are similarly broad, stating that "placement decisions be made by a group of persons, including persons knowledgeable about the child, the meaning of the evaluation data, and the placement options."

multiple chemical sensitivity (MCS)
Allergic condition or syndrome characterized by severe reactions to chemicals commonly found in homes, schools and workplaces.

In *Placentia-Yorba Linda Unified School District,* 22 IDELR 305 (SEA CA 1995), an administrative decisionmaker held that a student with a medical diagnosis of MCS was not eligible for **special education** and **related services** on the basis of having an **"other health impairment"** because she was not lethargic, attended school regularly and in no way showed limited strength, vitality or alertness resulting from her disability.

multiple disabilities
1. Generally, a combination of 2 or more disabilities that result in the individual with the disabilities having significant difficulties in functional living. 2. Defined, as a term of art, in IDEA regulations at 34 C.F.R. § 300.7(b)(6) as: "concomitant impairments (such as mental retardation-blindness, mental retardation-orthopedic impairment, etc.), the combination of which causes such severe educational problems that they cannot be accommodated in **special education** programs solely for one of the impairments. The term does not include **deaf-blindness**."

multiple intelligences
Howard Gardner's theory of **intelligence,** popular among educators, in which he claims there are several relatively independent intelligences: logical-mathematical, linguistic, musical, spatial, bodily-kinesthetic, interpersonal and intrapersonal.

multiplier
In connection with awarding of **attorneys' fees,** an upward adjustment of the amount computed under the **lodestar method** based on fac-

tors such as novelty of the claim or probability of success; explicitly prohibited under the IDEA (20 U.S.C. § 1415(e)(4)(C)), but permitted for the calculation of **Section 1988** fees awards, including those for successful **Section 1983** claims asserted in connection with IDEA claims.

multipurpose system
Augmentative communication device with educational, vocational or recreational applications as well as for communication; commercial **high-tech electronic communication aids** include: the Liberator, Dynavox and the Touch Talker/ Light Talker.

multisensory approach
In connection with reading instruction, use of visual, auditory and tactile or kinesthetic **[kinesthesis]** pathways to present instructional content. See also **Lindamood-Bell "Auditory Discrimination in Depth Program"; Project Read.**

muscle tone
The resistance of muscle tissues to being stretched; when deficient, tone may be either **flaccid** or **spastic.**

muscular dystrophy (MD)
An hereditary disease for which there is no cure in which muscle tissue is replaced by fatty tissue, resulting in weakness and wasting away of muscle tissues; progressive deterioration of functioning and a loss of vitality; several different types, including **Duchenne disease,** myasthenia gravis and progressive atrophy.

myotonic dystrophy
See **Steinart's disease.**

N

NIDRR National Institute on Disability and Rehabilitation Research

NRT norm-referenced test

narcissistic personality disorder Personality disorder characterized by a need to be perfect and grandiosity.

An individual with such a disorder believes that his or her happiness is the responsibility of others and that he or she has a right to get anything desired. As a result, he or she may exhibit inappropriate behavior in the face of disappointment. Nevertheless, a student with such a disorder may not be IDEA-eligible. For example, the hearing officer in *Murrieta Valley Unified School District,* 23 IDELR 997 (SEA CA 1995), found that a 15-year-old student with a diagnosed narcissistic personality disorder met none of the 5 possible criteria for a **serious emotional disturbance** under IDEA regulations at 34 C.F.R. § 300.7(b)(9), even though

he experienced several episodes of violent behavior and "psychotic breaks" at home at times when he felt thwarted or frustrated.

narrative recording An **observational recording method** for the **systematic observation of behavior** in which the trained observer records all the child's behaviors or actions during the unit of time in which his or her behavior is being observed. See also **running record.**

The objective of narrative recording is to fully describe the child's behavior without resort to quantitative recording procedures.

nasogastric tube (NG tube) feeding Providing nutrition through a tube extending from an individual's nose and throat to the stomach when that individual is unable to ingest adequate nutrition or take medication orally. See also **gastrotomy tube feeding.**

National Assessment of Educational Progress (NAEP) Federally supported
program that tracks the performance of American students in core academic subjects and produces a national survey of students' achievements over time, known as the nation's "report card."

> There is an ongoing controversy in the educational field about the extent to which students receiving **special education** services must be included in the survey and the **accommodations** or adaptations that should be allowed to permit their meaningful participation.

National Institute on Disability and Rehabilitation Research (NIDRR) The branch of the **Office of Special Education and Rehabilitative Services (OSERS)** that provides leadership and support for a comprehensive national program of rehabilitation research, the prime goal of which is to enable individuals with disabilities to live independently.

native language 1. Defined, as a term of art, in the

Bilingual Education Act (codified at 20 U.S.C. § 3283(a)(2)) as: "when used with reference to an individual of limited English proficiency, ... the language normally used by that individual, or in the case of a child, the language used by the parents of the child." 2. Defined, as a term of art, in Part H almost identically as in BEA as "when used with reference to an individual of limited English proficiency, ... the language or **mode of communication** normally used by the parent of a child eligible under this part." 3. Incorporated by reference in Parts B of the IDEA at 20 U.S.C. § 1401(a)(22).

> Part B regulations require that written notice to parents, when required, must be provided in the parent's native language or other mode of communication. 34 C.F.R. § 300.500(a)(1). Further, tests and other evaluation materials must be provided and administered in the child's native language or other mode of communication. Part B regulations at 34 C.F.R. § 300.532(a)(1). Despite the regulatory definition of "native language," it seems reasonable to administer tests in English, assuming the student is bilingual, even if his or her parents are **limited-English proficient.** For example, an administrative decisionmaker held in *Greenfield Public School,* 21 IDELR

345 (SEA MA 1994), that there was no obligation to conduct testing in Cantonese to a bilingual 9-year-old student who had displayed **age-appropriate** levels in testings and assessments conducted in English since the age of 3.

natural environment In connection with the provision of **early intervention services** to **children with disabilities** under Part H, the type of setting, such as the home, preschool or child care setting, which is natural or normal for the child's age peers who have no disabilities.

Part H regulations at 34 C.F.R. § 303.12 establish the natural environment as the location for the provision of early intervention services that is the **least restrictive environment (LRE),** provided that "[t]o the extent appropriate, early intervention services must by provided in the types of settings in which infants and toddlers without handicaps participate." While there are some similarities between the LRE requirement of Part B and the natural environment requirement of Part H, those requirements are not identical. *Letter to Zimenoff,* 23 IDELR 439 (OSEP 1994).

natural language teaching paradigm In connection with **educational methodology** for developing language and communication skills in children with **autism** and **language disorders,** generally understood as instructional models based on natural situations and environments.

negative reinforcement A **behavior modification** principle in which a student is motivated to perform a desired behavior in the future because he or she wishes to avoid an undesired event that was contingent upon past performance of the undesired behavior, such as avoiding a reprimand. As opposed to **positive reinforcement.**

Nemeth code Used by blind individuals for academic work in mathematics and science. See also **Grade II Braille; Grade III Braille.**

neocortex The portion of the brain considered to be the source of **cognition.** Also called cerebral cortex.

neologism New, meaningless word that a child may create by scrambling the sounds or syllables of words he or she knows.

nephritis Disease involving inflammation of the kidney; identified as a health problem that could be an "**other health impairment**" for purposes of IDEA eligibility in Part B regulations at 34 C.F.R. § 300.7 (b)(8).

neurasthenia A syndrome of tiredness, headache, weakness, lack of initiative and similar symptoms that are not the result of an identifiable organic cause, but may be indicative of a depressive disorder.

neurological assessment An examination that specifically focuses on mental status, cranial nerves, motor functions, deep tendon reflexes, sensation and gait abilities; when used more in a psychiatric context, also refers to an examination of an individual's thinking ability, such as whether there are hallucinations or delusions and mood state. See also **neuropsychological assessment.**

neurological hard signs Indicia of neurological disease, such as abnormalities in reflex, that are generally considered definitive of dysfunction and capable of confirmation with diagnostic procedures such as MRIs. As distinguished from **neurological soft signs.**

neurological impairment An injury or disease of the **central nervous system (CNS),** such as **cerebral palsy.**

neurological soft signs Subtle deficits, such as awkwardness, disturbances of balance, hyperkinesis, and problems with **fine motor [skills]** coordination, linked with or thought to indicate **brain injury** or dysfunction, but not medically documented symptoms of neurological disease. As distinguished from **neurological hard signs.**

Unlike neurological hard signs, diagnosis of the presence of neurological soft signs is strictly low-tech, involving observation of the child in normal activities, such as walking, or by seeing how he or she performs simple tasks, such as putting a finger on his or her nose.

neuropsychological assessment 1. Typically uses specialized psychometric test instruments designed to examine specific functions and compare them against specific norms in order to help identify impairments in mental function and therefore, by inference, impairments in brain function; often a related attempt to lateralize or localize the damage, that is, to identify which side of the brain (right or left hemisphere) or the specific part of the brain (such as the **temporal lobes**) is at fault. 2. Used as a tool to evaluate how much a child's educational performance may be influenced by unusual functions of the **central nervous system (CNS)**, systematically assess a child's skills and determine appropriate programming.

Neuropsychological assessments are conducted by neuropsychologists and include assessments of attention, language, **memory,** perception, sensory and motor functions. A complete neuropsychological assessment requires gathering and analyzing information about a child's physical, social and psychological development and education, using sources such as parental observations, **systematic observation of behavior,** and testing that includes the **Halstead-Reitan Neuropsychological Test Battery** and the **Luria-Nebraska Neuropsychological Battery.** It typically takes about 15 hours to complete.

neuropsychological model A specific orientation

of the **medical model** that focuses on evaluation of **central nervous system** functioning as a key to understanding behavior.

neuropsychology Discipline concerned with functional assessment and mapping, or correlating, of human behavior to specific areas of the brain; encompasses assessment of cognitive processing [**cognition**] and affective dimensions of behavior [**affect**]. See also **lobes of the brain.**

next friend In connection with **special education** litigation, a **parent** bringing an action on behalf of his or her child; the parent is not considered a party to the action, but rather an officer of the court.

nexus inquiry In connection with disciplining students with disabilities, the inquiry that must be made to determine whether there is a causal relationship between the action complained of and the student's disability before a **long-term suspension** is imposed. See also **manifestation determination.**

The philosophy underlying the nexus inquiry requirement is that a child should not be denied educational services because of actions that should be expected to result from his or her disability. Courts have, however, established different standards of required relatedness to be applied in the course of the inquiry. Courts all support the view expressed by the Fifth Circuit Court of Appeals in 1981 (in *S-1 v. Turlington,* 1980-81 EHLR 552:267 (5th Cir. 1981)) that the mere fact that a student knows right from wrong does not make his or her misconduct unrelated to the disability. Beyond that, courts differ about the required degree of connectedness. The Ninth Circuit Court of Appeals, for example, stated in *Doe v. Maher,* 1985-86 EHLR 557:353, 359 n.8 (9th Cir. 1986), that "[a] handicapped child's conduct [is related to his disability] only if the handicap significantly impairs the child's behavior controls.... [I]t does not embrace conduct that bears only an attenuated relationship to the child's handicap."

non-academic and extracurricular services and activities Defined, as a term of art, in IDEA regulations at 34 C.F.R. § 300.306(b) and Section 504 regulations at 34 C.F.R. § 104.37(a)(2) as including "**counseling services,** athletics, transportation, health services, recreational activities,

special interest groups or clubs sponsored by the **public agency,** referrals to agencies that provide assistance to individuals with disabilities, and employment by students, including both employment by the public agency and assistance in making outside employment available."

Generally, school districts are required under Section 504 and the ADA to provide non-academic services and extracurricular activities "in such manner as is necessary to afford handicapped students an equal opportunity for participation in such services and activities." 34 C.F.R. § 104.37(a)(1). Uniform application of eligibility requirements for such activities as a rule complies with the law. Nonetheless, if modifying non-essential eligibility requirements would allow a student with a disability to participate, the school district will have to modify the rule. The distinction between essential and non-essential requirements can be problematic; court decisions are not uniform in their approach. See, e.g., the decisions in *Pottgen v. Missouri State High School Activities Association,* 21 IDELR 929 (8th Cir. 1994) and *Sandison v. Michigan High School Athletic Association, Inc.,* 21 IDELR 658 (E.D. Mich. 1994).

nondiscriminatory norm-referenced test Test that has modifications of test medium, administration or content so that it measures the same abilities and skills among the disabled and nondisabled.

nonsectarian school A **private school** whose **curriculum** and operation are independent of religious orientation and influence in all but incidental ways.

non-sheltered employment The range of employment opportunities for graduates of **special education** programs who can function in workplaces other than **sheltered employment** situations, including **competitive work, enclaves** within industry, **mobile work crews** and **supported employment.**

nonspecific deficiencies associated with impairments of the central nervous system Language disorder associated with children with, for example **mental retardation** or **Down syndrome,** characterized by difficulty with developing meaningful sounds, building vocabulary and acquiring **grammar.**

nonsupplanting 1. In connection with Part B funding, the requirement set out in the IDEA at 20 U.S.C. § 1414(2)(b)(ii) that such funding be used to supplement and increase the level of state and local funds spent on educating **children with disabilities,** not to replace those expenditures. Also referred to as local-level nonsupplanting and distinguished from **State-level nonsupplanting requirement.** 2. In connection with Part H funding, the requirement set out at 20 U.S.C. § 1478(b)(5)(B) that Part H funds supplement and increase, rather than take the place of, state and local funds for eligible children. See also **maintenance of effort.**

normal curve In connection with a **standardized test,** the typical distribution of how scores deviate from the **mean.** Also called a bell curve or bell-shaped curve.

normal curve equivalent In connection with a **standardized test,** statistical operations that score an examinee's test results in relationship to the performance of other examinees,

197

either nationally or locally, on an equal-interval bell curve scale. See also **standard score.**

normal in-school disciplinary proceedings Includes use of study **carrel, time-out,** detention or restriction of privileges.

According to the U.S. Supreme Court in *Honig v. Doe,* 1987-88 EHLR 559:231 (1988), imposition of such discipline with students with disabilities does not trigger the **procedural safeguards** of the IDEA.

norm group The defined group of test-takers whose scores are used to compute individual test-taker's scores on **norm-referenced tests;** typically a large group of students, generally a national age or grade group.

norm-referenced test (NRT) Comparison of one student's performance, as measured by the test score, with the performance of the norm group, allowing fine distinctions among students and identification of where a student stands in relation to that group; typically developed by commercial test companies.

When compared to **criterion-referenced tests,** norm-referenced tests are almost always broader in content and most typically used to test aptitude and interest and assess personality, although, like criterion-referenced tests, they may be used for achievement testing as well.

norms Performance standards established by a **reference group** to describe average or typical performance; usually determined by testing a representative group and then calculating the group's test performance.

nursing services An **early intervention service** under Part H defined, as a term of art, in Part H regulations at 34 C.F.R. § 303.12(d)(6) as including: "(i) the assessment of health status for the purpose of providing nursing care, including the identification of patterns of human response to actual or potential health problems; (ii) provision of nursing care to prevent health problems, restore or improve functioning, and promote optimal health and development; and (iii) administration of medications, treatments, and regimens prescribed by a licensed physician."

nutrition services An **early intervention service** under Part H defined, as a term of art, in Part H regulations at 34 C.F.R. § 303.12(d)(7) as including: "(i) conducting individual assessments in—(A) nutritional history and dietary intakes; (B) anthropometric, biochemical, and clinical variables; (C) feeding skills and feeding problems; and (D) food habits and food preferences; (ii) developing and monitoring appropriate plans to address nutritional needs of children eligible under this part, based on the findings in [the assessments conducted as required above]; and (iii) making referrals to appropriate community resources to carry out nutritional goals."

Nutrition services, along with **case management services,** are referred to as **"additional services"**—services not traditionally provided under Part B, despite being required under Part H.

nystagmus Visual impairment involving rapid involuntary movement of the eyeballs that affects **fine motor skills** and may cause difficulty in reading.

O

OCD obsessive-compulsive disorder

OCR Office for Civil Rights

ODD oppositional defiant disorder

OERI Office of Educational Research and Improvement

OESE Office of Elementary and Secondary Education

OHI other health impairment

OSEP Office of Special Education Programs

OSERS Office of Special Education and Rehabilitative Services

OT occupational therapy

OTA Office of Technology Assessment

observation 1. As a method of **assessment** generally, see **systematic observation of behavior.** 2. In connection with determining whether a student has a **specific learning disability,** a required part of an **evaluation** under Part B regulations at 34 C.F.R. § 300.542.

While Section 300.542(a) states that "[a]t least one team member other than the child's regular teacher shall observe the child's academic performance in the regular classroom setting" the regulations do not specify a required amount of observation time or when the observation must take place.

observational learning See **modeling.**

observational recording method Any one of various methods in which professionals observe the behavior of a child in connection with a **systematic**

observation of behavior; 4 most commonly used in the school setting are: (a) **narrative recording;** (b) **interval recording;** (c) **event recording;** and (d) **ratings recording,** with choice of method a matter of professional judgment that considers, among other things, the frequency and intensity of the behavior to be observed.

observer drift In connection with the **systematic observation of behavior,** the failure of the observer to maintain consistent standards for observing and recording whether or not a behavior has occurred, usually attributed to factors such as fatigue and intervening distractions. See also **guinea pig effect; halo effect.**

obsessive-compulsive disorder (OCD) An anxiety disorder characterized by recurrent thoughts that the individual does not wish to think about (obsessions) or repetitive ritualistic behavior that the individual feels compelled to perform (compulsions) or both; individuals recognize that the thoughts or actions are not productive, but are unable to exert rational control to stop them.

A student with an OCD may be eligible for **special education** and **related services** as seriously emotionally disturbed **[serious emotional disturbance]** when the disorder compromises educational performance by interfering with normal thinking and making it difficult for students to attend to school work. OCD usually presents in adolescence or early adult years, but also has been observed in children. The 17-year-old student in *Sanger v. Montgomery County Board of Education,* 23 IDELR 955 (D. Md. 1996), for instance, had displayed a variety of obsessive-compulsive symptoms on a continuous basis since infancy. Typically, OCD presents in children or youth as a co-morbid **[co-morbidity]** disorder. For example, the 2nd grade boy in *W.B. v. Matula,* 23 IDELR 411 (3d Cir. 1993), had **Tourette's syndrome, attention deficit hyperactivity disorder** and a severe form of obsessive-compulsive disorder.

obstacle perception The ability of a blind individual to use sound waves and echoes to recognize when he or she is approaching an object. See also **echolation device; mobility aids.**

obtained score 1. Test score based on the premise that, even under circumstances that appear to be identical, a child will not receive the same score on each occasion he or she takes a particular test. 2. A construct arrived at by adjusting the child's **true score** to account for the probability and extent of error in scoring.

occipital lobes The regions of the brain in the back part, in which flows visual information; involved in processing basic visual functions such as object recognition and, to some extent, determining where those objects are. See also **lobes of the brain.**

occupational activities As part of a program of **vocational education,** alternatives may include paid work experience during the day, paid work experience after school hours, unpaid work observations, and in-school vocational laboratory.

occupational therapy (OT) 1. In connection with services for **children with disabilities** generally, the improvement of **sensory integration,** handling of objects, posturing of one's body and increasing daily living functioning. 2. A **related service** under Part B of the IDEA defined, as a term of art, in IDEA regulations at 34 C.F.R. § 300.16(b)(5) as including: "(i) Improving, developing or restoring functions impaired or lost through illness, injury, or deprivation; (ii) Improving ability to perform tasks for independent functioning when functions are impaired or lost; and (iii) Preventing, through early intervention, initial or further impairment or loss of function." (3) An **early intervention service** under Part H of the IDEA defined, as a term of art, in Part H regulations at 34 C.F.R. § 303.8 as including: "services to address the functional needs of a child related to the performance of self-help skills, **adaptive behavior** and play, and sensory, motor, and postural development [that include] (i) identification, assessment and intervention; (ii) adaptation of the environment, and selection, design and fabrication of assistive and **orthotic** devices to facilitate development and promote the acquisition of functional skills; and (iii) prevention or minimization of the impact of initial or future impairment, delay in development, or loss of functional ability."

ocular control training

Exercises to strengthen eye muscles to improve eye coordination and vision.

Office for Civil Rights (OCR)

The office within the **United States Department of Education** charged with assuring compliance with federal statutes that prohibit discrimination based on race, color, national origin, sex, age or disability; responds to complaints with investigations and issues **letters of findings (LOF)** as a result of those investigations; empowered to conduct administrative hearings that may result in suspension, termination or refusal to grant **federal financial assistance** to **public agencies.**

Office of Educational Research and Improvement (OERI)

The office within the **United States Department of Education** that gathers, analyzes and disseminates to the public statistical and other types of information concerning American education.

Office of Elementary and Secondary Education (OESE)

The office within the **United States Department of Education** that provides financial assistance to **state educational agencies (SEAs)** and **local educational agencies (LEAs)** for maintenance and improvement of both public and private **preschool, elementary school** and **secondary school** education.

Office of Special Education and Rehabilitative Services (OSERS)

The office within the **United States Department of Education** that supports programs to assist in the education of **children with disabilities** and the **rehabilitation** of youths and adults with disabilities; contains 3 offices: **Office of Special Education Programs (OSEP), the Rehabilitation Services Administration (RSA),** and the **National Institute on Disability and Rehabilitation Research (NIDRR).**

Office of Special Education Programs (OSEP)
The branch of the **Office of Special Education and Rehabilitative Services (OSERS)** responsible for administering programs relating to the free appropriate public education to all eligible beneficiaries, including interpreting the requirements of the IDEA statute and regulations and issuing policy letters. See also **Office of Special Education Programs Policy Letters.**

> OSEP oversees programs to expand and improve **special education,** administers **grants** to **state educational agencies** to help state and local districts serve **children with disabilities** and monitors state programs to ensure that students with disabilities receive appropriate education and that their rights and those of their **parents** or **guardians** are protected.

Office of Special Education Programs Policy Letters
Letters issued by OSEP in response to letters sent by individuals, organizations and entities who request OSEP's interpretation of the requirements of the IDEA statute and regulations in the context of a particular factual situation.

Courts are not bound by the interpretations in Policy Letters, although they generally give them deferential consideration. Two areas in which OSEP's interpretation of the IDEA in Policy Letters has created controversy is the continuation of educational services to properly expelled students with disabilities and the nature of school districts' obligations to parentally placed **private school students with disabilities.**

Office of Technology Assessment (OTA)
An office formerly within and reporting to Congress charged with providing information and analysis concerning emerging technologies and their uses, probable benefits and potential adverse impacts; since disbanded.

off-task behavior
In connection with **systematic observation of behavior,** a child behaving inappropriately for the situation; e.g., in the classroom, calling out rather than raising his or hand to signal a desire to speak. As distinguished from **on-task behavior.**

one-tier administrative system
The IDEA due process system in those states in which there is only 1 state-level

205

administrative **due process hearing,** whose decision an **aggrieved party** may appeal by commencing a **civil action** in federal court; codified in the IDEA at 20 U.S.C. § 1415 (e)(2). As opposed to **two-tier administrative system.**

ongoing support services In connection with **supported employment,** may include the use of a **job coach;** follow-up services such as regular contact with the employer, the individual, or his or her parents to reinforce and stabilize the job placement; **social skills** training; and facilitation of natural supports.

on-task behavior In connection with the **systematic observation of behavior,** a child behaving appropriately for the situation; e.g., when a child is in the classroom, raising his or her hand to signal a desire to speak rather than calling out. As distinguished from **off-task behavior.**

open-ended question In connection with **alternative assessment,** a question that allows a student to respond in a variety of ways of his or her own choosing, as opposed to a question with a specific menu from which to choose the correct response. See also **selection response test.**

open-ended task In connection with **alternative assessment,** student performance of a task that there is no one right way to perform; requires the student to exercise judgment in assessing the specific actions to be performed and how to perform them.

open head injury Generally, **traumatic brain injury** in which the brain is exposed because the dura is breached. As distinguished from a **closed head injury.**

The child may be eligible for IDEA services under eligibility requirements set out at 34 C.F.R. § 300.7(b)(12) when the injury results in impairments in 1 or more areas, such as: **cognition;** language; **memory;** attention; reasoning; **abstract thinking;** judgment; problem-solving; sensory, perceptual and **motor activities;** psychosocial behavior; physical functions; information processing; and speech.

oppositional defiant disorder (ODD) 1. Generally, a

disruptive **behavioral disorder** that often is an antecedent to a **conduct disorder,** equally prevalent among boys and girls after the onset of adolescence. 2. A disruptive behavioral disorder meeting the diagnostic criteria of the DSM-IV defined as: "A. A pattern of negativistic, hostile, and defiant behavior lasting at least 6 months, during which four (or more) of the following are present: (1) often loses temper; (2) often argues with adults; (3) often actively defies or refuses to comply with adults' requests or rules; (4) often deliberately annoys people; (5) often blames others for his or her mistakes or misbehavior; (6) is often touchy or easily annoyed by others; (7) is often angry and resentful; (8) is often spiteful or vindictive. B. The disturbance in behavior causes clinically significant impairment in social, academic or occupational functioning. C. The behaviors do not occur exclusively during the course of a psychotic or mood disorder. D. Criteria are not met for Conduct Disorder and, if the individual is age 18 years or older,

criteria are not met for Antisocial Personality Disorder."

optacon **Assistive technology device** composed of a tiny camera and a raised dot matrix that converts images photographed by the camera into raised letters (Greek alphabet, not **Braille**) that can be read by touch; can be used to read any text on paper; requires high touch sensitivity and long training.

oral/aural method Communication method for deaf individuals involving speaking, **lip reading,** listening (to extent residual hearing can be amplified) and writing, but excluding **sign language** or **finger spelling.** See **deaf education.**

oral pharyngeal disorder **Communication disorder** resulting from malformation of the pharynx (tube that extends through ear canals and mouth to lead to esophagus).

organic brain syndrome In connection with a **physical or mental impairment,** as defined in Section 504 regulations at 35 C.F.R. § 104.35, a somewhat archaic term referring to a **mental disorder** due to unspecified brain disease, usually a dementia, with more specific diagnosis usually possible.

orientation 1. The method by which a blind individual uses his or her remaining senses to determine where in the environment he or she is situated. See also **mobility training.** 2. Component of signs in **sign language** involving the relation of the individual's hand to his or her body.

orthopedic impairment 1. Generally, a disability that limits mobility and ambulation. 2. Defined, as a term of art, in IDEA regulations at 34 C.F.R. § 300.7(b)(7) as: "a severe orthopedic impairment that adversely affects a child's educational performance. The term includes impairments caused by congenital anomaly (e.g., **clubfoot,** absence of some member, etc.), impairments caused by disease (e.g., poliomyelitis, bone tuberculosis, etc.) and impairments from other causes (e.g., **cerebral palsy,** amputations, and fractures or burns that cause **contractures**)."

Children with orthopedic impairments usually require educational programming that includes **physical therapy** and **occupational therapy** and mobility and/or communication aids. Because some students with orthopedic impairments may not have accompanying intellectual, learning or psychological disabilities, there may be questions about their eligibility for **special education** and **related services** under the IDEA. This was the case in the federal district court case of *Yankton School District v. Schramm,* 23 IDELR 42 (D.S.D. 1995). While the school district maintained that an adolescent with **cerebral palsy** who had achieved excellent overall success in school was not entitled to **transition services** under the IDEA, the court held otherwise. Finding that the reduced homework to accommodate for writing slowness and instruction in modified keyboarding techniques constituted special education the student needed as a result of the disability, the court held the student to be IDEA-eligible.

orthotics Devices to augment the function of body parts and increase mobility and ability to perform **activities of daily living,** such as a splint or **braces.** As distinguished from **prosthesis.**

Orton-Gillingham method
A reading instructional method that is a **multisensory approach** designed as

a tutorial method focusing very heavily on **phonics.**

Because the Orton-Gillingham method is a highly structured and repetitious technique for teaching reading, it generally is used only with children who have **learning disabilities.** The basis of the method is an intensive, sequential phonics-based approach to teach the basics of word formation before whole meanings by use of visual, auditory and **kinesthetic [method]** modalities. Specifically, the method stresses the repeated associations of individual **phonemes** with their sound, name and cursive formation. It starts with drill cards for visual recognition of an initial set of letters, goes on to focus on letter sound and formation (traced, copied and drawn free-hand from memory), and finally blends the learned letters to form simple words. The process begins again as the student moves to the next set of letters.

ostomy Surgically created opening from the intestine and urinary tract and through the skin which provides for elimination of body wastes. Also called a stoma.

ostomy management and care Includes keeping the **ostomy** and surrounding skin in good condition and, when a bag rather than a **catheter** is in use, replacing a bag that is leaking; may be a **school health service.**

other health impairment (OHI) 1. Defined, as a term of art, in IDEA regulations at 34 C.F.R. § 300.7(b)(8) as: "having limited strength, vitality or alertness, due to chronic or acute health problems such as a heart condition, **tuberculosis, rheumatic fever, nephritis, asthma, sickle cell anemia, hemophilia, epilepsy, lead poisoning, leukemia,** or **diabetes** that **adversely affects a child's educational performance."**

Neither the IDEA nor the regulations define "limited alertness." According to OSEP, a child with **attention deficit disorder** may be eligible on the basis of having limited alertness despite his or her heightened alertness to environmental stimuli generally if that results in limited alertness to academic tasks. *Letter to Cohen,* 20 IDELR 73 (OSERS 1993).

Otis-Lennon School Ability Test Test designed to measure the learning skills most closely associated with the ability to learn new things and enjoy academic success; contains items in 5 clusters: (a) verbal comprehension, (b) verbal reasoning, (c) pictorial reasoning, (d) figural reasoning and (e) quantitative reasoning.

outcome-oriented process In connection with defining the **transition services** mandated under the IDEA (20 U.S.C. § 1412(2)(B)), generally understood to mean a process reasonably calculated to produce positive post-school outcomes for the transitioning student with a disability.

overcorrection A **behavior management** technique in which a child who performs an inappropriate behavior is required to do a corresponding or related appropriate behavior several times; a **punishment.**

overlap services Services, such as **physical therapy** or **occupational therapy,** that are **related services** under Part B of the IDEA and **early intervention services** under Part H of the IDEA.

> While all related services under Part B must be provided **free** to parents, under Part H some services may be subject to fees (20 U.S.C. § 1476(b)(9)). The question then becomes, in a **birth-mandate state:** Must all early intervention services be provided free or can some services be subject to fees? According to *OSEP Policy Memorandum 90-14,* 16 EHLR 708 (OSEP 1990), the answer depends on whether the service

is an **overlap service** or an **additional service.** To the extent that overlap services have been provided free to **infants and toddlers with disabilities** under Part B (in accordance with an **individualized education program**), they must continue to be provided under Part H, in accordance with an **individualized family service plan.** However, if the services are additional services that have been provided through programs other than Part B and paid for by other public agencies, the **Office of Special Education Programs (OSEP)** expects that the services would continue to be provided and paid for through those other funding sources.

oxygen supplementation Provision of oxygen from a portable oxygen tank through a nasal **catheter,** face mask or catheter mask. See also **ventilator.**

P

PECS Picture Exchange Communication System

PIAT Peabody Individual Achievement Test

PKU phenylketonuria

PPVT-R Peabody Picture Vocabulary Test-Revised

PTI Pictoral Test of Intelligence

palilalia Complex verbal tic consisting of repetition of one's own words. As distinguished from **echolalia.**

palpebral fissures Eye openings.

paraprofessional In connection with **special education,** a staff member other than a teacher engaged in education in the classroom who is, under state law, typically required to have specific training and meet state-mandated qualification standards.

Paraprofessionals may be assigned to provide 1-on-1 assistance to students with cognitive disabilities who are placed in a **regular education** classroom. However, as was illustrated in the Sixth Circuit Court of Appeals' decision in *Hudson v. Bloomfield Hills Public Schools,* 23 IDELR 612 (E.D. Mich. 1995), too much assistance can be counterproductive. In that case, the paraprofessional assigned to a **trainably mentally retarded** 14-year-old girl who lacked age appropriate conversational skills and had difficulty with peer relationships was the only person with whom the student would really talk. When the staff tried to put a little distance between them, the student rebelled by slamming her book shut or by fidgeting with the pages to draw her paraprofessional's attention.

parent In connection with entitlement to parental rights under the IDEA, defined, as a term of art, in IDEA Part B regulations at 34 C.F.R. § 300.13 and Part H regulations at 34 C.F.R. § 303.18 as: "a parent, a **guardian,** a **person acting as a parent of a child** or a **surrogate parent** who has been appointed in accordance with [§ 300.514 of Part B regulations or § 303.405 of Part H regulations]. The term does not include the State if the child is a ward of the state."

The IDEA does not address whether a divorced parent who does not live with the child should be accorded parental rights and responsibilities under the law. Thus, the **Office of Special Education Programs (OSEP)** has stated that the issue should be resolved under state law. *Letter to Dunlap,* EHLR 211:462 (OSEP 1987). Generally, state courts (or federal courts interpreting state law) that have published opinions addressing this issue have denied parental rights to non-custodial parents in the absence of a specific grant of authority by the court or in a court-approved settlement agreement.

parent advocate See **lay advocate.**

parentally placed students See **private school students with disabilities.**

parent counseling and training 1. Generally consists of counseling to educate parents about their child's disability, to help parents resolve emotional stress resulting from coping with the child's disability, and training for more effective communication with the child and at-home management of problem behavior consistent with the approach used at school. 2. A **related service** defined, as a term of art, in Part B regulations at 34 C.F.R. § 300.16(b)(6) as: "assisting parents in understanding the special needs of their child and providing parents with information about child development." See also **family training, counseling, and home visits.**

parietal lobes The portions of the brain in front of the **occipital lobes** and behind the **frontal lobe,** which are heavily involved in touch input and in processing higher order aspects of visual-spatial function. See also **lobes of the brain.**

Parson's Visual Acuity Test A **screening** test for visual problems used with children who have **severe disabilities** that impede communication of what they see.

Part A of the IDEA Contains the general provisions of the IDEA, including definitions; entitled "General Provisions" and codified at 20 U.S.C. §§ 1400-1409.

Part B of the IDEA Sets out the state formula grant program that requires each state receiving **federal financial assistance** under the IDEA to develop a **State plan** to ensure provision of **free appropriate public education (FAPE)** to all disabled children residing within the state and contains a series of **procedural safeguards** designed to protect the interests of children with disabilities; entitled "Assistance for Education of All Children with Disabilities" and codified at 20 U.S.C. §§ 1411-1420.

Part C of the IDEA A discretionary program that addresses funding of regional resource centers to provide consultation, technical assistance and training services, as well as the special needs of particular groups of **children with disabilities;** entitled "Centers and Services to Meet Special Needs of Individuals with Disabilities" and codified at 20 U.S.C. §§ 1421-1427.

Part D of the IDEA A discretionary program that concerns training personnel for educating **children with disabilities;** entitled "Training Personnel for the Education of Individuals with Disabilities" and codified at 20 U.S.C. §§ 1431-1435.

Part E of the IDEA A discretionary program that authorizes funding of research and demonstration projects to improve services for **children with disabilities;** entitled "Research in the Education of Individuals with Disabilities" and codified at 20 U.S.C. §§ 1441-1444.

Part F of the IDEA A discretionary program designed to promote instructional media for persons with disabilities, such as captioned films for the deaf; entitled "Instructional Media and Materials for Individuals with Disabilities" and codified at 20 U.S.C. §§ 1461-1462.

Part H of the IDEA A discretionary program that authorizes federal formula **grants** to states for the development and implementation of statewide systems to provide **early intervention services** for infants and toddlers with disabilities; entitled "Infants and Toddlers with Disabilities" and codified at 20 U.S.C. §§ 1471-1485.

partially sighted Central **visual acuity** measured as between 20/70 and 20/200 in the better eye, as corrected. See also **Snellen chart.**

participating agency 1. In connection with **education records,** defined, as a term of art, in Part B regulations at 34 C.F.R. § 300.560 as: "any agency or institution that collects, maintains, or uses **personally identifiable information,** or from which information is obtained, under this part [Part B]." 2. In connection with **transition services,** a governmental agency other than the school district that is financially and legally responsible for providing transition services to the student, such as state departments of vocational rehabilita-

tion, developmental disabilities councils and the Social Security Administration.

passing from grade to grade Not in every instance the sole indicia of whether a child with a disability is receiving a **free appropriate public education (FAPE),** although credible evidence supports that conclusion in the ordinary course.

In holding that Amy Rowley was not entitled to an **interpreter,** the U.S. Supreme Court in *Board of Education of Hendrick Hudson Central School District v. Rowley,* 1981-82 EHLR 553:656, 668 n.25 (1982), relied in large part on the fact that Amy was passing from grade to grade in a public school program. The Court was careful, however, to set some limits on the scope of its holding. It stated in a footnote that: "We do not hold today that every handicapped child who is advancing from grade to grade in a regular public school system is automatically receiving a 'free appropriate public education.'"

passive-aggressive Expressing hostility by uncooperative behavior, such as, in the school environment, failing to complete work, working slowly or ignoring assigned responsibilities.

Peabody Individual Achievement Test (PIAT)

Peabody Individual Achievement Test (PIAT) Individually administered **screening** test for children between the ages of 6 through 18 years to measure achievement in mathematics, reading recognition, reading comprehension, spelling and general information; multiple-choice format for some sections is useful with children with **expressive language disorders.**

Peabody Picture Vocabulary Test-Revised (PPVT-R)

Peabody Picture Vocabulary Test-Revised (PPVT-R) Standardized individually administered multiple-choice test that measures the **receptive language** communication ability of individuals between the ages of 30 months through adulthood who have adequate hearing ability.

pedagogical signed systems

pedagogical signed systems See **sign language.**

peer tutoring

peer tutoring **Individualized instruction** provided by a child close to the same age but functioning on a higher level as an adjunct to classroom instruction.

Peer tutoring is a common **accommodation** or programming element for students with **learning disabili**ties who are eligible under Section 504 but not the IDEA.

pendency of a proceeding

pendency of a proceeding In connection with a dispute about identification, **evaluation,** educational placement or the provision of **free appropriate public education (FAPE),** the period of time during which a child with a disability must remain in his or her **present educational placement,** starting when the request for a hearing is filed and generally continuing for as long as the review proceedings continue. See also **stay-put provision.**

IDEA regulations at 34 C.F.R. § 300.513 make it clear that the pendency period includes both "the administrative or judicial proceeding concerning a complaint" in the absence of an agreement otherwise. But 2 federal districts courts—*Manchester School District v. Williamson,* 17 EHLR 1 (D.N.H. 1990) and *Anderson v. District of Columbia,* 15 EHLR 441:508 (D.C. Cir. 1989)—have held that the pendency of a proceeding does not include a judicial appeal of the trial court's decision.

pendent jurisdiction

pendent jurisdiction A judicial doctrine that permits a claim that could not otherwise not be heard in federal court to be heard by a federal court when such claim shares a common nucleus of operative, or pertinent fact, with a federal claim that is within the court's jurisdiction. See also **State standards, incorporation of.**

percentile rank or score
The percentage of students whose score in a test falls below a given score; e.g., if a student's test score has a percentile rank of 60%, 60% of the students who took the test had a score lower than that student's score.

> There is no relation between percentile rank difference and **raw score** range. For example, a 10% difference in percentile rank could equal a 1 point raw score difference.

perception Ability to process and comprehend information one receives from his or her senses.

perceptual-motor disorder Generally, a deficiency in sensory perception of one's environment resulting in problems correctly receiving, processing or responding to sensory information from one's environment, in turn causing problems with comprehension, **memory** and the perceptual-motor skills needed for reading, writing and mastering arithmetic.

performance assessment
As defined by the former **Office of Technology Assessment (OTA)**: "testing methods that require students to create an answer or product that demonstrates their knowledge and skills in various ways such as conducting experiments, writing extended essays and doing mathematical computations." Also called per-formance-based assessment or authentic assessment. As distinguished from **selection response test.**

performance criteria Characteristics of a student's performance evaluated in **performance assessment,** often expressed as a **rubric.**

performance deficit In connection with assessment of a student's ability to produce prosocial behaviors, the inability to produce the correct behavior outside a testing situation, despite ability to role-play the correct behavior during testing. As distinguished from a **skill deficit.**

performance scale Scale of **Wechsler Intelligence Scales for Children-III (WISC-III)** in which student performs tasks to assess nonverbal reasoning and visual-motor coordination; 6 subtests include: (a) picture completion, (b) picture arrangement, (c) block design, (d) object assembly, (e) coding and (f) mazes (optional). See also **verbal scale.**

performance scale IQ **Standard score** with a **mean** of 100 and **standard deviation** of 15, derived from a combination of 5 of the 6 subtests that comprise the **performance scale** of the **Weschler Intelligence Scales for Children-III (WISC-III)**; discrepancy between a student's verbal and performance IQ is often used to screen for whether a child has a learning or language disability. See also **full scale IQ; verbal scale IQ.**

Perkins Brailler The most widely used braille writer in the United States, a tool to teach young blind children to write in **Braille.** See also **Grade I Braille.**

perseverate Continuing to perform a behavior beyond its normal endpoint and having difficulty switching tasks; associated with children with **autism** and **severe mental retardation.** As distinguished from compulsive behavior exhibited by an individual with an **obsessive-compulsive disorder.**

perseverative behaviors Similar behaviors repeated over and over, associated with children with **autism** or **severe mental retardation.**

persistent vegetative state Caused by diffuse damage to the **cerebellum,** a coma-like state in which the individual appears to possess some arousal capability and exhibits some evidence of alertness and ability to respond to the environment. See also **zero reject principle.**

The hearing officer in *Weston Public School,* 1987-88 EHLR 509:154 (SEA MA 1987), held that a 19-year-old youth who had been in a persistent vegetative state for nearly 15 years was entitled to **special education** and that the services recommended for him—systematic effort to increase the student's relatedness to his environment and to train him to respond selectively to designated stimuli—were educational services.

person acting as a parent of a child

A person entitled to assert parental rights under the IDEA under the definition of a **"parent"** in IDEA regulations at 34 C.F.R. § 300.13.

The IDEA regulations do not further define what it means to "act as a parent," but a Note to the regulation gives as an example "a grandmother or stepparent with whom the child lives, as well as persons who are legally responsible for a child's welfare."

personal assistance services

An **independent living service** under the **Vocational Rehabilitation Services and Other Rehabilitation Services Act** and a support service under the **Developmental Disabilities Assistance and Bill of Rights Act of 1975** defined, as a term of art, at 29 U.S.C. § 706(11) and 42 U.S.C. § 6001(18), respectively, as: "a range of services . . . designed to assist an **individual with a disability** to perform daily living activities on and off the job that the individual would typically perform if the individual did not have a disability, [s]uch services . . . designed to increase the individual's control in life and ability to perform everyday services on or off the job."

personality assessment

Systematic description and measurement of an individual's characteristics; 4 kinds of **assessment** methodologies: (a) **interview,** (b) objective (with **standardized tests** and self-reported tests), (c) projective (e.g., Rorschach test) and (d) behavioral (**systematic observation of behavior**).

personally identifiable information

1. In connection with information contained in **education records,** that information to which students and parents have a protectable privacy interest under the **Family Educational Rights and Privacy Act (FERPA)** and privacy and access rights under Part B and Part H of the IDEA. 2. Defined, as a term of art, in FERPA regulations at 34 C.F.R. § 99.3 as including, but not limited to: "(a) The student's name; (b) The name of the student's **parent** or other family member; (c) The address

of the student or the student's family; (d) A personal identifier, such as the student's social security number or student number; (e) A list of personal characteristics that would make the student's identity easily traceable; or (f) Other information that would make the student's identity easily traceable." 3. Defined, as a term of art, slightly differently in Part B regulations at 34 C.F.R. § 300.500(c) as including: "(1) The name of the child, the child's parent, or other family member; (2) The address of the child; (3) A personal identifier, such as the child's social security number or student number; or (4) A list of personal characteristics or other information that would make it possible to identify the child with reasonable certainty." As distinguished from **directory information.** See also **Buckley Amendment.**

personnel standards In connection with **special education,** the requirement in the IDEA (at 20 U.S.C. § 1413(a)(14)) that states establish and maintain standards to ensure that only adequately and appropriately trained personnel provide special education or **related services.**

pervasive developmental disorder (PDD) The general description of the class of disorders described in the DSM-IV as "characterized by severe deficits and pervasive impairment in multiple areas of development ... including impairment in reciprocal social interaction, impairment in communication, and the presence of stereotyped behavior, interests or activities"; specific pervasive developmental disorders are: **autistic disorder (autism); Asperger's disorder; Childhood Disintegrative Disorder;** and **Rett's disorder.**

phenylketonuria (PKU) A hereditary metabolic disorder thought to be a common cause of **mental retardation.**

philtrum Groove between the upper lip and nose.

phonation Sound production in terms of loudness, pitch and vocal quality.

phoneme The smallest unit of an individual's speech that distinguishes one utterance from another, like a syllable; the English language has 24 consonant and 12 vowel phonemes. See also **morpheme.**

> The word "cat," for example, contains three phonemes: the /k/, /a/ and /t/ sounds.

phonemic awareness

Ability to recognize **phonemes** and put their sounds together to form words and phrases quickly, accurately and automatically; essential for decoding. See also **decoding skills; phonological awareness.**

> Phonemic awareness is the foundation for all higher level reading skills. The majority of children with **reading disorders** cannot master this skill without special instruction.

phonics

The relationship of speech sounds to their written symbols; an instructional method for teaching reading by helping students recognize words by sounding them out; as opposed to the **whole language method** of reading instruction. See also **balanced approach; Orton-Gillingham method; Project Read.**

phonological awareness

Awareness of how words sound and how they are represented in written language or print; ability to identify and manipulate the sounds of language.

> Many children with **learning disabilities** cannot readily learn how to relate letters of the alphabet to the sounds of language. These students must be explicitly taught the process of phonological awareness.

phonological disorder

A **learning disorder** the diagnostic criteria for which is defined in the DSM-IV as: "A. Failure to use developmentally expected speech sounds that are appropriate for age and dialect (e.g., errors in sound production, use, representation, or organization such as, but not limited to, substitutions of one sound for another ... or omissions of sounds such as final consonants). B. The difficulties in speech sound production interfere with academic or occupational achievement or with social communication. C. If **mental retardation,** a speech-motor or sensory deficit or environmental deprivation is present, the speech difficulties are in excess of those usually associated with these problems."

> Generally, a phonological disorder is a learning disorder resulting in difficulty making use of phonological information when processing written and oral

language. Severity can range from little impact on intelligibility to complete unintelligibility. Major components involve **deficits** in **phonemic awareness,** sound-symbol relations, **storage of phonological information** and **retrieval of phonological information** from **long-term memory.**

phonological dyslexia A **learning disability** characterized by difficulty sounding out words.

phonology Study of rules of language associated with **phonemes** and language structure. See also **linguistic systems.**

physical education Defined, as a term of art, in IDEA regulations at 34 C.F.R. § 300.17(b)(2) as: "(i) the development of (A) physical and motor fitness; (B) fundamental motor skills and patterns; and (C) skills in aquatics, dance, and individual and group games, and sports (including intramural and life-time sports). . . . (ii) **special education, adaptive physical education,** movement education, and motor development."

physical or mental impairment In connection with establishing eligibility for protection and services under Section 504, defined, as a term of art, in Section 504 regulations at 34 C.F.R. § 104.3(j)(2)(i) as: "(A) any physiological disorder or condition, cosmetic disfigurement, or anatomical loss affecting one or more of the following body systems: neurological; muscoskeletal; special sense organs, including speech organs; respiratory; cardiovascular; reproductive; digestive; genito-urinary; hemic and lymphatic; skin; and endocrine; or (B) any mental or psychological disorder such as **mental retardation, organic brain syndrome,** emotional or mental illness, and **specific learning disabilities."**

Courts generally have concluded that to fall within the ambit of Section 504 an individual's qualifying physical disability must substantially impair performance, as opposed to being a physical characteristic, such as left-handedness or crossed eyes. With regard to mental impairments, generally courts defer to identification of a condition as an impairment by medical authorities. Individuals with **learning disabilities** have been recognized as eligible under Section 504. See, *Hessler v. State Board of Education of Maryland,* 1982-83 EHLR 554:455 (4th Cir. 1983).

physical restraint May be an appropriate **aversive inter-**

    221

vention when a child with a disability cannot be stopped from injuring himself or herself, others or property in a less restrictive way; typically involves some type of wrestling hold, but specific method will depend on the child's size, strength and then-emotional state.

When the need for physical restraint is reasonably predictable, the child should have a **protocol** describing the conditions under which such restraint will be used included in his or her **behavior management plan.**

physical therapy 1. Generally, use of equipment and **modalities,** such as heat packs and hydrotherapy, and exercise to restore physical functioning, rehabilitate muscles and improve coordination. 2. A **related service** defined, as a term of art, in Part B regulations at 34 C.F.R. § 300.16(b)(7) as: "services provided by a qualified physical therapist." 3. May be considered **special education** rather than a related service under state law (34 C.F.R. § 300.17(a)(2)). 4. An **early intervention service** defined, as a term of art, in Part H regulations at 34 C.F.R. § 3030.12(d)(9) as including: "(i) screening of infants and toddlers to identify movement

dysfunction; (ii) obtaining, interpreting, and integrating information appropriate to program planning, to prevent or alleviate movement dysfunction and related functional problems; and (iii) providing services to prevent or alleviate movement dysfunction and related functional problems."

The Third Circuit Court of Appeals' decision in *Polk v. Central Susquehanna Intermediate Unit 16,* 1988-89 EHLR 441:130 (3d Cir. 1988), widely known for its formulation of the "more than **de minimus educational benefit**" standard for determinations of **free appropriate public education (FAPE),** concerned whether direct or consultative physical therapy was appropriate programming for a 14-year-old student with severe physical disabilities and the mental capacity of a toddler. The court explained the significant role physical therapy plays in the special education programming for students with severe disabilities:

"For children like [the student] with severe disabilities, related services serve a dual purpose. First, because these children have extensive physical disabilities that often interfere with development in other areas, physical therapy is an essential prerequisite to education. For example, development of motor abilities is often the first step in overall educational development. . . . Second, the physical therapy itself may form the core of a severely disabled child's special education. . . . In [the student's] case, physical therapy is not merely a conduit to his education but constitutes, in and of itself, a major portion of his special education, teaching him basic skills such as toileting, feeding, ambulation, inter alia."

pica behavior Consumption of dirt, clay, laundry starch and related non-food items with little or no nutritional value and potential for self-injury; associated with students with **autism** or **mental retardation.**

Pictoral Test of Intelligence (PTI) Standardized **intelligence test** for children between the ages of 3 and 8 years, useful in evaluating children with sensory or motor disabilities.

Picture Exchange Communication System (PECS) A functional communication training approach to teaching children with **autism** to communicate needs by emphasizing use of pictures.

place of public accommodation As defined in **Title III of the Americans with Disabilities Act (ADA)** at 42

U.S.C. § 12181(7), includes "a nursery, elementary, secondary, undergraduate, or postgraduate **private school** or other place of education."

platform switch See **button switch.**

policies In connection with Part H of the IDEA, defined, as a term of art, in Part H regulations at 34 C.F.R. § 303.19 as: "State statutes, regulations, Governor's orders, directives by the **lead agency,** or written documents that represent the State's position concerning any matter covered under this part."

portfolio assessment Systematic collection of a student's work samples, records of observations, test results and the like over a period of time, allowing evaluation of student growth and achievement.

positioning Adjusting, placing, turning, lifting and moving a student with a disability or assisting the student into an optimal position; can be a **related service.**

positioning devices Devices that help provide support

for body stability, the trunk and head, and upright posture; reduce pressure on the skin surface for an individual with a physical disability; or arrange instructional or play materials for maximum performance efficiency.

positive reinforcement Principle used in **behavior modification** in which a student is motivated to perform a desired **target behavior** by his or her receipt of a reward after performing the desired behavior. See also **negative reinforcement.**

postlingual deafness Profound hearing loss that occurs after the normal acquisition of language. As opposed to **prelingual deafness.**

post-school activities In connection with **transition services** under the IDEA, enumerated at 20 U.S.C. § 1401(a)(19) as including: **postsecondary education,** vocational training [**vocational education**], **integrated employment** (including **supported employment**), continuing and **adult education, adult services,** independent

living, and community participation.

postsecondary education In connection with **transition services** under the IDEA, a **post-school activity** that includes: technical trade schools and vocational centers, public community colleges, and 4-year colleges and universities.

potential maximizing standard The standard of appropriateness enunciated by the trial court and affirmed by the Second Court of Appeals, but rejected by the U.S. Supreme Court in *Board of Education of Hendrick Hudson Central School District v. Rowley,* 1981-82 EHLR 553:656, 660 (1982); described by the Court as follows: "an opportunity to achieve [a student's] full potential commensurate with the opportunity provided to other children."

Some states have adopted, for purposes of state education law, a potential maximizing standard that is the same or similar to the standard rejected by the Court in *Rowley.* Massachusetts, for example, has a "maximum development" standard; California also mandates provision of services designed "to achieve his or her full potential commensurate with the opportunity provided to other pupils." See also **State standards, incorporation of.**

Prader-Willi syndrome
Genetic disorder resulting in insatiable appetite, **central nervous system (CNS)** dysfunction and abnormal growth and development; associated with **mental retardation.**

pragmatics Linguistic system
concerned with functional language use, including the ability to engage in a conversation through appropriate use of nonverbal behaviors such as maintaining eye contact and taking turns speaking and listening to others.

An **individualized education program (IEP)** objective for pragmatics could include the ability to perform each of these functions: requesting, discussion of effect, expression of need, initiation of communication, question asking, greetings, taking conversational turns and describing.

praxis planning Ability to
plan and execute tasks requiring motor skills. Also called motor planning.

precision range In con-
nection with **IQ scores,** the range of scores resulting from consideration of the **standard error of measurement** and confidence level for a particular **instrument.**

predictive validity The ex-
tent to which a student's achievement on a test serves as an indicator of future scholastic achievement. See also **content validity; construct validity; concurrent validity; validity.**

preliminary injunction
Extraordinary equitable relief that a court may order upon a showing of necessity to preserve the relative positions of the parties and minimize the risk of irreparable harm until a decision of the merits is made. As distinguished from an **automatic injunction.** See also **injunction; temporary retraining order (TRO).**

The standard for granting a preliminary injunction is court-made, but generally is the same throughout the country and, in a general sense, the same for **special education** cases as any other. The Eighth Circuit Court of Appeals formulated its standard as follows: "When considering a motion for a preliminary injunction, a district court weighs the movant's [party requesting the injunction] probability of success on the merits,

225

the threat of irreparable harm to the movant absent the injunction, the balance between the harm and the injury that the injunction's issuance would inflict on other interested parties, and the public interest." *Dataphase System, Inc. v. CL System, Inc.,* 640 F.2d 109, 114 (8th Cir. 1981).

In connection with **special education,** courts have granted preliminary injunctions to, among other things, require a school district to fund a **residential placement** pending resolution of the dispute in situations where the **stay-put provision** is not implicated. For example, in *Taylor v. Honig,* 16 EHLR 1138 (9th Cir. 1990), the court affirmed the lower court's preliminary injunction ordering the school district to place a severely disabled adolescent, then an inpatient at a psychiatric hospital, at a private facility pending resolution of the dispute.

prelingual deafness Deafness at birth or before language acquisition.

The distinction between prelingual and **postlingual deafness** is extraordinary; the educational needs of a child who cannot learn language through hearing, as one normally does, are truly unique.

prelingual hearing loss Congenital loss or loss that occurs before age 3, as opposed to **prevocational hearing loss.**

preparatory individualized education program (IEP) A temporary or **interim IEP** that a school district implements before the required parties have met to design and approve the "actual" IEP.

A preparatory IEP is inconsistent with the IDEA. The school district in *Myles S. v. Montgomery County Board of Education,* 20 IDELR 237 (M.D. Ala. 1993), violated the IDEA when it provided programming under a "preparatory IEP" for about the first 2 weeks of the school year, the time period prior to the scheduled IEP meeting. In the absence of extraordinary circumstances, an agreed-upon IEP must be effect at the beginning of the school year. School districts are not excused from delay attributed to staff summer vacations.

preplacement evaluation
1. The **assessment** that a school district must conduct prior to the initial placement of a child with a disability in a program providing **special education** and **related services** under Part B; regulations at 34 C.F.R. § 300.531 mandate that a "full and individual evaluation of the child's educational needs . . . be conducted in accordance with the requirements of [34 C.F.R. § 300.532]." 2. The assessment that a school district

must conduct prior to initial placement of an individual with a disability who requires or may require special education or related services in a regular or special education program or any subsequent **significant change in placement** under 34 C.F.R. § 104.35(a) of Section 504 regulations, with such evaluation being conduced in accordance with the requirements set out in § 104.35(b) of the Section 504 regulations.

The requirements for preplacement evaluations for the IDEA (set out in 34 C.F.R. § 300.532) and Section 504 (set out in 34 C.F.R. § 104.35(b) and official commentary) are essentially the same. The Part B requirements are as follows: "State educational agencies and LEAs shall ensure, at a minimum, that: (a) Tests and other evaluation materials—(1) Are provided and administered in the child's **native language** or other **mode of communication,** unless it clearly is not feasible to do so; (2) Have been validated [**validity**] for the specific purpose for which they are used; and (3) Are administered by trained personnel in conformance with the instructions provided by their producer; (b) Tests and other evaluation materials include those tailored to assess specific areas of educational need and not merely those that are designed to provide a single general intelligence quotient; (c) Tests are selected and adminis-

tered so as best to ensure that when a test is administered to a child with impaired sensory, manual, or speaking skills, the test results accurately reflect the child's aptitude or achievement level or whatever other factors the test purports to measure, rather than reflecting the child's impaired sensory, manual, or speaking skills (except where those skills are the factors that the test purports to measure); (d) No single procedure is used as the sole criterion for determining an appropriate educational program for a child; (e) The evaluation is made by a **multidisciplinary team** or group of persons, including at least one teacher or other specialist with knowledge in the area of suspected disability; (f) The child is assessed in all areas related to the suspected disability, including, if appropriate, health, vision, hearing, social and emotional status, general **intelligence,** academic performance, communicative status, and motor abilities."

preprimary program Elementary education program for children too young to attend first grade; includes kindergarten (the year before 1st grade), and **preschool** (the years before kindergarten). Also called nursery school or prekindergarten.

prereferral intervention **Intervention** in the **regular education** classroom tried before

227

a student suspected of possibly having a disability is formally referred for a special education **preplacement evaluation;** 2 common approaches include **teacher assistance teams (TATs)** and **collaborative consultation.**

preschool The educational level from a child's birth until the time he or she is entitled to receive elementary education under state law.

preschool screening Generally, brief inexpensive examinations of children ages 3 to 5 years, performed to identify those who may be **at-risk** for difficulties with **academic achievement** or social adjustment later on.

present educational placement In connection with the **stay-put provision** of the IDEA, the placement in which the child must remain during the pendency of any administrative or judicial proceedings, as specified in Part B regulations at 34 C.F.R. § 300.513.

While the regulations do not define "present educational placement," according to the **Office of Special Education and Rehabilitative Services**

(OSERS), it is generally understood to mean the program of **special education** and **related services** being provided in accordance with the most recently approved **individualized education program (IEP).** *Letter to Baugh,* EHLR 211:481 (OSERS 1987).

pressure of speech **Thought disorder** characterized by motivation to speak so intense that, once the speaker gets started, he or she is difficult to interrupt. See also **flight of ideas.**

presumption in favor of inclusion The directive that school districts consider whether a child with a disability could be placed in a regular classroom with **supplementary aids and services** before considering other, more restrictive placements. See also **continuum of alternative placements; inclusion; mainstreaming.**

That the **least restrictive environment (LRE) mandate** of the IDEA creates a rebuttable presumption in favor of inclusion appears to be the position of the **United States Department of Education** and the 4 federal circuit courts of appeal (the Third, Fifth, Ninth and Eleventh) that have considered the issue since 1989. As articulated by the federal district court in *Oberti v. Board of Education of Borough of Clementon School District,* 19 IDELR 423 (D.N.J. 1992): "School districts ... must consider placing **children with disabilities** in regular classroom settings, with the use of supplementary aids and services, including classroom assistants, before exploring other, more restrictive alternatives."

prevailing party In connection with **attorneys' fees** awards under the IDEA, undefined in the statute (20 U.S.C. § 1415(e)(2)(B)), but established by legislative history and numerous judicial decisions to mean a **parent** who succeeds on any significant issue that achieves some of the benefits sought or whose initiation of a lawsuit was a catalytic, necessary or substantial factor in obtaining the relief sought; considered to be the same standard applicable to awarding of attorneys' fees to prevailing parties under **Section 1988.**

prevocational hearing loss Loss between the ages of 3 and 19 years, as opposed to **prelingual hearing loss.**

prevocational skills Prerequisite skills for **vocational education,** such as vocabulary, comprehension, ability to tell time and perform arithmetic calculations, ability to listen and make oneself understood, writing and internalization of work values.

prima facie case Generally, presentation by the party bringing the complaint or suit of sufficient evidence to compel the responding party or defendant to proceed with its case.

primary referral sources In connection with the Part H **child find** system, includes "hospitals, including prenatal and postnatal care facilities; physicians; parents; **day care services** programs; **local educational agencies;** public health facilities; other social services agencies; and other health care providers" (34 C.F.R. § 303.321(d)(3)).

private school Generally, a school that is not under federal or state control or supervision. Private schools that receive federal funds must comply with Section 504. Even if a private school does not receive **federal financial assistance,** it still may be subject to Section 504 if it is considered an indirect recipient of federal funding. See, e.g., *Bangor (ME) Public School District,* 20

IDELR 278 (OCR 1993). Further, IDEA regulations at 34 C.F.R. § 300.400 provide that if a private school enrolls a publicly placed student, that student retains all of the rights and protections granted to him or her under the IDEA to the same extent as a student with a disability attending public school.

private school students with disabilities

Defined, as a term of art, in IDEA regulations at 34 C.F.R. § 300.450 as: "[in connection with children to whom FAPE has been made available] **children with disabilities** enrolled by their parents in private schools or facilities other than children with disabilities [publicly enrolled in a private school or facility.]" Also referred to as parentally placed students. See also **comparable benefits; genuine opportunity for equitable participation; private school students with disabilities, EDGAR regulations concerning.**

private school students with disabilities, EDGAR regulations concerning

Regulations imposing responsibility on states and **local educational agencies (LEAs)** administering federally funded programs to provide students enrolled in **private schools** with a **genuine opportunity for equitable participation,** including an obligation to consider the needs of such students and the number of such students and to spend the same average amount of program funds on students enrolled in private schools that are spent on students enrolled in public schools; adherence to these regulations, codified at 34 C.F.R. §§ 76.650-76.652, is required for **private school students with disabilities** by IDEA regulations at 34 C.F.R. § 300.451.

private sources of support

In connection with **special education** funding, a funding source which may be a primary payer for services that are **related services** under the IDEA, to the extent there is an otherwise valid obligation to provide or pay for those services; generally includes insurers whose insureds are parents of a child with a disability. See also **similar third party.**

procedural due process

As a matter of U.S. Constitutional law, the mandate set out in the Fifth Amendment and

Fourteenth Amendment to the Constitution that certain procedural protections must be provided before the government may deprive any person of life, liberty or property. See also **minimum due process.**

procedural safeguards 1. The collective term used to refer to the formality requirements of Part B of the IDEA that are designed to allow **parents** to participate meaningfully in decisions concerning the appropriate educational program for their children; includes: (a) providing prior written notice whenever the school district proposes an action concerning the identification, **evaluation** or educational placement of a child with a disability or the provision of **FAPE** to him or her, or refuses to accede to a parental request with reference to any of those items (34 C.F.R. § 300.504(a)); (b) seeking parental **consent** before conducting a **preplacement evaluation** or making an initial placement in a program of **special education** and **related services** (34 C.F.R. § 300.504(b)); (c) affording parents an opportunity to challenge a school district action concerning the identification, evaluation or educational placement of a child with a disability or the provision of FAPE to him or her in a **due process hearing** (34 C.F.R. § 300.506); and (d) giving parents the right to inspect and review all **education records** concerning the issues identified above (34 C.F.R. § 300.502). 2. In connection with **children with disabilities** entitled to services under or the protection of Section 504, defined in regulations at 34 C.F.R. § 104.36 as including: "notice, an opportunity for the parents or guardian of the person to examine relevant records, an impartial hearing with opportunity for participation by the person's parents or guardian and representation by counsel, and a review procedure."

The principal guidance provided by the U.S. Supreme Court in the seminal *Board of Education of Hendrick Hudson Central School District v. Rowley,* 1981-82 EHLR 553:656, 670 (1982), is the instruction that a court's role in an IDEA lawsuit is to make a twofold inquiry, the first part of which is: "[H]as the State complied with the procedures set forth in the [IDEA]?" This first inquiry imposes a procedural litmus test. The Court perceived a congressional conviction that adequate compliance with procedural safeguards would, in most situations, assure substantive compliance with the intent of the IDEA.

process remediation Attempts to correct or strengthen **deficits** in cognitive processes such as perception, **memory** or attention.

productivity Defined, as a term of art, in the federal **Developmental Disabilities Assistance and Bill of Rights Act of 1975** at 42 U.S.C. § 6001(20) as: "engagement in income-producing work that is measured by increased income, improved employment status, or job advancement; or engagement in work that contributes to a household or community." See also **integration and inclusion.**

profession or discipline In connection with the personnel standards imposed by the IDEA on state and local **public agencies** and their agents providing **special education** or **related services** to **children with disabilities,** defined, as a term of art, in Part B regulations at 34 C.F.R. § 300.153(a)(3) as:

"a specific occupational category that—provides special education and related services to children with disabilities under [Part B]; has been established or designated by the State; and has a required scope of responsibility and degree of supervision."

profound mental retardation Terminology of DSM-IV generally associated with individuals with **mental retardation** whose **IQ scores** are less than about 20, who have marked deficiencies in **adaptive behavior** (very limited or no self-care ability) and no language development; usually associated with neurological disabilities and impairments in sensorimotor functioning; termed **severe/profound mental retardation** under some state educational codes.

Project Read An instructional method to teach reading which incorporates the principles of the **Orton - Gillingham method** by using visual, auditory, tactile and kinesthetic [kinesthesis] sensory approaches, but also addresses reading comprehension and writing.

promote movement from school to post-school activities The obligation of school districts under the **transition services** provisions of the IDEA (20 U.S.C. § 1410(a)(19)); described in legislative history as the obligation of school districts to "familiarize themselves with post-school opportunities and services available for students with disabilities in their communities and the State, and make use of this information in the transitioning planning for individual students" so they can facilitate **linkages** with other agencies whose services are anticipated to be needed by students.

prompting Instructional technique in which a cue—visual, auditory or physical—is presented in order to facilitate successful completion of a task or performance of a behavior.

properly proposed settlement offer In connection with the award of **attorneys' fees** to **prevailing parties** under the IDEA, a written settlement offer made by the local school district (or similar **public agency**) in accordance with the time frames set out in 20 U.S.C. § 1415(e)(4)(D)(i).

proprioceptive sense An individual's subconscious awareness of body position, either when he or she is in motion or still. See also **vestibular sense.**

prosocial behaviors In connection with instruction in **social skills** for students who have **conduct disorders** or **behavioral disorders,** includes: taking turns, working with others and following directions, displaying appropriate behavior towards peers and adults, showing interest and caring, settling conflicts without fighting, and presenting appropriate affect.

prosody The rhythm of speech that helps give oral communication meaning.

prosthesis Device that replaces a missing or malfunctioning body part or function, such as a communication prosthesis for an individual who

233

lacks adequate speaking or writing ability.

protective services Governmental services designed to prevent or remedy abuse, neglect or exploitation of children who may be harmed through physical or mental injury, sexual abuse or exploitation, and negligent treatment or mistreatment.

> Protective service activities may include investigation and **intervention, counseling services** for children and families, and arrangement of alternative living arrangements or **foster care services.**

protocol A plan for using individual tests in combination to adequately test for the **diagnosis** that is suspected or for alternative diagnosis; e.g., a protocol for assessing individuals suspected of having specific learning disabilities.

proximity of school to home A preferential factor in placement decisions, according to IDEA regulations at 34 C.F.R. § 300.552(a)(3), which states that "[e]ach **public agency** shall ensure that ... each disabled child's educational placement ... [i]s as close as possible to the child's home."

> Authoritative case law makes it clear that "[t]here is no basis under the IDEA or Section 504 ... for such a right of mandatory placement [in a neighborhood school]." *Urban v. Jefferson County School District R-1,* 21 IDELR 985 (D. Colo. 1994). School districts may permissibly concentrate resources at particular schools for particular needs and disabilities. They properly exercise their administrative discretion when they deploy resources in an efficient manner. See also *Murray v. Montrose County School District RE-1J,* 22 IDELR 558 (10th Cir. 1995).

psychoanalysis Specialized technique grounded in the **medical model** for treatment of mental/emotional disorders during which the individual verbalizes all his or her thoughts and feelings to an analyst who neither passes judgment nor tries to direct the encounters.

> Psychoanalysis is a long and tedious method of treatment, now in disfavor for philosophical, medical and economic reasons.

psychoeducational assessment Evaluation of a student's learning behavior for the purpose of designing an educational program and designating placement.

psychological assessment An evaluation of a child's unique affective characteristics that includes, but is not limited to, the administration and interpretation of psychological testing. As distinguished from a **neuropyschological assessment.**

Psychological Screening Battery Computer-aided **battery** designed to provide indications of psychopathology, with a special emphasis on depression and suicide ideation, and to indicate the possible need for a **neurological assessment** or **neuropsychological assessment.**

psychological services 1. A **related service** under Part B of the IDEA defined, as a term of art, in Part B regulations at 34 C.F.R. § 300.16(b)(8) as including: "(i) administering psychological and educational, and other **assessment** procedures; (ii) interpreting assessment results; (iii) obtaining tests, integrating, and interpreting information about child be-

havior and conditions relating to learning; (iv) consulting with other staff members in planning school programs to meet the special needs of children as indicated by psychological tests, interviews, and behavioral evaluations; and (v) planning and managing a program of psychological services, including psychological counseling for children and parents." 2. An **early intervention service** under Part H of the IDEA defined, as a term of art, in Part H regulations at 34 C.F.R. § 300.16(b)(8) as including: "(i) administering psychological and developmental tests, and other assessment procedures; (ii) interpreting assessment results; (iii) obtaining, integrating, and interpreting information about child behavior, and child and family conditions related to learning, mental health, and development; and (iv) planning, and managing a program of psychological services, including psychological counseling for children and parents, **family counseling,** consultation on child development, parent training, and educational programs." See also **psychological test.**

psychological test Test to gather information about an individual's personality characteristics, strengths and weaknesses, and the nature of his or her interactions with others; a more limited activity than a **psychological assessment.**

psychometrist An individual trained to administer and evaluate the results of certain tests, such as individually administered **intelligence tests** and **psychological assessments.**

In some states, individuals must have graduate degrees and be licensed as a "school psychometrist" or "educational diagnostician." In other states, individuals may be trained technicians with at least a bachelor's degree. According to the **Office of Special Education Programs (OSEP)** (in *Letter to Allen,* 21 IDELR 1130 (OSEP 1994)), state standards govern the educational, training and/or licensing requirements for individuals who conduct educational **evaluations.** It is not a violation of Part B to use psychometrists who do not have graduate degrees or are not licensed to administer tests as long as those individuals are supervised by trained personnel and the practice is consistent with state law and state personnel standards which comply with Part B. See also **highest requirements in the State applicable to a specific** profession or discipline; **psychometry.**

psychometry 1. Study of the quantitative assessment of an individual's psychological traits or mental capabilities, as derived from that individual's performance on **standardized tests** and other assessment modalities. 2. The method of using **psychological tests** to measure mental functions and infer underlying abilities.

psychomotor Behavior **domain** involving neurological control of muscle activity. As distinguished from cognitive and affective functioning.

psychopath Generally speaking, an individual who exhibits emotional instability or asocial behavior, but no intellectual impairment.

psychosocial adjustment How an individual relates to and interacts with other people in his or her environment; believed to be susceptible to **remediation** through reinforcement [**reinforcer**].

psychotherapy Application of psychological theories

and principles to the treatment of problems of abnormal behavior, emotions and thinking; goal of treatment is to help the individual gain an understanding of his or her problems.

Although IDEA regulations at 34 C.F.R. § 300.16(b)(4) limit covered **medical services** to those necessary for the purposes of **diagnosis** and **evaluation,** some courts and administrative decisionmakers have ruled that psychotherapy performed by psychiatrists for therapeutic purposes is a **related service.** When a student's educational program calls for **residential placement** in a mental health facility or hospital, there is a consensus that psychotherapy and other services performed by a licensed psychiatrist are covered **counseling services** (to the extent they relate to assisting a student to benefit from education) rather than **excluded medical services.** On the other hand, when outpatient psychotherapy is at issue, better reasoned decisions decline to provide coverage. See, e.g., *Metropolitan Government v. Tennessee Department of Education,* 1988-89 EHLR 441:450 (Tenn. Ct. App. 1989).

psychotropic drugs Drugs that affect brain processes directly and change behavior indirectly.

public In connection with the requirement of the IDEA that each child with a disability receive a **free appropriate public education (FAPE),** defined, as a term of art, in the IDEA at 20 U.S.C. § 1401(a)(18)(A) as: "public expense" whether at public schools or **private schools.**

public accommodation

Private entity prohibited from discriminating against individuals on the basis of disability under **Title III of the Americans with Disabilities Act;** defined, as a term of art, in ADA regulations at 28 C.F.R. § 36.104 as a "private entity that owns, leases (or leases to), or operates a **place of public accommodation**."

public agency 1. In connection with Part B of the IDEA, defined in Part B regulations at 34 C.F.R. § 300.14 as "include[ing] the **SEA, LEAs, IEUs,** and any other political subdivisions of the State that are responsible for providing education to **children with disabilities.**" 2. In connection with Part H of the IDEA, defined in Part H regulations at 34 C.F.R. § 303.30 as including: "the **lead agency** and any other political

237

subdivision of the State that is responsible for providing **early intervention services** to children eligible under this part and their families."

public awareness program In connection with Part H, the program a State must have to inform the public about the state's early intervention program, including how to make referrals or gain access to a comprehensive, multidisciplinary evaluation or other **early intervention services** (34 C.F.R. § 303.20).

public expense In connection with **independent educational evaluations** under the IDEA, defined, as a term of art, in Part B regulations at 34 C.F.R. § 300.503(a)(3)(ii) as: "the **public agency** either pays for the full cost of the **evaluation** or ensures that the evaluation is otherwise provided at no cost to the **parent**." See also **at no cost; free.**

public information In connection with a state's use of Part B funds for support services, interpreted by the **Office of Special Education and Re-**

habilitative Services (OSERS) in *Letter to Simon,* 20 IDELR 1459 (OSERS 1994), to mean generally any activity that is designed to inform the public about Part B requirements and is consistent with the purposes of Part B.

pull-out program **Resource room** instruction or services.

punishment As a term of art in **behavior management,** primarily identified with the use of aversive stimuli, or aversives.

punitive damages An award of damages to a plaintiff in a lawsuit that is over and above the actual loss he or she suffered as a result of the defendant's wrongful conduct to punish the defendant and make an example to deter others from behaving similarly; usually only awarded when a defendant's wrongful acts can be characterized fairly as outrageous.

Administrative decisionmakers are not authorized to award punitive damages. Generally, courts have refused to award punitive damages for violations of the IDEA. While courts have recognized the availability of punitive damages under Section 504, they also limit the possible circumstances under which such awards may be made for intentional discrimination or retaliation for exercising one's rights under Section 504.

P-value In connection with **standardized tests,** the percentage of examinees who responded correctly to a test item.

239

Q

quadriplegia Type of **spasticity (cerebral palsy)** affecting all 4 limbs.

qualified, in connection with education professionals 1. In connection with Part B, defined, as a term of art, in Part B regulations at 34 C.F.R. § 300.15 as: "a person [who] has met SEA [**state educational agency**] approved or recognized certification, licensing, registration, or other comparable requirements that apply to the area in which he or she is providing **special education** or **related services.**" 2. In connection with Part H, defined, as a term of art, in Part H regulations at 34 C.F.R. § 303.21 as: "a person [who] has met State approved or recognized certification, licensing, registration, or other comparable require-

ments that apply to the area in which the person is providing **early intervention services.**"

qualified individual with a disability In connection with the provision of education services under Section 504 in **elementary school** and **secondary school,** defined, as a term of art, in Section 504 regulations at 34 C.F.R. § 104.3(k)(2) as including an **individual with a disability** (as defined by Section 504): "(i) of an age during which nonhandicapped persons are provided such services, (ii) of any age during which it is mandatory under state law to provide such services to handicapped persons; or (iii) to whom a state is required to provide a free appropriate public education under [the IDEA]." See also **age range.**

qualitative assessment

Flexible, open-ended, holistic and nonstatistical assessment. See also **performance assessment.**

R

RATC Roberts Apperception Test for Children

RSA Rehabilitation Services Administration

racially or culturally discriminatory testing and evaluation materials Generally understood to mean materials whose scores and classifications, used in the evaluation of **children with disabilities** or suspected of having disabilities, are affected by language difficulties, deprivation of experience and deviation from the majority culture and value system that are unrelated to the disability or suspected disability; selection or administration of such tests and materials is prohibited under Part B regulations at 34 C.F.R. § 300.530(b).

In *Larry P. v. Riles,* 1983-84 EHLR 555:305 (9th Cir. 1984), the Ninth Circuit Court of Appeals affirmed the lower court's finding that the administration of **intelligence tests** in the school district's evaluation of African-American students for classification as **educable mentally retarded (EMR)** was culturally and racially discriminatory. Using the IQ test as the basis for classification, the district had a disproportionate enrollment of African-Americans in EMR classes, despite the lack of any genetic basis for such a result. The court found that the IQ test was not designed to eliminate cultural biases against African-American children and, in fact, was standardized and designed on the basis of an all-white population **reference group** despite general acceptance in the scientific community that the test tended to underestimate the academic ability of racial and ethnic minorities.

rapid decoding Ability to recognize written words rapidly and automatically; essential skill for **reading.** See also **decoding skills.**

rating scale Subjective assessment made on predetermined criteria in the form of a scale.

ratings recording Observational recording method for the **systematic observation of behavior** in which the trained observer rates observations of the behavior on a scale at the end of the observation period.

ratio IQ score Scoring used in connection with some **intelligence tests,** including the **Stanford-Binet Intelligence Scale;** computed by dividing a student's **mental age** by his or her chronological age.

ratio schedule of reinforcement In connection with **behavior modification, positive reinforcement** technique in which reinforcement is contingent upon a specific number of performances of the **target behavior.**

Raven Progressive Matrices Nonverbal test of reasoning ability that can be administered either individu-

ally or to a group; 3 different versions for children from age 5 through adults; in all versions test-takers use either verbal or visual perceptual skills to complete pictures of symbols arranged in specific patterns.

raw score Number of test items answered correctly; converted to **standard score** for meaningful interpretation.

reactivity See **guinea pig effect.**

readability formula Formula to assess and identify the **readability level** of a text.
> Various formulas are in use. While they differ in specifics, most are based on an analysis of items such as word length, sentence length or sentence structure. Such criteria have been subject to criticism for relying on surface characteristics of a text, independent of content.

readability level Difficulty level of a passage of text, usually expressed in terms of grade level.

reading Meaningful receptive communication from printed materials.
> Reading is a complex cognitive process that requires many **cognitive**

abilities and skills, such as attention, **memory,** associative connections between sensory modalities, **phonological awareness, rapid decoding** and general **intelligence.** For educational purposes, there are generally considered to be 4 distinct types of reading activities: (a) **developmental reading;** (b) study, or reading to learn content and achieve mastery of a subject; (c) **functional reading;** and (d) recreational reading or reading as a **leisure-time activity.**

reading disorder 1. Generally, the result of a deficit in any of the cognitive skills required to comprehend what one has read. 2. A **learning disorder** the diagnostic criteria for which is defined in the DSM-IV as: "A. Reading achievement, as measured by individually administered standardized tests of reading accuracy or comprehension, is substantially below that expected given the person's chronological age, measured **intelligence** and **age-appropriate** education. B. The disturbance in Criterion A significantly interferes with **academic achievement** or **activities of daily living** that require reading skills. C. If a sensory deficit is present, the reading difficulties are in ex-

cess of those usually associated with it."

reading remediation Identification and treatment of reading problems.

reading vocabulary The range of words one recognizes in print and understands in context; over time one's reading vocabulary exceeds one's **hearing vocabulary** and **speaking vocabulary.**

reasonable accommodation Generally, the requirement under Section 504 that a **recipient of federal financial assistance** provide accommodations or modifications that do not alter the fundamental nature of the program or service to individuals with disabilities when such accommodations make the individual qualified to participate in the program or benefit from the service.

Experts in the field question whether the reasonable accommodation principle is applicable when the issue is the provision of an appropriate education to a student with a disability. OCR has taken the position that Section 504 regulations covering elementary and secondary education establish the right to a **free appro-**

245

priate public education (FAPE) that cannot be limited or undercut by the reasonable accommodation concept. See, e.g., *Letter to Zirkel*, 20 IDELR 134 (OCR 1993).

receptive language Understanding communication from others. As distinguished from **expressive language.**

receptive language disorder Presents as an inability to understand spoken or written language that may affect **reading, writing** and problem-solving in arithmetic. See also **expressive language disorder.**

recipient of federal financial assistance In connection with Section 504, defined, as a term of art, in Section 504 regulations at 34 C.F.R. § 104.3(f) as including "state [educational agencies] and **local educational agencies,** including **intermediate educational units,** that receive federal funds [**federal financial assistance**]."

record In connection with **education records,** defined, as a term of art, in **Family Educational Rights and Privacy Act (FERPA)** regulations at 34

C.F.R. § 99.1 as: "any information recorded in any way, including, but not limited to, handwriting, print, tape, film, microfilm, and microfiche."

The regulation makes it clear that content, rather than storage medium, is the operative factor. Thus, it is clear that computer files are also education records, to the extent they contain **personally identifiable information.**

recreation 1. In connection with individuals with disabilities, generally means opportunities to participate in **leisure-time activities** in either individual or group activities. 2. A **related service** under the IDEA defined, as a term of art, in Part B regulations at 34 C.F.R. § 300.16(b)(9) as including: "(i) assessment of **leisure function;** (ii) recreation programs in schools and community agencies; and (iii) leisure education."

recreational therapist A professional trained to develop programs to assist individuals with disabilities plan and manage **leisure-time activities.**

redshirting a kindergartner Retaining a student who does not demonstrate readiness for learning to read in kindergarten or otherwise deferring entrance to first grade for another year.

reductive techniques **Behavior management** techniques, such as **extinction,** that reduce or eliminate undesired **target behaviors.**

reevaluation 1. Periodic evaluation of a student already identified as eligible for services under either Section 504 or the IDEA. 2. In connection with the IDEA, regulations at 34 C.F.R. § 300.534 require that a reevaluation meeting the **preplacement evaluation** requirements be conducted every 3 years, or "more frequently, if conditions warrant, or if the child's parent or teacher requests an evaluation." 3. In connection with Section 504, reevaluations are required under Section 504 regulations at 34 C.F.R. § 104.35(a) before any action is taken to make a **significant change in placement** and at periodic intervals under 34 C.F.R. § 104.35(d), although the regulation does not make clear how frequently

such reevaluations must be performed.

reference group The large group of age or grade peers used for comparison with an individual student's performance on a **standardized test.** Also called a standardization sample.

referral Identification for individual **evaluation** or treatment, made either individually or through systemic **screening.**

reflex activities Functional abilities of the **central nervous system** such as respiration, autonomic control, and basic motor reflexes and controls. As distinguished from **higher mental functions.**

regression-recoupment problem Loss of learned skills during the summer resulting in the need to relearn at the start of the new school year. All children experience regression during extended school breaks. When a child with a disability has a sufficiently severe regression-recoupment problem, **extended school year (ESY) services** are a component of his or her appropriate educational program. Regression-recoupment problems triggering the need for ESY services occur when:

247

(a) a child suffers an inordinate or disproportionate degree of regression during that portion of the year in which the customary 180-day school year is not in session, and (b) it takes an inordinate or unacceptable length of time for the child to recoup those skills (academic, emotional or behavioral) that have been lost upon returning to school.

"regressive" autism Common term used to describe children who develop normally until autistic symptoms start to emerge in the age range of 18 to 36 months.

regular education As distinguished from **special education,** an established **curriculum** of academic subjects offered in essentially the same fashion for all children and youth.

regulation Rules issued by executive branch of government to clarify, intepret or further enforcement of **statutes** that, when properly adopted, have the force of law; when the IDEA is concerned, the Department of Education is charged with issuing regulations, when federal law is concerned, it is codified in the Code of Federal Regulations (C.F.R.).

rehabilitation Programming or services to reduce **deficits** and attain maximum possible level of mental or physical functioning. As distinguished from **habilitation.**

Rehabilitation Act of 1973 Federal legislation establishing federally created rights for people with disabilities; most pertinently, Sections 501, 503 and 504, which prohibit federal agencies, federal contractors and **recipients of federal financial assistance** from discriminating against otherwise **qualified persons with disabilities** solely on the basis of disability; codified at 29 U.S.C. §§ 791 et seq.

rehabilitation counseling services A **related service** defined, as a term of art, in IDEA regulations at 34 C.F.R. § 300.16(b)(10) as: "services provided by qualified personnel in individual or group sessions that focus specifically on career development, employment preparation, achieving independence, and integration in the workplace and community of a student with a disability. The term also includes **voca-**

tional **rehabilitation services** provided to students with disabilities by vocational rehabilitation programs funded under the Rehabilitation Act of 1973, as amended."

Rehabilitation Services Administration (RSA)

The branch of the **Office of Special Education and Rehabilitative Services (OSERS)** that allocates **grants** to state **vocational rehabilitation agencies.**

rehabilitation technology

1. Defined, as a term of art, in the **Vocational Rehabilitation and Other Rehabilitation Services Act** at 29 U.S.C. § 706(13) as: "systematic application of technologies, engineering methodologies, or scientific principles to meet the needs of and address the barriers confronted by individuals with disabilities in areas which include education, **rehabilitation,** employment, **transportation, independent living skills,** and recreation." 2. Defined, as a term of art, in the **Developmental Disabilities Assistance and Bill of Rights Act of 1975** at 42 U.S.C. § 6001(22) as:

"systematic application of technologies, engineering methodologies, or scientific principles to meet the needs of and address the barriers confronted by individuals with **developmental disabilities** in areas that include education, rehabilitation, employment, transportation, independent living, and **recreation.** Such term includes rehabilitation engineering, **assistive technology devices** and **assistive technology services."**

rehabilitative services

1. Covered services under **Medical Assistance (Medicaid)** generally consisting of **speech pathology, physical therapy,** and **occupational therapy.** 2. Defined, as a term of art, in Department of Health and Human Services regulations at 43 U.S.C. § 440.130(d) as including: "any medical or remedial services recommended by a physician or other licensed practitioner of the healing arts, within the scope of his practice under State law, for maximum reduction of physical or mental disability and restoration of a recipient to his best possible functional level."

reinforcement of alternative behaviors A **behavior modification** technique designed to reduce a given behavior by ignoring that behavior and reinforcing specific alternative behaviors.

reinforcement of functional communicative behavior A **behavior modification** technique designed to reduce a specific undesirable behavior by ignoring that behavior while reinforcing an appropriate behavior.

reinforcement of incompatible behavior A **behavior modification** technique designed to reduce a specific behavior by ignoring that behavior and reinforcing specific behaviors that are physically incompatible with it.

reinforcement of low rates A **behavior management** technique in which a **reinforcer** is given for performing an undesired behavior at increasingly lower rates; usually used for behaviors that occur so frequently or are so ingrained in the student's behavior patterns that a large im-

mediate decrease in occurrences is unrealistic.

reinforcer A reward that, when following a behavior, increases the probability that the behavior will be repeated in the future.

related services 1. Generally, services required to assist a child with a disability to benefit from **special education.** 2. Defined, as a term of art, in the IDEA at 20 U.S.C. § 1401(a)(17) as: "**transportation,** and such developmental, corrective, and other supportive services (including **speech pathology** and **audiology, psychological services, physical [therapy]** and **occupational therapy, recreation,** including **therapeutic recreation, social work services, counseling services,** including rehabilitation counseling, and **medical services,** except that such medical services shall be for diagnostic and evaluation purposes only) as may be required to assist a child with a disability to benefit from special education, and includes the **early identification and assessment of disabling conditions in children."** 3.

Undefined in Section 504, although identified as acomponent of an appropriate education in Section 504 regulations at 34 C.F.R. § 104.33(b).

IDEA regulations at 34 C.F.R. § 300.16 also identify as related services **parent counseling and training** and **school health services,** but make it clear that the listing provided in the regulations is not exhaustive. Because the same term—**related services**—is used under both the IDEA and Section 504, commentators reason that the interpretations and principles that have evolved regarding related services under the IDEA should be applicable to those that should be provided under Section 504.

reliability With reference to a **standardized test,** the extent to which the test is dependable, stable and consistent when administered to the same individual on different occasions; types of procedures for evaluating reliability include: **test-retest reliability, alternate form reliability** and **internal consistency reliability.**

remand An appellate court's return of a case to the trial court for a new hearing or trial, limited additional hearings or some other further action.

According to the Third Circuit Court of Appeals in *Muth v. Central Bucks School District,* 1987-88 EHLR 559:295 (3d Cir. 1988), administrative review officers may not remand to the local level for the taking of additional evidence, for doing so would impermissibly compromise the finality of the local hearing officer's decision, absent appeal.

remedial reading Corrective instruction for a student who is not making adequate progress with regular reading instruction.

remediation Actions or instruction designed to correct or resolve a student's identified deficiencies so that he or she can perform closer to his or her age or ability level; as an **intervention** strategy, the opposite of **compensation strategies;** types of remediation strategies include **skills remediation** and **process remediation.**

remedy The action a judicial or administrative decisionmaker orders to redress violation of the rights of a party or to prevent the commission of a further violation.

In cases brought under Part B of the IDEA, courts are empowered to "grant such relief as the court determines is appropriate." 20 U.S.C. § 1415(e)(2). Remedies generally recognized as appropriate include injunctive relief **[injunction]** (ordering a party to do or not do something), **tuition reimbursement,** and **compensatory education.** Courts do not generally consider **compensatory damages** (over and above out-of-pocket expenses) or **punitive damages** appropriate remedies under the IDEA.

removal The right given all defendants in federal court actions under 20 U.S.C. § 1441(b) to transfer a case filed in state court to federal court when the law permits the case to be heard in either state or federal court.

The IDEA, at 20 U.S.C. § 1415(e)(2), gives parties the right to bring a **civil action** under the IDEA in either "any state court of competent jurisdiction [as determined under state law] or in a district court of the United States." Thus, a defendant (the losing party in a **due process hearing**) in an IDEA civil action filed in state court may remove to federal court.

Reporter's Test A screening test for expressive **aphasia,** used in conjunction with the **Token Test,** in which children are asked to verbally describe the ways in which the examiner is manipulating tokens.

"reptile brain" Portion of the brain responsible for primitive activities such as fighting and reproduction (mating).

residency 1. Generally speaking, where an individual lives, with his or her place of residence being the factor used to determine, among other things, entitlements to benefits. 2. In connection with **special education,** the requirement that triggers the obligation of a **local educational agency (LEA)** to fund the education of a child with a disability.

Neither the IDEA nor any other federal law precisely defines exactly what "residency" entails for purposes of responsibility for special education, making the determination a matter of state law. The **Office of Special Education Programs (OSEP)** has taken the position that it will consider the home school district of a child with a disability to be the district in which his or her parents reside, unless state law determines residency on another basis. *Letter to Mills,* EHLR 213:139 (OSEP 1988).

residential placement In connection with **special education,** a placement for educational purposes in which a student with a disability receives **residential treatment** in a residential treatment facility.

IDEA regulations at 34 C.F.R. § 300.302 require a school district to fund a residential placement—including room and board and nonmedical care—whenever such placement is "necessary to provide special education and **related services** to a child with a disability." There is no explicit provision elucidating when and under what circumstances a residential placement is "necessary." In *North v. District of Columbia Board of Education,* 1979-80 EHLR 551:557 (D.C. Cir. 1979), the Circuit Court for the District of Columbia Circuit made the first authoritative statement of the principal that, if the educational and noneducational needs of a student with a disability are intertwined, the school district is responsible for providing free residential placement rather than funding just those services that meet educational needs. When a student with a **serious emotional disturbance** is residentially placed, programming involves constant supervision and may include individual, group and family therapy, behavior therapy, and psychiatric services.

residential treatment Residential care and comprehensive treatment and services 24-hours per day for individuals, including **children with disabilities,** whose problems are so severe or otherwise such that they cannot be addressed while the individual remains at home

or receives services in the community; component services may include **substance abuse services;** individual, group and **family counseling; family therapy;** supervised recreational and social activities; training in **activities of daily living;** and vocational or prevocational training.

res judicata Legal principle under which a final decree or judgment on the merits of a case rendered by a court having jurisdiction over the matter is conclusive of the rights of the parties to that action with respect to all matters determined. See also **estoppel, collateral.**

resource room A specially equipped and staffed classroom in a regular school in which a student with a **mild disability** or one who is **gifted** spends part of his or her day receiving **individualized instruction** or **skills remediation,** with the balance of the day spent in a regular classroom; sessions are usually 20 to 45 minutes, and instruction may be given either individually or in small groups.

resource room teacher Specially trained teacher who

253

provides **direct instruction** to students in the **resource room** and consultative services to the students' regular classroom teachers.

respiratory management Application of procedures and devices to help a child with a disability breathe, including **tracheotomy care, suctioning,** oxygen supplementation and **assisted ventilation;** may be a **school health service.**

respite care In connection with **children with disabilities,** child care services, non-medical in nature, designed to temporarily relieve the family of stress resulting from continuous management and supervision or to meet a sudden family crisis; may be provided in or out of the home.

> Respite care is not considered a **related service** under Part B of the IDEA. See, e.g., *Rebecca S. v. Clarke County School District,* 22 IDELR 884 (M.D. Ga. 1995). However, it may be a covered service under state programming for individuals with developmental disabilities or **Medical Assistance (Medicaid).** Further, the **Office of Special Education Programs (OSEP)** identifies it as a Part H **early intervention service.**

See, e.g, *OSEP Policy Memorandum 92-2,* 18 IDELR 246 (1991).

response cost In connection with **behavior management,** a procedure in which a specific amount of an available **reinforcer** is contingently withdrawn following an undesired behavior.

response generalization The ability to apply a learned skill or behavior in similar situations.

retrieval In connection with **memory,** the process of conscious recognition and recall of information already learned and stored.

retrieval of phonological information In connection with **phonological awareness,** relates to how a child remembers pronunciation of words or portions of words, including individual letters. See also **long-term memory.**

Rett's disorder 1. A neurological disorder, occurring only in girls, that presents initially as some symptoms of **autism** after a period of normal development, typically associated with **severe mental retardation** or **profound mental retardation.** 2. A developmental disorder the diagnostic criteria for which is defined in the DSM-IV as: "A. All of the following: (1) apparently normal prenatal and postnatal development; (2) apparently normal **psychomotor** development; (3) normal head circumference at birth. B. Onset of all of the following after a period of normal development: (1) deceleration of head growth between ages 5 and 48 months; (2) loss of previously acquired purposeful hand skills between ages 5 and 30 months with subsequent development of stereotyped hand movements (e.g., hand wringing or hand washing); (3) loss of social engagement early in the course (although social interaction often develops later); (4) appearance of poorly coordinated gait or trunk movements; (5) severely impaired **expressive [language]** and **receptive language** development with severe psychomotor retardation." Also referred to as Rett's syndrome.

While hand-wringing is common among children who have Rett's disorder, biting and spitting are not.

Nonetheless, when a student with Rett's disorder did exhibit such behaviors uncontrollably, the school district did not discriminate against her on the basis of her disability when it required her to wear a shielding device consisting of a clear plastic sheet suspended from a tennis visor to prevent her from spitting on others. *LaCrosse (WI) Public School District,* 18 IDELR 189 (OCR 1992).

Reye's syndrome An acute, often fatal, childhood illness causally linked to ingestion of aspirin during a viral illness; survivors often have mental impairments.

rheumatic fever A disease largely affecting children and young adults involving acute episodes of fever and inflammation and swelling of the tissues around joints and also heart valves; identified as a health problem that could be an "**other health impairment**" for purposes of IDEA eligibility in Part B regulations at 34 C.F.R. § 300.7(b)(8).

ribbon switch In connection with **assistive technology devices,** a single **switch** device that is a flat flexible strip resembling a ribbon, activated when

255

an individual applies pressure at any point along the ribbon.

rigidity Severe form of spastic **cerebral palsy [spasticity],** usually **quadriplegia.**

Ritalin Pharmaceutical brand name of methylphenidate, a stimulant that has become a treatment of choice for ameliorating poor attention, social misbehavior and other manifestations of **attention deficit hyperactivity disorder (ADHD)** or **attention deficit disorder (ADD),** despite questions concerning its long-term benefits and questionable impact on academic success.

There is little controversy about the legal aspects of Ritalin use in schools. Schools cannot condition the receipt of **special education** and **related services** on parents' agreeing to the administration of Ritalin to their child. *Valerie J. v. Derry Cooperative School District,* 17 EHLR 1095 (D.N.H. 1991). If a physician does prescribe Ritalin for a student and dosage during school hours is required, then administration is a related service under Section 504. *Response to Mentink,* 19 IDELR 1127 (OCR 1993). Even if Ritalin is prescribed solely to help a student concentrate in school, the medication itself is not a related service, and a school district is not responsible for

its costs. *Somerville Public Schools,* 23 IDELR 932 (SEA MA 1996).

Ritvo-Freeman Real Life Rating Scale Used in diagnosis of **autism** in infants, using behavioral observations about the child's sensorimotor functions, social relationships, affect, sensory responses and language.

Roberts Apperception Test for Children (RATC) Picture card test used with children ages 6 through 15 years to assess perception of common interpersonal situations for purposes of personality assessment, treatment planning and assessment of effectiveness of treatment.

Roncker portability test In connection with the **least restrictive environment (LRE) mandate** of the IDEA, the test proposed by the Sixth Circuit Court of Appeals in *Cincinnati City School District Board of Education v. Roncker,* 1982-83 EHLR 554:381 (6th Cir. 1983), holding that if the particular needed services that appear to make a more restrictive setting more appropriate can be modified so that they can be transported to a less restrictive setting, such a modification and less restrictive placement is required. See also **Daniel R.R. test; Holland test; inclusion.**

rubric In connection with **performance assessment,** guidelines for evaluating a student's work that: (a) describe what is to be assessed; (b) establish a **scale** for scoring; and (c) set criteria for grading the assessed task on the scale.

running record In connection with the **systematic observation of behavior,** the observation technique that involves the **narrative recording** that results from recording behavior as it occurs, rather than retrospectively.

257

S

SAMI Sequential Assessment of Mathematics Inventories

SDMT Stanford Diagnostic Mathematics Test

SDRT Stanford Diagnostic Reading Test

SEA State educational agency

SED serious emotional disturbance

SEE Signing Exact English

SEM standard error of measurement

SIB Scales of Independent Behavior

SIT sensory integration therapy

SIT Slosson Intelligence Test

SLD specific learning disability

saccadic movement Ability to accurately move eyes from one object or word to another.

satiation In connection with **behavior management,** a moderately intrusive **intervention** in which a large amount, in terms of either frequency or quantity, of a **reinforcer** is given to or used with a student, causing it to lose its effectiveness and the resulting behavior to cease.

savant skills Extraordinary abilities or talents, such as mathematical, artistic or memorization, found in a minority of individuals with **autism.**

scale In connection with **performance assessment,** the range of possible scores.

Scales of Independent Behavior (SIB) A norm-referenced test that is part of the **Woodcock Johnson Psychoeducational Battery** and consists of a structured interview that measures 14 subscales of developmental and social independence.

The SIB is intended for use with students of all ages and indicated when a brief overall **screening** is appropriate. It is particularly suitable with young children and those with severe and profound disabilities.

scales of measurement
System for assigning values or scores to test results of all individuals who take the test; 4 types commonly used: (a) nominal, (b) ordinal, (c) interval and (d) ratio.

scanning In connection with **augmentative communication devices,** access method in which the individual scans or reviews the universe of possible inputs, shown in rows and columns, and activates a **switch** when he or she reaches the desired item.

Scanning devices are used by an individual with a disability who lacks sufficient motor ability to use **direct selection.** Time-saving variations permit group scanning or predictive scanning.

schizophrenia 1. **Mental disorder** resulting in pervasive deterioration in functioning, with onset typically in adolescence or early adulthood; characterized by: (a) disturbances in thought processes, (b) delusions and other disturbances in thought content, (c) flat or inappropriate **affect,** (d) bizarre behavior, (e) distorted sense of self and relationship to other people or environment and (e) hallucinations and other disturbances in perception (hearing voices). 2. Specifically identified as a **serious emotional disturbance (SED)** under IDEA regulations at 34 C.F.R. § 300.7(b)(9)(ii).

school choice A program that may be adopted by a state in its education law under which parents are permitted to select the public school which their children will attend. See also **charter school; magnet school.**

According to the **United States Department of Education,** federal law does not dictate whether the "sending" or the "receiving" district in an interdistrict choice program must assume the responsibility for financing **free appropriate public education (FAPE),** as long as the rights of the **children with disabilities** and their **parents** under the IDEA or Section 504 are not compromised by participation in the choice program. See, e.g., *Letter to Lutjeharms,* 16 EHLR 554 (OSERS 1990).

school health services A **related service** under Part B of the IDEA defined, as a term of art, in Part B regulations at 34 C.F.R. § 300.16(b)(11) as: "services provided by a qualified school nurse or other qualified person." See also **nursing services; special health care needs.**

> While courts have disagreed about whether certain services are, either per se or in combination with other needed services, **excluded medical services,** rather than school health services, it is generally agreed that the following are covered school health services: administration of insulin by injection, **clean intermittent catheterization, tracheotomy care, tube feeding,** changing of dressings or **ostomy management and care.**

school psychologist Educational professional whose function includes **assessment, intervention** and **counseling services,** with particular exper-

tise in the learning process. See also **psychometrist.**

School to Work Opportunities Act Federal **grant** program under which school districts who are **grantees** must provide career awareness, exploration and counseling for all students, including those with disabilities, beginning at the earliest possible age, but not later than the 7th grade; codified at 20 U.S.C. §§ 6101-6251.

scooter 3-wheeled vehicle sometimes used as an alternative to a wheelchair when an **individual with a disability** has little or no difficulty maintaining an upright position, but insufficient strength to handle a wheelchair.

scope of review Limitation imposed under enabling law on the issues a court may decide in adjudicating a case; in connection with **civil actions** under the IDEA (20 U.S.C. § 1415(e)), limited to those issues that were raised by the parties during the administrative process, as long as such issues could have been raised in those proceedings.

screening 1. The first step in the **assessment** process, a fast, efficient way to identify students who may have disabilities and should undergo further testing. 2. According to IDEA regulations at 34 C.F.R. § 300.500(b), includes "basic tests administered to or procedures used for all children in a school, grade or class."

> According to the **Office of Special Education Programs (OSEP)** the mass screenings used in connection with **child find** activities are not considered evaluations and thus are not subject to the prior parental notice and consent requirements that apply to **preplacement evaluations.** *Letter to Holmes,* 19 IDELR 350 (OSEP 1995).

seating and positioning Selecting and adapting a mobility or **seating system** to meet the needs of an individual with a mobility impairment, taking into account needs related to body stability, trunk/head support and the objective of maintaining an upright posture.

seating system Postural support to allow an individual who uses a wheelchair or other mobility device to be positioned comfortably and able to use the device; numerous off-the-shelf and custom-made systems.

secondary school A school comprising any span of grades beginning with the next grade following **elementary school** or **middle school** and ending with or below grade 12, including both junior and senior high school; a **day school** or residential school that provides secondary education as determined under state law.

second priority children In connection with use of Part B funds by **state educational agencies (SEAs)** and **local educational agencies (LEAs),** defined, as a term of art, in Part B regulations at 34 C.F.R. § 300.320(b) as: "**children with disabilities,** within each disability category, with the most severe disabilities, who are receiving an inadequate education." See also **first priority children.**

> Note 1 to 34 C.F.R. § 300.320 states that there should be no second priority children after September 1, 1978.

Secretary In connection with **special education,** the Secretary of the **United States**

Department of Education (ED).

Section 501 of the Rehabilitation Act of 1973 (Section 501) Federal legislation that prohibits federal agencies from discriminating against otherwise **qualified individuals with disabilities** solely on that basis; codified at 29 U.S.C. § 791.

Section 503 of the Rehabilitation Act of 1973 (Section 503) Federal legislation that prohibits federal contractors from discriminating against otherwise **qualified individuals with disabilities** solely on that basis; codified at 29 U.S.C. § 793.

Section 504 of the Rehabilitation Act of 1973 (Section 504) Federal legislation that prohibits **recipients of federal financial assistance,** including public schools, from discriminating against otherwise **qualified individuals with disabilities** solely on that basis; codified at 29 U.S.C. § 794.

Section 504 provides that "No otherwise qualified individual with a disability in the United States . . . shall, solely by reason of her or his disability, be excluded from the participation in, be denied the benefits of, or be subjected to discrimination under any program or activity receiving **Federal financial assistance** or under any program or activity conducted by any Executive agency. . . ."

Section 1983 Federal civil rights legislation which provides that: "Every person who, under color of any statute, ordinance, regulation, custom, or usage, of any State or Territory, subjects, or causes to be subjected, any citizen of the United States or other person within the jurisdiction thereof to the deprivation of any rights, privileges, or immunities secured by the Constitution and laws, shall be liable to the party injured in any action at law, suit in equity, or other proper proceeding for redress"; codified at 42 U.S.C. § 1983.

In part because of the uncertain availability of damages in cases claiming a deprivation of **free appropriate public education (FAPE),** parents have often joined Section 1983 to their IDEA or Section 504 claims. In 1984 (in *Smith v. Robinson,* 1982-83 EHLR 555:493 (1984)), the U.S. Supreme Court ruled that the IDEA was the exclusive **remedy** for a child with a disability claiming denial of FAPE. Congress overruled that decision in 1986 when it amended the IDEA by adding a new provision, 20 U.S.C. § 1415(f). That section makes it clear that claims alleging a denial of FAPE also may be brought under Section 504 and Section 1983, provided the complaining party first submits the claim to the administrative process of the IDEA. See also **exhaustion of administrative remedies.**

Section 1988 Federal civil rights legislation permitting courts to award **attorneys' fees** to **prevailing parties** in **Section 1983** actions; codified at 42 U.S.C. § 1988.

When enacting the **Handicapped Children's Protection Act (HCPA),** Congress intended that the same standard in effect for awards of attorneys' fees under Section 1988 be applied in the award of attorneys' fees under the IDEA. (1986 *U.S. Code Cong. and Admin. News* 1808).

seizure As commonly used, may refer to either abnormal electrical activity in the brain, which tends to be rhythmic, or the motor or other changes produced by such electrical activity. See also **epilepsy.**

Seizures may cause, for example, uncontrollable muscle spasms and loss of consciousness (a grand mal seizure).

seizure disorder See **epilepsy.**

selection response test Testing method that requires the child to respond in a manner that can be easily identified and graded as correct or incorrect, such as a multiple-choice test. As distinguished from **performance assessment.**

selective mutism A disorder identified in the DSM-IV as characterized by a consistent failure to speak in specific social situations despite being willing and able to speak in others. Also referred to as elective mutism or voluntary mutism.

self-care skills Activities in the **domain** of **adaptive behavior,** such as toileting, eating, grooming, bathing, shopping or housekeeping.

For a youngster with very **severe disabilities,** an appropriate education requires addressing the skills that will assist him or her to function as well as is reasonably possible in an independent fashion. For example, a federal district court ruled in 1990 that the education program for a 21-year-old brain-injured young adult was appropriate because it addressed her behavior problems, **social skills** and **self-care skills.** *Brown v. Wilson County School Board,* 16 EHLR 718 (M.D. Tenn. 1990). See also **special education.**

self-contained class or program
Located within a **regular education** school, a full-day or mostly full-day class or program for **children with disabilities,** usually composed of children in the same categorical grouping who cannot be educated appropriately in a regular classroom; characterized by highly individualized, closely supervised specialized instruction.

self-injurious behavior
Self-stimulation consisting of repetitively performing a behavior, such as eye-gouging, head banging, self-biting or face slapping, that injures oneself; typically presents in children with **autism** or **severe mental retardation.** See also **self-injurious behavior inhibiting system (SIBIS).**

> Some experts in autism postulate that self-injurious behavior is related to deficits in **sensory integration** or **sensory impairment.** See also **sensory extinction.**

self-injurious behavior inhibiting system (SIBIS)
A device that, when worn or attached, delivers a contingent mild electric shock in response to a **self-injurious behavior** such as head banging; an **aversive intervention** device obtainable only with a doctor's prescription.

> Assuming state law does not have a blanket prohibition against use of a SIBIS device, a school district must make a convincing showing of necessity and lack of alternatives to support use of the device as part of an appropriate program under either the IDEA or Section 504. For example, in *Salinas Union High School District,* 22 IDELR 301 (SEA CA 1995), a hearing officer found that the use of a SIBIS device may be a **related service** under the IDEA only in those instances when the necessity of its use for a particular student with a disability has been demonstrated.

self-management
Strategies which involve a student's management and control of his or her own behavior through the systematic application of behavioral principles, such as **self-monitoring,** self-reinforcement and self-evaluation.

self-monitoring
In connection with students who have **attention deficit disorder (ADD),** using such things as an audio tone or random beep to cue the student and allow him or her to determine how well he or she is attending to a task and then

recording on a check-off sheet whether he or she was exhibiting **on-task behavior** or **off-task behavior.**

self-stimulatory behavior Repeated nonfunctional and nonresponsive movements such as: (a) rocking to and fro, (b) arm or hand flapping, (c) eye rubbing; associated with students with **autism, severe mental retardation** or blindness. See also **stereotypic behaviors.**

semantics Linguistic system concerned with the rules of language governing the meanings of words in sentences. See also **phonics; syntax.**

sensor Alternative input interface used in a **scanning** system instead of a keyboard; variety of ways an individual who cannot use a keyboard can activate, including by touching, breathing or shaking.

sensory extinction Behavior conditioning technique for control of **self-stimulatory behavior** premised on the hypothesis that an individual who performs such behavior does so for the resulting sensory feedback; consists of removing that feedback to decrease future occurrences of the behavior, e.g., cushioning something that is banged to reduce noise.

sensory impairment Hypersensivity or hyposensitivity of 1 or more of the following: auditory sense, visual sense, **tactile sense,** taste, **vestibular sense,** olfactory sense and **proprioceptive sense**; often associated with individuals with **autistic disorders.**

sensory integration Generally, how an individual organizes, interprets and uses sensory information, including information from his or her **tactile sense, vestibular sense** and **proprioceptive sense** to move through space and coordinate movement.

One of the theories concerning **autism** or other **developmental disabilities** is that dysfunctional sensory integration resulting in over- or underresponsiveness to sensory input and inability to process sensory information results in or contributes to **autistic behaviors.**

sensory integration assessment Evaluation of an individual's ability to take in and process sensory information that may enable educators to make adaptations to the environment that make it more conducive to learning.

sensory integration therapy (SIT)

A treatment program, usually designed and provided by occupational therapists, to help a child perceived to have or having a **sensory integration** dysfunction modulate sensory input and process and respond to that input in a more purposeful manner.

SIT is provided in the context of play in order to motivate the child to work on skills that build muscle tone, perception, attention and coordination. When the child is hypersensitive to light touch and movement, therapy initially consists of providing firm touch and pressure through firm pillows and suspended equipment to help calm the child. While SIT is neither age- nor disability-specific treatment, it has become highly sought after by parents of preschool-age children with **autism,** who request that it be provided as **occupational therapy,** a **related service** under the IDEA (Part H and Part B).

sensory memory

Perception of information held in consciousness for a very brief period of time before either being rapidly lost or retained for further processing.

separation anxiety disorder

A disorder identified in the DSM-IV as characterized by developmentally inappropriate and excessive anxiety concerning separation from home or those individuals to whom the child is attached.

Sequential Assessment of Mathematics Inventories (SAMI)

Individually administered **norm-referenced test** measuring the mathematical ability of children in kindergarten through 8th grade in 8 areas, including mathematical language, geometric concepts, computation and word problems.

serial suspensions

A series of **suspensions** cumulatively totaling more than 10 school days per school year.

According to the **Office for Civil Rights (OCR),** serial suspensions may not be used to circumvent the 10 school day limit of the **Honig decision**. The consistent view of OCR, expressed in many **Letters of Findings (LOF),** is that cumulative suspensions totalling more than 10 school days in a school year may constitute a **significant change in placement** in those instances in which they create a pattern of exclusion, triggering the **reevaluation** requirement of Section 504 regulations at 34 C.F.R. § 104.35(a).

In 1995, in *OSEP Memorandum 95-16*, 22 IDELR 531 (OSEP 1995), the **Office of Special Education Programs (OSEP)** adopted OCR's position concerning serial suspensions as its own with respect to whether they trigger **procedural safeguards,** opining that whether a series of **short-term suspensions** constitutes a **change in educational placement** must be decided on a multifactorial student-by-student basis.

serious emotional disturbance (SED)

A disability that establishes eligibility under the IDEA, defined, as a term of art, in IDEA regulations at 34 U.S.C. § 300.7(b)(9)(i) as: "(i) . . . a condition exhibiting one or more of the following characteristics over a **long period of time** and **to a marked degree** that **adversely affects a child's educational performance**—(A) An inability to learn that cannot be explained by intellectual, sensory, or health factors; (B) An inability to build or maintain satisfactory interpersonal relationships with peers and teachers; (C) Inappropriate types of behavior or feelings under normal circumstances; (D) A general pervasive mood of unhappiness or depression; or (E) A tendency to develop physical symptoms or fears associated with personal or school problems. (ii) The term includes **schizophrenia.** The term does not apply to children who are **socially maladjusted,** unless it is determined that they have a serious emotional disturbance."

SED is purely a legal term of art created by regulators in connection with IDEA-eligibility criteria, with no DSM or other **medical model** equivalent. Further, there is no clear, unambiguous understanding of the regulatory definition that has universal agreement. Instead, educators and administrative and judicial decisionmakers wrestle with distinguishing eligible children and youth from those who are socially maladjusted or have unfortunate family or personal circumstances. Additionally, there is no consensus about whether being diagnosed as having a **conduct disorder** or an **oppositional defiant disorder** makes a child or youth per se eligible, ineligible or neither.

Most educational definitions suggest that both the disorder and the student's behavior patterns which cause academic problems for the student and his or her peers are important. There are many published administrative decisions concerning whether a student has a serious emotional disturbance, but few authoritative judicial decisions.

severe conduct disorder

A **conduct disorder** diagnosed on the basis of meeting far more than the minimum number of DSM-IV diagnostic criteria for a conduct disorder or meeting those criteria involving considerable harm to others. See also **mild conduct disorder; moderate conduct disorder.**

severe disability

Generally, extensive mental, physical and/or behavioral impairment or a combination of multiple impairments likely to be permanent in nature and greatly compromising an individual's ability to function independently in the community, perform self-care and obtain employment. Also called severe/profound impairments or **multiple disabilities**. See also **individual with a severe disability.**

severe discrepancy between achievement and intellectual ability

In connection with evaluation of a **specific learning disability,** eligibility requirement set out in IDEA regulations at 34 C.F.R. § 300.541(a)(2), which requires that a child be found to have "a severe discrepancy between achievement and intellectual ability in one or more of the following areas: oral expression, listening comprehension, written expression, basic reading skill, reading comprehension, mathematics calculation, or mathematics reasoning." See also **achievement on an individually administered standardized test substantially below that expected for a student of similar age, schooling and level of intelligence.**

There is a lack of consensus about the precise contours of the requisite degree of severity, but generally a severe discrepancy is understood to be based on the difference between scores on standardized **intelligence tests** and **achievement tests,** when the difference is reliable [**reliability**] and unusual in non-learning disabled children. Several complex formulas assess whether a difference is sufficiently severe. According to the **Office of Special Education and Rehabilitative Services (OSERS),** states are generally free to select a formula to determine the existence of a severe discrepancy between achievement and intellectual ability, provided that a **multidisciplinary team (MDT)** has the authority to override a purely mechanical application of the formula. *Letter to Murphy,* EHLR 213:216 (OSEP 1989).

severe hearing loss When measured by an **audiometer,** loss from 70 to 90 **decibels.**

severely disabled A nonrigorous term generally understood to describe individuals whose disabilities compromise **functional skills** to the extent that substantial assistance with **daily living activities** and ongoing supervision is required.

severe mental retardation Terminology of DSM-IV generally associated with individuals with **mental retardation** whose IQ scores are in the range of about 20-25 to 35-40; considered to have **severe/profound mental retardation** under some state educational codes.

> Most individuals with severe mental retardation can learn to talk by the time they reach **elementary school** and be trained for elementary self-care and sight reading of "survival words" [**sight word approach**]. They can live in the community if closely supervised.

severe/profound mental retardation An educational category developed by some states to describe children with **mental retardation** generally conforming to **severe mental** retardation or **profound mental retardation** under the classification of the DSM-IV.

severe/profound mental retardation, educational programming for Using **reinforcers** to emphasize **self-care skills,** such as feeding and dressing. See also **severely disabled; special education**.

severe spasticity Type of **cerebral palsy** in which one is unable to sit, walk or stand without support (**brace, cane** or the like) and has poor overall body control

shaping Behavior modification technique involving reinforcement [**reinforcers**] of approximations of desired **target behaviors;** as distinguished from **modeling.**

> 1-on-1 **discrete trial training** for children with **autism** uses both shaping and **chaining** procedures to increase performance of desired behaviors such as eye contact, use of **expressive language** and **social** skills.

sheltered employment Employment in a workplace, such as a **sheltered workshop,** in which disabled individuals work in a self-contained unit without integration with non-disabled workers. As distinguished from **competitive work.**

Sheltered employment is not specifically identified as a **post-school activity** in the IDEA in connection with **transition services.** Nonetheless, it may be a suitable option for some students with more significant disabilities.

sheltered workshop A facility engaged in production or service for the primary purpose of providing gainful employment as an interim step for those individuals with disabilities who cannot be readily absorbed in the competitive labor market; exempted from minimum wage requirements of Fair Labor Standards Act. Also called a work activity center. See also **sheltered employment.**

short-term instructional objectives In connection with the **statement of annual goals** required to be included in an **individualized education program (IEP),** subskills of an annual goal written in a sequential order to reflect a progression through the various skills needed to meet the annual goals and that describe the setting, material or behavior to be learned and the degree of proficiency that will be considered satisfactory performance. See also **mastery learning.**

short-term memory Memory that typically persists for only seconds to minutes; distinguished from short-term stores, which are the actual memory processes that hold memories for short periods of time. See also **chunking; long-term memory.**

short-term suspension Generally, any **suspension** of 10 school days or less. See also **serial suspensions.**

shunt Surgically implanted tube that drains excess fluid from the brain, used in connection with, e.g., children with **hydrocephalus.** See also **shunt management.**

shunt management A **specialized health care need** that consists of observing a student with a **shunt** for signs and symptoms of malfunctioning; can be provided by an aide; may be a **school health service.**

271

sickle cell anemia A genetic blood disorder, generally prevalent among African-Americans, that causes low vitality and pain; identified as a condition that may result in IDEA-eligibility under the category of "**other health impairment**" under regulations at 34 C.F.R. § 300.7(b)(8).

sight vocabulary In connection with students with limited reading ability, basic words the student can recognize as whole words, without requiring understanding of word formation or general reading **decoding skills.**

sight-word approach Method used to allow mastery of a **reading vocabulary** as part of **functional reading** programming.

signation Component of signs in **sign language** involving movements of the hand.

sign communication See **sign language.**

significant change in placement A trigger for imposition of the obligation of a school district to conduct a re-evaluation under Section 504 (34 C.F.R. § 104.35(a). See also **serial suspensions.**

> The term is not defined in the regulations, but the Ninth Circuit Court of Appeals aptly defined it as "a significant change in program or services." *Doe by Gonzales v. Maher,* 1985-86 EHLR 557:353 (9th Cir. 1986).

significant relief In connection with **attorneys' fees** under the IDEA, the quantum, or type, of relief that a **parent** must obtain in order to be a **prevailing party** entitled to an award; established by judicial interpretation to usually require something more than success on a procedural issue, but not necessarily success on all contested issues or even on the primary issue.

Signing Exact English (SEE) A manual English-based communication system for instructing deaf individuals. As distinguished from non-English based **sign language.**

sign language A visual-gestural system of language for deaf or hearing-impaired individuals involving facial expressions, handshapes, body movements and gestures; components of signs in sign communication are: (a) **tabula,** (b) designator (hand shape), (c) **signation,** (d) **orientation,** (e) lexicon and (f) **unique syntax.** See also **American Sign Language (ASL).**

A hotly disputed issue in the educational community and between parents and school districts has been whether deaf students should be taught exclusively in sign language, or using oral methods of communication. See also **educational methodology; oral/aural method; Total Communication.**

similar third party In connection with **special education** funding, generally understood to be a **private source of support** similar to an insurance company; used, but undefined, in IDEA regulations at 34 C.F.R. § 300.301(b).

The court in *Guardianship Estate of Zarse v. Illinois Department of Mental Health & Developmental Disabilities,* 1988-1989 EHLR 441:260 (Ill. App. Ct. 1988), interpreted the term to encompass a health maintenance organization or a self-insured employee welfare benefit plan.

simple motor tic Includes eye-blinking, head jerking and grimacing, often associated with **Tourette's disorder.** See also **complex motor tic.**

simple vocal tic Includes throat clearing, grunting and sniffing, often associated with **Tourette's disorder.** See also **complex vocal tic.**

sip and puff switch In connection with **assistive technology devices,** a dual **switch** that is activated by blowing into an apparatus resembling a drinking straw.

skill deficit In connection with **assessment** of a student's ability to produce **prosocial behaviors,** the inability to produce the correct behavior in a testing situation. As distinguished from a **performance deficit.**

skills In connection with the annual goals and **statement of annual goals, including short-term objectives,** of an **individual education program (IEP)** generally understood to be the intended outcomes of **special education** instruction and **support services;** the planned or calculated benefits of the educational program of a child with a disability. *Allamakee Community School District & Keystone AEA 1,* 24 IDELR 516 (SEA IA 1996).

skills remediation Attempts to correct or strengthen particular academic skills, such as **decoding skills** in reading.

slate and stylus Writing method for blind individuals similar to paper and pencil.

> The slate is attached to a back plate. Holes or "windows" on the front of the guide are used to emboss dots on a piece of paper with the stylus, a conically ground steel point attached to the handle. As compared to the **Perkins Brailler,** it is more portable but slower.

Slingerland Screening Test Screening tests for **specific learning disability** administered either individually or in groups to evaluate: **visual perception and discrimination, visual memory, visualmotor integration, auditory discrimination,** auditory visual coordination, auditory motor coordination and comprehension.

Slosson Full-Intelligence Test A quick **screening** test consisting of verbal, performance and memory subtests, used to determine if further evaluation is needed.

Slosson Intelligence Test (SIT) Instrument used for **screening** or estimating a child's **cognitive ability** and as a quick index of general verbal **intelligence;** designed for children and youth between the ages of 2 and 18; when used for children over 4 years of age, questions and responses are given verbally.

slow learner A nonspecific term generally understood to be a student whose global academic abilities are delayed in comparison to his age peers, resulting in overall slower academic progress.

> Slow learners usually are children with lower than average intelligence, rather than children with at least average intelligence who have **specific learning disabilities.** Thus, slow learners are not eligible for **special education** services on this basis because their performance is consistent with their intellectual abilities.

Snellen chart Eye chart used to screen for **visual acuity** in terms of ability to see at a distance. See also **field of vision.**

social competence 1. Globally, an individual's ability to both positively engage in socially appropriate behavior and refrain from behaving inappropriately such that he or she is able to deal effectively on an everyday basis with his or her environment and responsibilities. 2. Narrowly, the complex set of verbal and nonverbal behaviors from which an individual selects appropriate responses in a specific interpersonal situation.

socialization Acquisition of complex set of skills required to interact effectively with others; educational programming for some disabled students includes direct training for same. See also **social skills; social skills, educational programming for acquisition of.**

socially maladjusted In connection with determining eligibility for **special education** and **related services** under the IDEA, students whose behaviors are very similar to those exhibited by students considered to have a **serious emotional disturbance** for purposes of IDEA eligibility, but who are nonetheless specifically excluded from eligibility on the basis of their behavior in accordance with Part B regulations at 34 C.F.R. § 300.7(b)(9)(ii). See also **conduct disorder; oppositional defiant disorder.**

"Socially maladjusted" is not defined in the IDEA and has no widely accepted definition in any professional field. Further, few courts or administrative decisionmakers have provided help on this issue. Published cases that do exist seem to be fact-specific and extremely difficult to use as guidance. The federal district court case of *Doe v. Sequoia Union High School,* 1983-84 EHLR 555:263 (D. Vt. 1983), e.g., held that a student was socially maladjusted rather than seriously emotionally disturbed. The young woman had numerous truancies and deteriorating grades, was allegedly using drugs and had joined a "punk" subculture. Central to the court's decision was the student's generally acceptable level of achievement in **regular education** when she was not under the influence of drugs and alcohol.

social mastery center Includes a designated room staffed by teachers which can be utilized or accessed by students for social, emotional and behavioral consultation activities on an individual as-needed basis.

social perception 2 components: (a) an awareness of other people's emotions and (b)

275

an understanding of one's own behavior; **deficits** associated with individuals with **pervasive developmental disorder, autism** and, in some cases, **specific learning disabilities.**

social promotion School district policy of advancing a student from grade to grade despite failure in most or all academic subjects.

> The primary determining factor for a social promotion decision is usually age, but size and perceived social maturity or level of independence also may be factors. Applying a policy of social promotion to students with disabilities may constitute a denial of **free appropriate public education (FAPE).** For instance, in *Hall v. Vance County Board of Education,* 1985-86 EHLR 557:155 (4th Cir. 1985), the Fourth Circuit Court of Appeals held that a student with a **learning disability** who was passed from year to year due to a policy of social promotion, despite not making significant academic progress, was denied FAPE.

social skills Ability to respond to situations involving others in ways that tend to result in positive results, such as forming and maintaining friendships and being socially accepted.

While nondisabled students typically acquire social skills gradually through experience, some **children with disabilities** require purposeful instruction. Thus, social skills building may be part—sometimes a critical part—of the **curriculum** for some children with disabilities, such as students with **autism** or **behavioral disorders**.

social skills, educational programming for acquisition of Includes social decoding (understanding social cues), social communication, and appropriate nonverbal behavior (e.g., smiling and maintaining eye contact); instructional methodology includes reinforcements [**reinforcers**] with **consequences,** cues and corrections, task analysis and **chaining.**

> Programming varies, of course, based on the unique individual needs of the child. For instance, appropriate programming for development of social skills for a 5-year-old boy with **autism** may include direct (1-on-1) instruction, generalization of drills into group activities, **integration** with shadowing in **regular education** kindergarten and unsupervised activities in the kindergarten classroom. See, e.g., *Allamakee Community School District & Keystone AEA 1,* 24 IDELR 516 (SEA IA 1996). Programming for a 14-year-old youth with a **learning disability,**

speech and language impairments and **attention deficit hyperactivity disorder (ADHD),** on the other hand, may include participation in a social skills classroom. See, e.g., *Eric J. v. Huntsville City Board of Education,* 22 IDELR 858 (N.D. Ala. 1995).

social work services An early intervention service under Part H of the IDEA defined, as a term of art, in Part H regulations at 34 C.F.R. § 303.12(d)(11) as including:

"(i) making home visits to evaluate a child's living conditions and patterns of parent-child interaction; (ii) preparing a psychosocial developmental assessment of the child within the family context; (iii) providing individual and family-group counseling with parents and other family members, and appropriate social skill building activities with the child and the parents; (iv) working with those problems in a child's and family's living situation (home, community, and any center where early intervention services are provided) that affect the child's maximum benefit from early intervention services; and (v) identifying, mobilizing, and coordinating community resources and services to enable the child and family to receive maximum benefit from early intervention services."

social work services in schools 1. Generally, individual, group and family casework and community liaison services. 2. A **related service,** defined, as a term of art, in Part B regulations at 34 C.F.R. § 300.16(b)(12) as including "(i) Preparing a social or developmental history on a child with a disability; (ii) Group and individual counseling with the child and family; (iii) Working with those problems in a child's living situation (home, school and community) that affect the child's adjustment in school; and (iv) Mobilizing school and community resources to enable the child to learn as effectively as possible in his or her educational program."

A school social worker's competencies must include counseling, crisis intervention, knowledge and communication of special education programs and rights and working with parents of disabled children to help them continue educational programming at home.

sovereign immunity 1. Generally, the legal doctrine

that bars lawsuits by individuals against governmental entities. 2. Embodied in the Eleventh Amendment of the U.S. Constitution as providing that: "[t]he Judicial power of the United States shall not be construed to extend to any suits in law or equity, commenced or prosecuted against one of the United States by Citizens of another State, or by Citizens or Subjects of any Foreign State."

In *Dellmuth v. Muth,* 15 EHLR 441:443 (1989), the Supreme Court ruled that reimbursement awards against a state for violations of the IDEA were barred by the Eleventh Amendment. But in 1990 Congress amended the IDEA (then the EHA) to overrule that case, providing that a state is not immune under the Eleventh Amendment from lawsuits and imposition of legal (money) or equitable remedies for violations of the IDEA.

Spalding method Instructional method for reading instruction based on a **multisensory approach,** may be used singly or combined with the **Orton-Gillingham method** in the instruction of students with **learning disabilities** in reading.

spasm Involuntary muscle contraction.

spastic In connection with **muscle tone,** overly resistant to passive stretching. As contrasted with **flaccid.**

spasticity Type of **cerebral palsy** characterized by tight limb muscles and resulting lack of muscle control, characterized in terms of how many limbs are affected and intensity as: **mild spasticity, moderate spasticity, monoplegia, triplegia, quadriplegia,** and **hemiplegia.**

"Speak Easy" An **augmentative communication device** with 14 channels that can be programmed to provide responses to questions, allowing a nonverbal child with a disability to communicate by pushing different buttons.

speaking vocabulary The range of words one is able to use in meaningful speech. See also **hearing vocabulary; reading vocabulary.**

special education 1. Generally, public education for a student with a disability consisting of other than the regular **curriculum,** although **regular education** placement or materials also may qualify as special education if it meets the individual needs of the child. 2. Defined, as a term of the art, in the IDEA at 20 U.S.C. § 1410(a)(16) as: "**specially designed instruction, at no cost** to the **parents** or **guardians,** to meet the unique needs of a child with a disability, including (A) instruction conducted in the classroom, in the home, in hospitals and institutions, and in other settings; and (B) instruction in **physical education**." 3. Undefined in Section 504, although it is presumed by commentators that the term has the same meaning as it does in the IDEA.

Special education is not limited to a typical school environment. Rather, under both the IDEA and Section 504, it must be provided in a variety of other settings, such as institutions and hospitals to the extent necessary to provide a **free appropriate public education (FAPE)** to all eligible children with disabilities. Because the IDEA is premised on the uniqueness of the educational needs of each child with a disability, it is conceptually difficult to further define just which curricula, methods, materials and resources comprise special education. Arguably, special education can most usefully be defined in terms of what it is *not*—educational pro-

grams designed and implemented without regard to the individual circumstances of any one particular student.

special education law, six basic principles of

Common core aspirations and beliefs underlying the **special education** requirement of both the IDEA and Section 504: (a) **zero reject principle,** (b) nondiscriminatory evaluation and classification, (c) individualized **appropriate** programming, (d) **least restrictive environment (LRE),** (e) **procedural safeguards** and (f) parental participation.

special health care needs

In connection with **special education,** health services, technology or some other form of health-related support services or program modifications that a student with a disability needs in order to receive an appropriate educational program in the **least restrictive environment**. As distinguished from **specialized health care needs.** See also **school health services.**

special instruction

An **early intervention service** under Part H of the IDEA defined, as a term of art, in Part H regulations at 34 C.F.R. § 300.12(12) as including: "(i) the design of learning environments and activities that promote the child's **acquisition** of skills in a variety of developmental areas, including cognitive processes and social interaction; (ii) **curriculum** planning, including the planned interaction of personnel, materials, and time and space, that leads to achieving the outcomes in the child's **individualized family service plan**; (iii) providing families with information, skills, and support related to enhancing the skill development of the child; and (iv) working with the child to enhance the child's development."

specialized health care needs A child's need for specialized health care procedures for life or health support during the school day, such as dependence on the use of a **ventilator, tracheotomy tube,** oxygen and nutritional supplements. See also **school health services.**

specially designed instruction Included in the

definition of **special education** in Part B regulations at 20 U.S.C. § 1410(a)(16) as that instruction that "meet[s] the unique needs of a child."

The term is not further defined in the IDEA and, according to the **Office of Special Education Programs (OSEP),** it requires no special definition by way of clarification. Rather, it should be understood according to its plain meaning to be **individualized instruction.** *Letter to Teague,* 20 IDELR 1462 (OSEP 1994). Thus, its nature varies to address the unique needs of the individual child and can be related to, and in support of, regular academic instruction, **vocational education,** or instruction in **daily living skills,** community living skills or **prevocational skills.**

specific academic aptitude or talent Ability to perform in an outstanding manner in a specific academic area or discipline, such as mathematics; usually identified by outstanding performance on a standardized aptitude test or **achievement test.**

specific language deficiencies associated with impairments of the central nervous system Understood as **deficits** in language ability in children with normal **intelligence** and adequate sensory and **motor activity** skills, including **dysphasia, aphasia** and **dyslexia.**

specific learning disability (SLD)

1. Generally, a neurologic disability resulting in an inability or compromised ability to achieve academically that is not related to, or the cause or result of low intellectual ability or sensory impairment. 2(a). Defined, as a term of art, in IDEA regulations at 34 C.F.R. §§ 300.7(b)(10) as: "a disorder in one or more of the basic psychological processes involved in understanding or in using language, spoken or written, that may manifest itself in an imperfect ability to listen, think, speak, read, write, spell, or to do mathematical calculations. The term includes such conditions as perceptual difficulties, **brain injury, minimal brain dysfunction, dyslexia** and **developmental aphasia.** The term does not apply to children who have learning problems that are primarily the result of visual, hearing, or motor disabilities, of **mental retardation,** of emotional disturbance [**emotional disorder**], or of environmental, cultural, or economic disadvantage." (b) 34 C.F.R. § 300.541 states that a child has an SLD if, and only if: "(a)(1) The child does not achieve commensurate with his or her age and ability levels, in one or more of the areas listed in paragraph (a)(2) of this section, when provided with learning experiences appropriate for the child's age and ability levels; and (2) [The **multidisciplinary team**] finds that a child has a **severe discrepancy between achievement and intellectual ability** in one or more of the following areas—(i) oral expression; (ii) listening comprehension; (iii) written expression; (iv) basic reading skills; (v) reading comprehension; (vi) mathematical calculation; or (vii) mathematical reasoning. (b) [The multidisciplinary team] may not identify the child as having a specific learning disability if the severe discrepancy between ability and achievement is primarily the result of—(1) a visual, hearing or motor impairment; (2) mental retardation; (3) emotional disturbance; or (4) environmental, cultural or economic disadvantage." See also **learning disorder.**

     281

More than half the states have adopted a modified or supplemented version of the federal definition (above) that generally has the following 4 definitional components: (a) difficulties in **academic achievement** in reading, writing, math, **receptive language** or **expressive language**; (b) disorders in attention, concentration, understanding, conceptualization, written or oral language or information processing; (c) exclusionary or rule-out criteria, in the sense that difficulties are not caused by other disorders or factors; and (d) significant discrepancy between actual achievement and achievement one would expect of a child with that level of intelligence. As is the case in eligibility determinations under the federal standard, **etiology** is either not relevant or only minimally relevant in most states.

specimen test A sample set of testing materials made available by a commercial test publisher, possibly including a copy of the basic test and administration guidelines.

speech and language impairments Defined, as a term of art, in IDEA regulations at 34 C.F.R. § 300.7(b)(11) as: "a **communication disorder** such as **stuttering,** impaired **articulation,** a **language [disorder]** impairment or a **voice [disorder]** impairment that ad-

versely affects a child's educational performance." See also **speech disorder.**

speech disorder A com**munication disorder** involving impairments in **articulation,** language, voice or **fluency** such that the impairment interferes with an individual's ability to communicate, calls unfavorable attention to the individual, or otherwise causes a social problem for him or her.

speech-language pathologist Professional who studies normal speech and language and provides a program of **diagnosis** and **remediation** to individuals with **speech disorders.**

speech-language pathology 1. Generally, services concerned with prevention, identification and treatment of disorders in speech, language, oral and pharyngeal sensorimotor function. 2. An **early intervention service** under Part H of the IDEA defined, as a term of art, in Part H regulations at 34 C.F.R. § 303.12(d)(14) as including: "(i) identification of children with communicative

6

or oral pharyngeal disorders and delays in development of communication skills, including the diagnosis and appraisal of specific disorders and delays in those skills; (ii) referral for medical or other professional services necessary for the **habilitation** or **rehabilitation** of children with communicative or oral pharyngeal disorders and delays in development of communication skills; and (iii) provision of services for the habilitation, rehabilitation, or prevention of communicative or oral pharyngeal disorders and delays in development of communication skills."

speech pathology A **related service** under the IDEA defined, as a term of art, in IDEA regulations at 34 C.F.R. § 300.16(b)(13) as including "(i) Identification of children with speech or language impairments; (ii) **Diagnosis** and appraisal of specific speech and language impairments; (iii) Referral for medical or other professional attention necessary for the **habilitation** or prevention of communicative impairments; and (iv) Counseling and guidance of parents, children,

and teachers regarding speech and language impairments."

speech reading See **lip reading.**

speech synthesizer An **assistive technology device** that converts text into artificial speech.

speech therapy See **speech pathology.**

spina bifida A congenital malformation of the **central nervous system (CNS)** in which the lower end of the CNS fails to close completely and the contents of the spinal column protrude from a sac in the lower back; usually results in paralysis of the lower extremities, lack of bladder and bowel control and **hydrocephalus.**

In *Irving Independent School District v. Tatro,* 1983-84 EHLR 555:51 (1984), the U.S. Supreme Court ruled that **clean intermittent catheterization (CIC)** was a **related service** for an 8-year-old student with spina bifida.

staffing See **IEP meeting.**

stammer A **speech disorder** resulting in jerky speech characterized by involuntary stops

283

and repetitions. As distin-guished from **stuttering.**

standard deviation In connection with **standardized tests,** statistical term used for measurement of the dispersion around the **mean** score in a sample or population.

standard error of measurement (SEM) In connection with a **standardized test,** quantification of the amount of error in test scores, with a large SEM indicating a greater level of uncertainty.

standardization sample See **reference group.**

standardized test A form of measurement in which the test questions, instructions and test conditions are always the same; usually commercially developed, widely disseminated and machine-scored.

> Standardized tests may be normed against a specific population by administering the test to that population and then calculating **means, standard deviations,** standardized scores, and percentiles. Standardized tests may also be criterion-based. See also **criterion-referenced test.**

standard of review, civil actions See **intermediate standard of review.**

standard score In connection with **norm-referenced tests,** score resulting from statistical operations performed on **raw scores;** types include **normal curve equivalent, stanine** and **scale** scores.

standing The legal doctrine that, to bring a lawsuit as a plaintiff, one must either be an injured party or one who is in danger of becoming injured due to the actions of the defendant(s).

> In connection with **civil actions** brought under the IDEA (20 U.S.C. § 1415(e)(2)) only **aggrieved parties** have standing.

standing table Equipment with a half-circle cut-out and gate in its back that allows an individual who ordinarily uses a wheelchair to stand.

standing wheelchair Powerized wheelchair that can lift the user to a standing position.

Stanford-Binet Intelligence Scale (4th ed.) Individual testing of **intelligence** by assessment of the general mental and **cognitive abilities** implicated in abstract reasoning of children (and adults) from age 2; 15 subtests in 4 different areas (verbal reasoning, abstract/visual reasoning, quantitative reasoning, and **short-term memory**), although not all subtests are used for each: (a) vocabulary, (b) comprehension, (c) absurdities, (d) verbal relations, (e) pattern analysis, (f) copying, (g) matrices, (h) paper folding and cutting, (i) quantitative, (j) number series, (k) equation building, (l) bead memory, (m) memory for sentences, (n) memory for digits and (o) memory for objects.

Stanford Diagnostic Mathematics Test (SDMT) Test

designed to measure progress in basic mathematics concepts and skills and to identify need for instructional strategies; covers whole numbers, fractions, decimals, percent, equations, problem solving, tables and graphs, geometry and measurement; 4 levels of tests for all different school ages and grades.

Stanford Diagnostic Reading Test (SDRT) Tests com-

prehension, **decoding skills,** vocabulary and reading rate with separate scores in connection with textual, functional and recreational **reading,** allowing a student's specific strengths and weaknesses in reading to be considered in **ability grouping;** 4 levels of tests for all different school ages and grades.

stanine In connection with **standardized tests, standard score** system that measures student performance on a 9-point scale, with a range of 1 to 9, a **mean** of 5 and a **standard deviation** equal to 2.

State As a matter of federal education law, generally any of the 50 States, the Commonwealth of Puerto Rico, the District of Columbia, American Samoa, the Virgin Islands, the Northern Mariana Islands, or the Trust Territory of the Pacific Islands (**Education Department General Administrative Regulations (EDGAR)** at 34 C.F.R. § 77.1(b).

State approved or recognized certification, licensing, registration or other comparable requirements

In connection with the personnel standards of Part B and Part H of the IDEA (20 U.S.C. § 1413(a)(14) and 20 U.S.C. § 1476(b)(13), respectively), defined, as a term of art, identically in IDEA regulations at 34 C.F.R. § 300.153(a)(3) for Part B and 34 C.F.R. § 303.361(a)(4) for Part H as: "the requirements that a State legislature has enacted or has authorized a State agency to promulgate through rules to establish the entry-level standards for employment in a specific profession or discipline in that state."

State complaint procedures

Required to be established under the IDEA (20 U.S.C. § 2831(a)) to resolve complaints concerning the education of **children with disabilities**; may be raised on either a systemic or individual child basis; Part B regulations at 34 C.F.R. §§ 300.660- 300.662 set out the federally imposed requirements.

Parents of children with disabilities have 2 separate means of resolving disputes with **public agencies** concerning the identification, **evaluation,** placement or provision of **free appropriate public education (FAPE)**: the complaint management system or an impartial **due process hearing.** According to the **Office of Special Education Programs (OSEP),** the complaint management system may be a less costly and more efficient way to resolve a dispute than an impartial hearing, making it an option parents should consider. *OSEP Memorandum 94-16,* 21 IDELR 85 (OSEP 1994). Making the complaint procedures more attractive is OSEP's assertion that there are no express or implied limitations in the IDEA on the actions that a **state educational agency (SEA)** may take to ensure compliance with the IDEA or remediate denials of FAPE. *Letter to Murray,* 19 IDELR 426 (OSEP 1992).

state educational agency (SEA)

Central agency in a state responsible for overseeing public education; defined, as a term of art, in the IDEA at 20 U.S.C. § 1401(a)(7) and in **Education Department General Administrative Regulations (EDGAR)** at 34 C.F.R. § 77.1(b) as: "State Board of Education or other agency or officer primarily responsible for the state supervision of public elementary and secondary schools, or if there is no such officer or agency, an officer or agency designated by the Governor or by State law."

The state, through its SEA, has the ultimate responsibility for ensuring that eligibility requirements for federal funding are met. As a result, the state's obligation can extend to actually providing an appropriate placement for a child with a disability when his or her **local educational agency (LEA)** is unable, or unwilling, to do so. See, e.g., *Doe v. Maher,* 1985-86 EHLR 557:353 (9th Cir. 1986).

State-level nonsupplanting requirement The requirement set out in the IDEA at 20 U.S.C. § 1413(a)(9) that, unless the **Secretary** grants an exception, funds provided to States under Part B are used to supplement and increase the level of other federal, state and local funding expended for **special education** and **related services** for IDEA-eligible children. As distinguished from the **local education agency (LEA)** level **nonsupplanting** requirement set out in 20 U.S.C. § 1414(a)(2)(B). See also **maintenance of effort.**

statement of annual goals, including short-term objectives Required portion of the **individualized education program (IEP)** for a student with a disability setting out the highest skill level the child is reasonably expected to attain in 1 year, with **short-term instructional objectives** describing measurable instructional steps that build upon the student's present performance and progress toward reaching an annual goal. See also **mastery learning.**

statement of present levels of educational performance Required portion of the **individualized education program (IEP)** for a student with a disability that should include: (a) student's **academic achievement;** (b) student's testing scores (with an evaluation of the scores); (c) description of the student's emotional maturity, self-help skills, adaptive skills, and development; (d) a physical report; and (e) statement of student's **prevocational skills** and **vocational skills.**

State plan The document a state must submit to the **Secre-**

tary of the **United States Department of Education** to obtain funds under the IDEA.

According to 20 U.S.C. § 1413 the State plan must include timetables and descriptive information concerning facilities, personnel and services that must be provided to comply with the state's obligations to children with disabilities.

State standards, incorporation of

The requirement in the IDEA at 20 U.S.C. § 1410(a)(18)(B) that **special education** and **related services** provided to a child with a disability must meet the standards of the **state educational agency (SEA).**

The incorporation of state standards into the definition of **free public appropriate education (FAPE)** recognizes that education has traditionally been considered a matter of state, rather than federal, concern. In *Board of Education of Hendrick Hudson Central School District v. Rowley,* 1981-82 EHLR 553:656 (1982), the U.S. Supreme Court emphasized that the federal standard for an **appropriate** education constitutes a floor, not a ceiling, upon the right of a disabled child to educational services. In effect, any higher or more rigorous state standards, to the extent they are not inconsistent with the IDEA, are incorporated into the law.

statistical significance

Extent to which statistical findings have meaning and are not just a product of happenstance; customarily measured in terms of percentage of time the findings would occur by chance.

statute Written enactment of legislation, the law (e.g., the IDEA, Section 504); when federal law, codified in the United States Code (U.S.C.).

statute of limitations The time frame within which a plaintiff must file his or her suit.

Neither the IDEA nor Section 504 contains an express statute of limitations. Generally, courts have held that the applicable limitations period is that contained in the state statute that most closely applies in similar types of actions.

stay-put provision 1. The provision of the IDEA requiring that a **public agency** maintain a child with a disability in his or her **present educational placement** while an administrative dispute or subsequent judicial proceeding is pending, unless the parties otherwise agree; set out in 20 U.S.C. § 1415(e)(3) as: "[d]uring the pendency of any proceeding conducted pursuant to this section, unless the State or local educational agency and the **parents** or **guardian** otherwise agree, the child shall remain in the **then current educational placement** of such child, or if applying for initial admission to a public school, shall, with the **consent** of the parent or guardian, be placed in the public school program until all such proceedings have been completed." 2. Substantially similar provision for Part H, set out in Part H regulations at 34 C.F.R. § 303.425. Also referred to as an **automatic injunction** or pendency placement.

> Neither Section 504 nor its regulations have a stay-put provision, although Section 504 regulations at 34 C.F.R. § 104.35(a) require school districts to conduct a **reevaluation** before taking any action with respect to a **significant change in placement.** The most controversial use of the stay-put is in connection with the **long-term suspension** or **expulsion** of students with disabilities. See **Honig decision.**

Steinart's disease Presents as varying degrees of **mental retardation,** poor muscle development, bilateral facial paralysis and general muscle weakness; typical symptoms in younger children include mus-

cle weakness, **psychomotor** delay, drooping eyelids and open drooling mouths. Also called myotonic dystrophy.

stereotyped movement See **stereotypic behavior.**

stereotypic behavior **Motor activity** such as body rocking, head rolling and head banging; typical of children with **autism,** other **developmental disabilities** or **severe mental retardation.**

> Under one school of thought, individuals with disabilities perform stereotypic behaviors to compensate for hypothesized sensory deprivation. See also **sensory impairment.**

stereotypic movement disorder Identified in the DSM-IV as characterized by repetitive, seemingly driven and nonfunctional **motor activity** that markedly interferes with normal activities and, for certain individuals, may result in self-injury.

sterognosis Ability to recognize an object by touch; impaired ability to do so is considered a **neurological soft sign.**

stimming Colloquial term for engaging in **self-stimulatory behavior(s).**

stimulants Class of medications commonly used for the treatment of inattention, impulsivity and restlessness in school-age children. See also **Ritalin**.

> Most stimulants prescribed for school-age children are administered orally 1 to 3 times per day, implicating administration as a **school health service** during the school day. The medication is absorbed quickly, with behavioral changes usually seen within 30 to 60 minutes of ingestion and typically lasting 3 to 8 hours.

stimulus generalization Ability to apply a skill or behavior learned in one setting in another setting or at different times or with different people.

stimulus oversensitivity Tendency of some individuals with **autism** to focus with an inappropriate intensity on 1 aspect of an object, such as the color of a box.

stoma See **ostomy**.

storage of phonological information In connection with **phonological awareness,** involves creating a sound-based representation of written words in working memory while reading.

strabismus Commonly known as crossed eyes.

strength model of remediation Technique of using a child's strongest intellectual abilities to remediate **deficits** in skill areas.

strephosymbolia Reversal of letters associated with **dyslexia.**

structured play A play group environment in which a therapist prompts a child with a disability and teaches him or her to participate in social activities such as taking turns and sharing. See also **pragmatics; prosocial behaviors**.

> Some professionals who work with young children with **autism** believe that **social skills** cannot be learned by 1-on-1 **discrete trial training** and accordingly, participation in a structured play group is a necessary adjunct to the **Lovaas program.**

structured recess Systematic recess **intervention** program for students who require a high level of structure during the recess period; involves instruction in specific game rules and appropriate play behavior.

study skills Techniques and approaches to assist students to become effective learners.

> Assistance to help improve study skills often is provided as special instruction in a **resource room** setting to children with **learning disabilities.**

stuttering A **speech disorder** resulting in both blocking and repetition of single sounds, with secondary behaviors including blinking, head-jerking or facial grimaces. As distinguished from **stammer.**

sua sponte (Latin) Ruling made by a court on its own, without a request made by a party to consider and rule on the issue.

> In the class action suit *Beth V. v. Carroll* the plaintiff class of disabled children brought a private lawsuit complaining that the State complaint procedures did not meet the requirements set out in the IDEA. Although the State did not challenge the plaintiff's right to bring such an action, the court issued an order raising, sua sponte, the threshold question of whether such a private right of action existed and required the parties to brief the issue. No. 93 Civ. 4418, 1994 WL 594267 (E.D. Pa. Oct. 25, 1994). After briefing, the court found in favor of the State, ruling that the IDEA did not provide the plaintiffs with a private right of action to sue for enforcement of the State complaint procedure. 22 IDELR 675 (E.D. Pa. 1995).

substance abuse services Services or activities whose primary purpose is to reduce or eliminate substance abuse or chemical dependence; may include a range of individual or **family counseling** methods or detoxification and may be provided in a variety of settings.

> In *Field v. Haddonfield Board of Education,* 18 IDELR 253 (D.N.J. 1991), the district court held that a drug treatment program was not a **related service** for an adolescent with a **serious emotional disturbance**.

subtest scatter In connection with test **batteries,** the variability among an individual's subtest scores.

suctioning Removal of secretions in the nose, mouth or **trachea** with a **catheter** and a suctioning machine; a **special health care need** that may be a **related service.**

　　291

sui generis (Latin) One of a kind, peculiar.

In *Garcia v. California State Department of Education Hearing Office,* 24 IDELR 547 (E.D. Cal. 1996), the court termed the disposition by motion of an IDEA **civil action** sui generis, for it is unique to the IDEA and is not governed by a generally applicable federal court procedure or rule.

summary judgment Judgment granted before trial in favor of a party that demonstrates that there are no genuine issues of material fact and the party is entitled to judgment as a matter of law.

In *Hunger ex rel. Hunger v. Leininger,* 20 IDELR 1242 (7th Cir. 1994), the Seventh Circuit Court of Appeals ruled that a district court may enter summary judgment in favor of a party in a **civil action** filed under the IDEA **sua sponte** without prior notice to either party, as long as the party that did not prevail never indicated an intent to move for the admission of additional evidence and the administrative record below showed no genuine issue of material fact and a correct application of the law. Justifying its decision, the court observed that a judge is not required to conduct a trial when there is no material issue of fact just because the "parties lack the wit to notice the absence of any triable issues."

supplementary aids and services Modifications to

the **regular education** program that must be made to ensure the satisfactory participation of a student with a disability, according to Part B regulations at 34 C.F.R. Part 300, Appendix Part C, question 48; common examples include a 1-on-1 aide, curriculum adaptations, and **assistive technology device.**

The **least restrictive environment (LRE) mandate** of the IDEA requires that a child with a disability must be educated with children who are not disabled to the maximum extent appropriate and may only be placed in a separate **self-contained class or program** "when the nature or severity of the disability is such that education in regular classes with the use of supplementary aids and services cannot be achieved satisfactorily." 20 U.S.C. § 1412(5)(B).

supported employment 1. Generally, **competitive work** in an integrated work setting with **ongoing support services** for individuals with **severe disabilities**. 2. Defined, as a term of art, in the **Vocational Rehabilitations and Other Rehabilitation Services Act** at 29 U.S.C. § 706(18)(A) as: "competitive work in integrated work settings for individuals with the most severe disabilities— ... for whom competitive employment has not traditionally occurred or; for whom competitive employment has been interrupted or intermittent as a result of a severe disability; and who, because of the nature and severity of their disability, need intensive supported employment services for the period [defined in another section of the statute]."

> There are 3 generally accepted supported employment models: (a) **enclaves,** (b) **mobile work crews** and (c) supported **competitive work.**

support services In connection with a state's use and distribution of IDEA funds, defined, as a term of art, in IDEA regulations at 34 C.F.R. § 300.370(b)(2) as including: "implementing the comprehensive system of personnel development of §§ 300.380-300.383 [of the IDEA regulations], recruitment and training of hearing officers and surrogate parents, and **public information** and parent training activities relating to FAPE for children with disabilities."

surface dyslexia **Learning disability** characterized by impaired whole word recognition.

surrogate parent An individual assigned by a school district (or similar **public agency**) to assume the rights and responsibilities of a **parent** under the IDEA when no parent can be identified for a particular child, as set out in IDEA regulations at 34 C.F.R. § 300.514.

> Although the IDEA itself does not require appointment of a surrogate parent when a parent whose whereabouts are known acts in a manner inconsistent with the best interests of the child with a disability, insofar as his or her educational needs are concerned the law does permit states to allow the appointment of surrogate parents in such circumstances, according to the **Office of Special Education Programs (OSEP).** *Letter to Isham,* EHLR 211:445 (OSEP 1987).

survival reading See **functional reading.**

survival skills Essential components of **functional skills** frequently demanded in everyday independent living in a community, such as shopping, reading a menu and balancing a checkbook.

suspension A temporary cessation of educational services, generally having a maximum duration of 3 to 15 school days.

293

State educational statutes regulate the allowable length of a suspension, the reasons for which a suspension can be ordered and the procedure that must be followed to implement. See also **long-term suspension; minimum due process; short-term suspension**.

suspension in excess of 10 school days See **long-term suspension.**

sweep check Screening test for hearing acuity.

switch In connection with an **assistive technology device,** an on/off mechanism functioning as an input control on electronic and assistive devices, such as **augmentative communication devices,** and computers.

A switch can be activated in the manner in which the user has the best and most consistent movement, such as by use of a finger, hand, arm, head, mouth, eyelid, eye-gaze, knee, foot, **headstick** or **mouthstick.**

switch and scanning system In connection with an **assistive technology device,** allows an individual with a disability to select an image as it automatically moves at an adjustable speed among selected images, symbols or boxes on a screen, pausing at each long

enough for the user to select it by activating a **switch.**

syntax Linguistic system concerned with the rules of language governing the arrangement of words in sentences.

synthetic touch The way in which a blind individual forms an impression of a whole object from his or her tactile experience of it parts.

systematic exclusion Behavior management technique involving immediate and consequential removal from school as a result of unacceptable behavior; on a continuum of alternatives, degree of restrictiveness is between **in-school suspension** and out-of-school **suspension.**

systematic observation of behavior An observational method of **assessment** in which "a trained observer watches behavior in a natural setting, records or classifies each behavior objectively as it occurs or shortly thereafter, ensures that the obtained data are replicable, and converts the data into quantitative informa-

tion." J.M. Sattler, *Assessment of Children* (3d ed.) (Jerome M. Sattler 1986), 473.

T

TACL-R Test of Auditory Comprehension of Language-Revised

TAT teacher assistance team

TBI traumatic brain injury

TDD telecommunications device for the deaf

TEACCH Treatment and Education of Autistic and Related Commumunications Handicapped Children

TMR trainable mentally retarded

TOWL Test of Written Language

TPN total parenteral nutrition

TRO temporary restraining order

TRS telecommunications relay services

TT text telephone

tabula Component of signs in **sign language** involving the location or place (palm, fingers or the like) where the sign is made.

tactile defensiveness Extreme sensitivity to touch; associated with some children with **autism.** See also **sensory impairment; sensory integration therapy (SIT).**

tactile sense Sense of touch over body surface, including pressure, temperature and pain. See also **sensory integration therapy (SIT).**

tactual signing Using **sign language** or **finger spelling**

into the palm as a means of communication with an individual with **deaf-blindness.**

talented A designation used in many states for **exceptional** children eligible for special educational programming, typically defined as having exceptional ability in an area such as art, music or performing arts. See also **gifted and talented; Gifted and Talented Children's Education Act.**

target behavior Specific undesired behavior(s) identified in a student's **behavior management plan** for modification, reduction or elimination; also refers to desired skills, the acquisition of which is a goal of **behavior modification** educational programming for a child with a disability.

task analysis A teaching strategy in which goals are broken down into smaller concrete elements and sequenced; in connection with **special education,** the basis for sequential instruction tailored to each child's pace of learning. See also **mastery learning.**

taste aversion An **aversive intervention** involving a substance with an unpleasant taste, commonly mouthwash or vinegar, administered immediately following an aggressive or injurious behavior.

teacher assistance team (TAT) Prereferral intervention involving creation of a team of 4 teachers, including the referring teacher, in which the teachers brainstorm ideas for teaching or managing a student who is having problems in the regular classroom.

technologically dependent As defined by the former **Office of Technology Assessment (OTA),** an individual who requires a medical device to compensate for the loss of a vital body function and substantial and ongoing nursing care to avert further disability or death. See also **excluded medical services; medically fragile.**

telecommunications device for the deaf (TDD) Machine which functions as a telephone for deaf individuals by employing graphic communications in the transmission of coded signals through the nationwide telecommunications system; uses video or print to display communications transmitted over telephone lines and a modem to type out a message displayed on the other end either on a monitor or on paper. Now referred to as **text telephone (TT)**.

telecommunications relay services (TRS) Telephone transmission services that give individuals who have hearing or speech disabilities the ability to engage in communication by wire or radio with a hearing individual, including services that enable 2-way communication between an individual who uses a **text telephone** or other non-voice terminal device and an individual who does not use such a device. See also **hearing carry over (HCO) services; voice carry over (VCO) services.**

telescoping In connection with programming for **gifted** students, covering the same material in the regular **curriculum** in less time. See also **acceleration.**

temporal lobes Lobes of the brain on both sides just above the ears which contain many important functions related to speech perception, language, **memory** and emotion.

temporary restraining order (TRO) An extraordinary equitable **remedy,** granted only after a strong showing of necessity, in order to preserve the status quo (current state of affairs) during the usually short period of time from when a lawsuit is initiated until the court holds a hearing on the party's application for a **preliminary injunction.**

> Courts are empowered to grant TROs in disputes under the IDEA. Generally, the standards for granting a TRO are the same as those courts use in deciding whether to issue a preliminary injunction.

ten-day rule As enunciated by the U.S. Supreme Court in *Honig v. Doe,* 1987-88 EHLR 559:231 (1988), the authority school officials have under the IDEA to temporarily suspend [**suspension**] a student with a disability for up to 10 school days without triggering **procedural safeguards.** See also long-term suspension; short-term suspension.

test age See **mental age (MA).**

Test of Auditory Comprehension of Language-Revised (TACL-R) Individually administered **screening** instrument that assesses the **receptive language** ability of children between the ages of 3 and 11 years; 3 sections—word classes and relations, grammatical **morphemes,** and elaborated sentences—all involve showing the child sets of 3 pictures and providing a verbal clue to elicit the selection of the picture that relates to the clue.

Test of Written Language (TOWL) Used to evaluate a student's written product in terms of proficiency in word usage, punctuation, spelling and sentence production.

test-retest reliability 1. In connection with a **standardized test,** an assessment of **reliability** based on administering the same test to the same group of individuals twice within a short period of time. 2. In connection with observation of behavior, the consistency of behavior over time and in different situations.

testwiseness Sophisticated test-taking skills resulting from extensive experience taking tests.

> The extent of the disability of a child whose performance on an assessment **instrument** is boosted by testwiseness may be understated, making the design of appropriate programming more challenging.

text telephone (TT) Machine employing graphic communication in the transmission of coded signals through a wire or radio communication system used for telephonic communication by individuals with hearing impairments or deafness; considered more current usage for **telecommunications device for the deaf (TDD).**

then current educational placement The placement in which a student should receive **special education** and **related services** during the **pendency of a proceeding** under the **stay-put provision** of the IDEA, codified at 20 U.S.C.

§ 1415(e)(3); referred to in IDEA regulations at 34 C.F.R. § 30.513 as the student's **present educational placement.** Neither the IDEA statute nor legislative history provide guidance on how to identify the then current educational placement. As stated by the Sixth Circuit Court of Appeals in *Thomas v. Cincinnati Board of Education,* 17 EHLR 113, 118 (6th Cir. 1990): "Because the term connotes preservation of the status quo, it refers to the operative placement actually functioning at the time the dispute first arises. If an IEP has been implemented, then that program's placement will be the one subject to the stay put provision. And where . . . the dispute arises before any IEP has been implemented, the 'then current educational placement' will be the operative placement under which the child is actually receiving instruction at the time the dispute arises." Thus, identification of the then current placement is not usually difficult. But what happens when that placement is no longer appropriate, is contrary to state law provisions or is not desired by either party? Such instances require case-by-case review and may add fuel to the already contentious relations between the school district and the parents.

therapeutic group home
In connection with mental health services for children and adolescents, a community-based homelike setting providing intensive treatment services to a small number of residents (usually 5 to 10) who need 24-hour-per-day supervision, but may be able to avoid hospitalization if provided psychiatric services in a less restrictive setting.

therapeutic recreation
Use of either individual or group play or physical activity to improve a variety of **deficits** in the physical, emotional, cognitive or social **domains;** structured physical or social activities prescribed and programmed by a recreational therapist to meet objectives of enjoyment of **leisure-time activities** and improvement in **motor activity** skills, strength and **social skills;** a component of the **related service** of **recreation** under Part B regulations at 34 C.F.R. § 300.16(b)(9)(ii).

Thorndike's Laws
The principles enunciated by the educational psychologist E. L. Thorndike that are the foundation for reading instruction with **basal readers:**

Law of Readiness: The order in which one learns a sequence of material matters.

301

Law of Exercise: Practice leads to automaticity.

Law of Effect: Positive reinforcement (reward) increases learning.

Law of Identical Elements: Learning is specific, with little transfer of learning to different tasks.

thought disorder Dysfunction that results in deviations from the logical progression of thought and a steady comprehensible manner of speech; types of deviations include: **circumstantiality, clang associations, flight of ideas, perseverative behaviors,** and **pressure of speech.**

tic Recurrent, rapid and abrupt movement or vocalization caused by contraction of small muscles, such as eye blinking or grunting; generally 4 types: **simple motor tic, complex motor tic, simple vocal tic** and **complex vocal tic.**

tic disorder Characterized by vocal and/or motor tics (simple or complex) that are not the result of one's general medical condition or a medication side-effect; 3 DSM-IV-identified specific tic disorders: transient tic disorder, chronic motor tic

disorder, and **Tourette's disorder** (syndrome).

When an individual has a tic disorder the tics are involuntary, in the sense that the movements can be controlled briefly, but the effort to restrain results in a build-up of tension that can be released only by ceasing the effort to control. See also **complex motor tic; complex vocal tic; simple motor tic; simple vocal tic.**

timeline for free appropriate public education
1. In connection with the IDEA, the **age range** of children for which a state must make a **free appropriate public education** available, set out in IDEA 20 U.S.C. § 1412(2)(B) and generally between the ages of 3 and 18 years. 2. In connection with Section 504, see **qualified persons with disabilities.**

An extension of the timeline may be made when a student who reaches the maximum age of eligibility under the IDEA is entitled to **compensatory education** as a **remedy** for a prior denial of FAPE. See, e.g., the decision of the Third Circuit Court of Appeals in *Lester H. v. Gilhool*, 16 EHLR 1354 (3d Cir. 1990), in which the court explicitly rejected the argument that the awarding of such relief to a student who has reached the end of the IDEA's mandated age range contravenes the statutory timelines for FAPE.

time-out Behavior management technique involving the contingent removal of a student from an activity through isolation from the group or from the environmental stimulus which has prompted the misbehavior; continuum of time-out alternatives includes time-out area in the classroom, time-out chair, and removal to another room or time-out room.

time sheet In connection with awards of **attorneys' fees** under the IDEA, an itemized daily accounting showing how the fee was computed and including the date, amount of time, identity of attorney and his or her hourly rate, and a description of each service performed.

Courts considering awards of attorneys' fees under the IDEA and Section 1988 generally require contemporaneous records of time and expenses. See, e.g., the Second Circuit's ruling in connection with Section 1988 in *New York State Association for Retarded Children v. Carey,* 711 F.2d 1136 (2d Cir. 1983).

tinnitus Persistent ringing in the ears.

Title II of the Americans with Disabilities Act Federal law that prohibits discrimination against individuals on the basis of disability by any agency or unit of local or state government, including public schools, colleges and universities; codified at 42 U.S.C. §§ 12131-12133.

Discrimination under Title II encompasses denial of access to public facilities and services on the basis of disability. In theory, access to services and activities offered by elementary and secondary schools should already be in place, as those **public agencies** have been subject to Section 504 of the Rehabilitation Act since 1973. Nevertheless, the ADA serves as a reinforcement of those now decades-old obligations.

Section 504 regulations contain **free appropriate public education** requirements that are similar to (although not identical with) those of the IDEA. The **Office for Civil Rights (OCR),** which is charged with the enforcement of both Section 504 and the ADA in public elementary or secondary education programs, interprets Title II of the ADA as having FAPE requirements consistent with those of Section 504. *OCR Senior Staff Memorandum,* 19 IDELR 859 (OCR 1992).

Title III of the Americans with Disabilities Act Federal law requiring places of **public accommodation,** including **private schools** which

303

do not receive **federal financial assistance,** to make reasonable modifications in their practices, policies or procedures, or provide **auxiliary aids and services** for students with disabilities, provided to do so does not fundamentally alter the nature of the program or result in an **undue burden;** codified at 42 U.S.C. §§ 12181-12189.

to a marked degree In connection with establishing eligibility for Part B on the basis of a **serious emotional disturbance** under Part B, the intensity requirement for the presentation of qualifying characteristics set out in regulations at 34 C.F.R. § 300.7(b)(9).

The term is undefined in the regulations, but as a general matter, according to the **Office of Special Education Programs (OSEP),** refers to the frequency, duration or intensity of a student's behavior, in comparison to his or her peers. *Letter to Anonymous,* EHLR 213:147 (OSEP 1989).

token economy system A method for management of classroom misbehavior in which students are given a mark, or token, for rewards redeemable at a later time as a

method to reinforce identified **target behavior(s).**

Token Test Screening test for children between the ages of 3 and 12 years for receptive **aphasia** in which children are asked to manipulate tokens in response to verbal directions. See also **Reporter's Test.**

tolling In connection with a **statute of limitations,** the period of time during which the statute of limitations is suspended, or is not running; the statute of limitations does not begin to run until the tolling period has expired.

Total Communication An approach for teaching deaf children involving the simultaneous use of signing and other manual forms of communication, along with speech and **lip reading;** usually does not include **American Sign Language.** See also **educational methodology.**

total parenteral nutrition (TPN) Administration of nutrients through an intravenous route as a substitute for oral, nasogastric or gastrotomy feeding when all of those methods are ineffective or hazardous; may be a **school health service.**

Tourette's disorder
1. Congenital neurological disorder with typical symptoms and associated behaviors including **tics** and involuntary and repeated rapid and sudden movements or vocalizations, sometimes obscene **[corpolalia].** 2. Classified in the DSM-IV as a **tic disorder** characterized by multiple motor tics and one or more facial tics performed many times daily; associated with **obsessive-compulsive disorders, attention deficit hyperactivity disorder (ADHD), learning disabilities, behavioral disorders** or **conduct disorders.** Also called Tourette's syndrome.

> In its much-discussed decision in *Clyde K. ex. rel. Ryan K. v. Puyallup School District,* 21 IDELR 664 (9th Cir. 1994), the Ninth Circuit ruled that removal from the regular classroom environment may be appropriate when the classroom behavior of a student with a disability is so disruptive it becomes unmanageable. In that case, the 15-year-old young man had Tourette's disorder and ADHD. As a result of these disabilities, he frequently disrupted class by, among other things, taunting other students with name-calling and profanity, insulting teachers with vulgar comments, and directing sexually-explicit remarks at female students.

trachea Cartilaginous tube extending from the larynx to the lungs serving as an individual's air passage. See also **tracheotomy; tracheotomy care; tracheotomy tube.**

tracheotomy Surgical opening into the **trachea** through the neck into which a **tracheotomy tube** is inserted to facilitate breathing.

tracheotomy care Includes **suctioning** to remove secretions that accumulate in the **tracheotomy tube,** changing the tube and the ties by which it is attached, and caring for the skin around the opening; may be a **school health service.**

tracheotomy tube A hollow tube inserted into an opening made in the **trachea** and extending into the lungs to permit air movement in and out of the lungs.

tracking See **ability grouping.**

trainable mentally retarded (TMR)
An educa-

tional category used by some states to describe children with **mental retardation** generally conforming to classification as **moderate mental retardation** under the DSM-IV.

Children identified as TMR may achieve up to a 2nd-grade academic level with supervision. They are likely to need moderate supervisory assistance as adults, although most develop some **self-care skills** and **vocational skills** in **sheltered employment.**

trainable mental retardation, educational programming for

Based on use of concrete materials, **modeling** and other **behavior modification** strategies, rather than verbal instruction initially. Instruction focuses on basic academic **survival skills** such as recognizing coins, telling time and **sight-word [approach] reading. Self-care skills,** simple **vocational skills** and **leisure-time activities** also are typically part of the program.

transition

In connection with **special education,** the change from secondary education to postsecondary programs, work and independent living. See also **post-school activities; transition services.**

transition activities that promote movement to postsecondary education

In connection with **transition services,** includes identifying or visiting appropriate institutions, taking the Scholastic Aptitude Test, investigating financial aid options, applying to schools, identifying needed accommodations at particular institutions and contacting the Disabled Student Services offices at individual campuses.

transition services

Defined, as a term of art, in both the IDEA at 20 U.S.C. § 1401(a)(19) and the **Vocational Rehabilitation and Other Rehabilitation Services Act** at 29 U.S.C. § 706(35) as: "a coordinated set of activities for a student designed within an **outcome-oriented process,** which promotes movement from school to **post-school activities,** including **postsecondary education,** vocational training, **integrated employment** (including **supported employment**), continuing and **adult education, adult services,** independent living, or community participation. The coordinated set of activities shall be based upon the student's needs, taking into account the student's preferences and interests, and shall include instruction, community experiences, the development of employment and other post-school adult living objectives, and, when appropriate, acquisition of **daily living skills** and functional **vocational evaluation."**

As a result of amendments to the IDEA in 1990, school districts are required to provide transition services to IDEA-eligible students with disabilities. Essentially, the IDEA requires that **individualized education programs (IEPs)** for older students include a **coordinated set of activities** designed to move **special education** students successfully from school to post-school settings, such as colleges, vocational training, independent living and employment. This mandate was created due to Congressional concern that high-school-age students in special education were at risk of dropping out of school or otherwise leaving the school setting unprepared for adult life and responsibility. The aspiration was that the future prospects for a student with a disability would be brighter if the school district took responsibility for determining what services he or she needed to assist in the attainment of post-school goals.

transportation 1. A **related service** under Part B of the IDEA defined, as a term of art, in Part B regulations at 34 C.F.R. § 300.16(b)(14) as including: "(i) Travel to and from school and between schools; and (ii) Travel in and around school buildings; and (iii) Specialized equipment (such as special or adapted buses, lifts, and ramps), if required to provide special transportation for a child with a disability." 2. An **early intervention service** under Part H of the IDEA, defined, as a term of art, in Part H regulations at 34 C.F.R. § 303.23 as including: "the cost of travel (e.g., mileage, or travel by taxi, common carrier, or other means) and related costs (e.g., tolls and parking expenses) that are necessary to enable a child eligible under this part and the child's family to receive early intervention services."

traumatic brain injury (TBI) 1. Damage to brain tissue caused by an external, mechanical force and resulting in disabling conditions that may impair orthopedic, visual, neurological, cognitive or emotional functioning and could include long-term comatose

    307

state [**coma**]. 2. 1 of the 13 disabilities for eligibility under the IDEA, defined, as a term of art, in 34 C.F.R. § 300.7(b)(12) as: "an acquired injury to the brain caused by an external physical force, resulting in total or partial functional disability or psychosocial impairment, or both, that adversely affects a child's educational performance. The term applies to **open [head injuries]** or **closed head injuries** resulting in impairments in one or more areas, such as **cognition;** language; **memory;** attention; reasoning; **abstract thinking;** judgment; problem-solving; sensory, perceptual and **motor abilities;** psychosocial behavior; physical functions; information processing; and speech. The term does not apply to brain injuries that are congenital or degenerative, or brain injuries induced by birth trauma."

Treatment and Education of Autistic and Related Communications Handicapped Children (TEACCH) Intensive **intervention** program for young children with **autism** and related conditions developed at

the University of North Carolina in Chapel Hill and offered by **public agencies** throughout the country, that incorporates strategies and modifications in **self-contained classes** with low teacher-student ratios; often supplemented by similar strategies provided by parents in the home setting.

Increasingly, parents are resorting to due process under either Part B or Part H to dispute whether TEACCH provides **free appropriate public education (FAPE)** or adequate **early intervention services** for preschoolers with autism. For a variety of reasons, parents are contending that the **Lovaas program,** involving intensive 1-on-1 services in the home setting is the only adequate programming for their children. Education and medical professionals have, in effect, divided into 2 camps: those who support TEACCH and those who advocate Lovaas. Without making an argument for one or the other, we note that because the TEACCH program includes classroom instruction it is less expensive than Lovaas, which typically calls for 30 to 40 hours per week of 1-on-1 instruction in the home. Administrative opinions that explain the salient features of TEACCH and compare it to Lovaas from a legal perspective include *Pitt County Board of Education,* 2 ECLPR 247 (SEA NC 1994) and *Board of Education of the Ann Arbor*

Public School, 24 IDELR 621 (SEA MI 1996).

treatment records In connection with **education records,** defined, as a term of art, in regulations implementing the **Family Educational Rights and Privacy Act (FERPA)** at 34 C.F.R. § 99.3 as "records made or maintained by a physician, psychiatrist, psychologist or other recognized professional or paraprofessional acting within the scope of his or her license that are made, used or maintained only in connection with treatment of the student and disclosed only to individuals providing treatment."

tremor Involuntary rhythmical movement of a part of the body.

trial training In connection with educational programming for autistic children, each attempt in a series of repeated attempts to teach a desired skill. See also **applied behavioral analysis; discrete trial training; Lovaas program.**

triplegia Rare form of **spasticity [cerebral palsy]** affecting only one limb.

true score In connection with a **standardized test,** the hypothetical score that reflects the child's ability, as otherwise determined. See also **obtained score; raw score.**

tube feeding Administration of nutrients through either **gastrotomy tube feeding** or **nasogastric tube feeding;** generally considered a **school health service.**

tuberculosis Airborne infectious disease compromising respiratory functioning and other bodily systems; identified as a health problem that be an "**other health impairment**" for purposes of IDEA eligibility in Part B regulations at 34 C.F.R. § 300.7(b)(8).

The leading case addressing whether an individual with a contagious disease has a **physical or mental impairment** within the meaning of Section 504 is *School Board of Nassau County v. Arline,* 1986-87 EHLR 558:228 (1987), in which the U.S. Supreme Court held that an employee with tuberculosis could allege that her discharge, if the result of discrimination on the basis of her disease, violated Section 504.

tuition reimbursement A **remedy** that either courts or due process hearing officers may award to parents as reimbursement for expenses incurred for a **unilateral placement** for their child with a disability that is ultimately determined to have been necessary because the placement and program proposed by the school district was inappropriate.

In *Burlington School Committee v. Massachusetts Department of Education,* 1984-85 EHLR 556:389 (1985), the U.S. Supreme Court held that the authority granted to courts in IDEA **civil actions** under 20 U.S.C. § 1415(e)(2) "to grant such relief as the court determines is appropriate" encompassed the authority to award retroactive reimbursement of **private school** tuition. The Court reasoned that it was an appropriate remedy because it "merely requir[ed the school district] to belatedly pay expenses that [it] should have paid all along." While thus making it clear that tuition reimbursement is an available remedy under the IDEA, the Court left open the possibility that a weighing of the equities in any particular instance could result in a failure to award full reimbursement, despite the denial of **free appropriate public education (FAPE).**

two-tier administrative system The IDEA due process system in those states in which a party must appeal the decision of a local (school district) level impartial **due process hearing** officer to a state level administrative review officer before commencing a **civil action;** a state's authority to adopt such a system is codified in the IDEA at 20 U.S.C. § 1415(c). See also **one-tier administrative system.**

U

undue burden The condition under which a **private school,** or other private entity that is a place of **public accommodation,** may be relieved of its obligation under **Title III of the Americans with Disabilities Act** to provide an **individual with a disability** with necessary **auxiliary aids and services**; defined in ADA regulations at 28 C.F.R. § 36.104 as encompassing significant difficulty or expense. As distinguished from **undue hardship.**

undue hardship Under Section 504 generally, the condition under which a **recipient of federal financial assistance** is not required to make a **reasonable accommodation** to allow a **qualified individual with a disability** to participate in the programs it offers or services it provides.

> Since the **Office for Civil Rights (OCR)** emphatically rejects the injection of a reasonable accommodation concept as a limitation on a school district's obligation under Section 504 to provide a **free appropriate public education (FAPE)** to **children with disabilities** (*Letter to Zirkel,* 20 IDELR 134 (OCR 1993)), it follows that such public entities are not required or permitted to raise a defense of undue hardship to a claim of denial of FAPE.

unilateral placement Enrollment by a **parent** of a child with a disability in a **private school** or facility. See also **private school students with disabilities.**

> When the child's school district has failed to offer a **free appropriate public education (FAPE),** the parent may be entitled to **tuition reimbursement.** When the school has offered FAPE, the child is entitled

311

only to the more limited services specified under Part B regulations at 34 C.F.R. §§ 300.403(a), 300.450-300.452. See also **genuine opportunity for equitable participation.**

unique syntax Component of **sign language** involving the order in which signs are made.

United States Department of Education (ED or DOE) The administrative agency of the federal government charged with the management and implementation of federal legislation concerning education and the oversight and enforcement of state and local agencies' compliance with such legislation.

V

VABS Vineland Adaptive Behavior Scales

VCO voice carry over services

VOCA voice output communication aid

validity 1. With reference to an **assessment,** the degree to which the interpretations and uses of the assessment results are supported by empirical evidence and logical analysis. 2. With reference to a **standardized test,** the extent to which the test measures what it is intended to measure, the degree of accuracy of either predictions or inferences based on the test score; different types of validity include **content validity, construct validity, predictive validity,** and **concurrent validity.** As distinguished from **reliability.**

Under Part B, the tests and other materials used in a **preplacement evaluation** must, among other things, have "been validated for the specific purpose for which they are used." 34 C.F.R. § 300.352(a)(2). According to an administrative decisionmaker, tests validated by their publishers meet the validation requirement of the regulations. *Board of Education of Duanesburg Central School District,* 20 IDELR 641 (SEA NY 1993).

ventilator Mechanical device to assist individuals in performing pulmonary functions. See also **ambu bagging; ventilator-dependent.**

Ventilator management involves checking settings, monitoring the device for mechanical failures and the individual for signs of respiratory distress, and performing maintenance activities such as unplugging mucus and **suctioning** of the connecting tube.

ventilator-dependent Being able to breathe only with an

313

external aid, such as a **ventilator;** having no spontaneous respiratory effort ability.

When a child is ventilator-dependent, he or she typically has multiple health conditions, resulting in a complex amalgam of **specialized health care needs.** For example, the 12-year-old student involved in a district court decision in favor of the parents in *Cedar Rapids Community School District v. Garret F.,* 24 IDELR 648 (N.D. Iowa 1996), became quadriplegic and ventilator-dependent as a result of an accidental injury. Required health services, in addition to ventilator management, included **clean intermittent catheterization, suctioning** of his **tracheotomy tube,** assistance with eating and drinking, **positioning,** and blood pressure monitoring.

School districts have argued, with mixed success, that such a student's needs, in the aggregate, are **excluded medical services,** rather than **school health services.** See also **medically fragile; technologically dependent.**

verbal scale Scale of the **Wechsler Intelligence Scales for Children-III (WISC-III)** in which student responds verbally to auditorily presented information to measure verbal comprehension and **expressive language** skills; 6 subtests include: (a) information, (b) similarities, (c) comprehension, (d) arithmetic, (e) vocabulary, and

(f) digit span (optional). See also **performance scale; verbal scale IQ.**

verbal scale IQ Standard score with a **mean** of 100 and a **standard deviation** of 15 derived from a combination of 5 of the 6 subtests that comprise the **verbal scale** of the **Weschler Intelligence Scales for Children-III (WISC-III).** See also **full scale IQ; performance scale IQ.**

The verbal orientation of most school training makes this score a good predictor of likely level of academic success. This same orientation, however, exposes it to criticism as being racially or culturally discriminatory.

versabraille A computer with a Braille keyboard and 20 electronic **Braille cells** used selectively to raise Braille characters.

vestibular sense System in the inner ear that detects movement and changes in the position of one's head; dysfunctions may cause either hyper- or hyposensitivity to movement.

The vestibular sense, along with the **tactile sense** and **proprioceptive sense,** combine with other bodily functions to help individuals understand and make appropriate responses to information received through the senses about the environment. When a child has, for example, a hypersensitive vestibular system, his or her ability to balance is compromised, possibly contributing to letter reversals in reading and writing. **Sensory integration therapy (SIT)** to enhance the child's vestibular functioning may be a **related service**.

Vineland Adaptive Behavior Scales (VABS) **Behavioral assessment** concerning the **social competence** of children from birth through age 19 consisting of information provided by a person who knows about the disabled student's competence in 5 behavioral **domains:** (a) communication skills, (b) **self-care skills,** (c) **socialization,** (d) **motor activity** and (e) **maladaptive behavior.**

VABS consists of more than 250 questions querying the respondent about whether the child performs various age-appropriate activities or exhibits specific maladaptive behaviors.

viseme In connection with **lip reading,** the smallest unit of visible speech. See also **homophene; phoneme.**

vision therapy Assists a child with **low vision** to develop residual vision, use **low vision aids** effectively and enhance auditory skills. See also **visual training.**

visual acuity The degree to which the eye can distinguish fine detail at varying distances, also termed the clarity of vision; 2 types: far distance visual acuity and near distance visual acuity.

Far distance visual acuity usually is measured on a **Snellen chart,** although there are alternative tests for nonreaders with limited ability to identify letters. Normal far distance visual acuity is between 20/20 and 20/40. Near distance visual acuity has no standard measurement instrument.

visual efficiency Variety of visual skills, such as eye movement ability, that allows an individual to adapt to the physical environment, respond to visual stimuli and process visual information.

visual figure-ground skill The ability to distinguish between foreground and background.

visual impairment 1. Impairment, including myopia,

315

hypropia, astigmatism, and visual field defect, that limits either **visual acuity** or **field of vision**. 2. 1 of the 13 disabling conditions for IDEA eligibility defined, as a term of art, in 34 C.F.R. § 300.7(b)(13) as: "an impairment in vision [including partial sight and blindness] that, even with correction, adversely affects a child's educational performance."

visual memory Memory that holds visual information.

visual-motor integration Ability to relate visual stimuli to motor responses in an accurate and appropriate manner; impaired ability associated with **learning disabilities.** See also **visual-motor integration therapy.**

visual-motor integration therapy Remediation in the areas of general coordination, balance, hand-eye coordination, eye movement, form recognition and **visual memory.**

visual perception and discrimination Ability to recognize visual stimuli and to differentiate among them.

Most academic activities, including mathematics and reading, require good visual-perception skills.

visual-spatial deficit Reading disorder involving difficulty linking letters together to form whole words.

visual tracking impairment Inability to follow a moving object.

visual training Therapy to enhance **visual efficiency** and remediate **visual impairments** that emphasizes development of smooth eye movement skills such as **fixation ability, saccadic movement,** eye focusing, eye-aiming, binocular vision, **hand-eye coordination,** visualization and **visual memory.**

vital signs Temperature, pulse, respiration and blood pressure.

The monitoring of any or all vital signs may be required as a **school health service** when appropriate.

vocabulary knowledge In connection with education, ability to recognize words and understand their meanings; 3 types of vocabulary knowledge: **hearing vocabulary,**

speaking vocabulary and **reading vocabulary.**
Vocabulary knowledge is crucial to communication, reading and writing instruction. The amount of such knowledge an individual has is associated with his or her **receptive language** skills and, possibly, general **intelligence** and reasoning ability.

vocational education
1. Includes preparing the student to work, in terms of developing good work habits and values, planning for occupational opportunities, and making career decisions; basic program components include: remedial basic skills, specific job training, personal and social adjustment skills, on-the-job training, and career information. 2. Defined, as a term of art, in IDEA regulations at 34 C.F.R. § 300.17(b)(3) as: "organized educational programs that are directly related to the preparation of individuals for paid or unpaid employment, or for additional preparation for a career requiring other than a baccalaureate or advanced degree."

vocational evaluation
Assessment to determine the eligibility and appropriate programming for students receiving **vocational education,** including **assessment** of skills, aptitudes, interests, work ethic and **social skills.**

vocational rehabilitation agency
State agency that helps individuals with physical or mental disabilities obtain employment through counseling, medical and psychological services, job training, and other individualized services.

Vocational Rehabilitation and Other Rehabilitation Services Act
Federal legislation providing **federal financial assistance** to state agencies that provide **vocational rehabilitation services** and services to foster independent living for eligible individuals with disabilities (see **vocational rehabilitation services, eligibility for**); established in Title I of the Rehabilitation Act of 1973 and codified at 29 U.S.C. §§ 701 et seq.

vocational rehabilitation counseling
Services to assist individuals with disabilities to live and work independently; provided by professionals who have completed a recognized formal educational curriculum.

vocational rehabilitation services The range of job-readiness and job training services, both individual services and group services, that may be required for individuals with disabilities under the **Vocational Rehabilitation and Other Rehabilitation Services Act,** as specifically identified in 29 U.S.C. § 723.

> The long list of services closely resembles the list of **special education** and **related services** under Part B of the IDEA: **evaluation, personal assistance services, individualized instruction, assistive technology devices,** treatment for **mental disorder** and **emotional disorder, interpreters,** readers, transportation, and **transition services.**

vocational rehabilitation services, eligibility for As established under the **Vocational Rehabilitation and Other Rehabilitation Services Act** at 29 U.S.C. § 706(8)(A), 3 criteria as follows: (a) the presence of a **physical or mental impairment,** (b) with such impairment constituting a substantial impediment to employment, and (c) the ability to benefit from the receipt of **vocational rehabilitation services** with respect to an **employment outcome.**

vocational skills Abilities and competencies needed to obtain and maintain employment in an area and at a level consistent with one's maximum capability and interests.

voice carry over (VCO) services In connection with telecommunications for persons with hearing or speech impairments, a reduced form of **telecommunications relay services (TRS)** in which an individual with a hearing disability is able to speak directly to the user on the other end and reply, with the help of a communications assistant who types the responses of the speaking individual.

voice disorder A **communication disorder** presenting as inappropriate voice quality, pitch or loudness.

voice output communication aid (VOCA) Electronic **augmentative communication system** or specially adapted personal computer that allows the user to produce synthesized speech; generally contains a broader range of symbols or characters to be selected for expressive communication.

voice recognition system

In connection with **assistive technology devices,** a system to replace the keyboard as a computer input device. See also **alternative input interface.**

voice synthesizer

1. In connection with **assistive technology devices** for the blind, a device that, in conjunction with a computer, converts text displayed on screen into sound; variety of reading options. 2. Also used to convert information input by an **individual with a disability** via a **switch** or keyboard into sound.

> A voice synthesizer allows children with **cerebral palsy** who cannot communicate orally but have sufficient motor skills to input information via appropriate switches to a computer with software that converts the input into sound.

voluntary mutism

See **selective mutism.**

voucher

Document or chit issued by a state that a parent uses in a **school choice** program which permits election of **private schools.**

W

WAIS Wechsler Adult Intelligence Scales

WISC-III Wechsler Intelligence Scales for Children-III

WPPSI Wechsler Preschool and Primary Scales of Intelligence

WRAT Wide Range Achievement Tests

waiver Intentional and voluntary relinquishment of a known right.

The IDEA places an express obligation on states to provide **free appropriate public education (FAPE)** to all eligible children and to otherwise comply with the provisions of the law. The right to demand the provision of FAPE belongs in the final instance to the federal government. Therefore, according to the **United States Department of Education,** neither an individual student nor **parent** may agree to waive their right to FAPE and release a **state educational agency (SEA)** or **local educational agency (LEA)** from its obligation to provide FAPE under the IDEA to publicly enrolled students. See, e.g., *Letter to Contrucci,* EHLR 211:380 (OSERS 1986). The same is true for the right to FAPE under Section 504. See, e.g., *Berlinbrothersvalley (PA) School District,* EHLR 353:124 (OCR 1988).

water mist An **aversive intervention** involving the use of a water mist delivered by means of a spray bottle to terminate an undesired behavior, typically one that is aggressive or injurious.

weapon In connection with the **Gun-Free Schools Act** and the **Jeffords Amendment,** a **firearm,** as that term is defined in federal law at 18 U.S.C. § 921.

As a result of borrowing this definition, the special procedures designed

321

to promote school security when dealing with dangerous students with disabilities do not apply to students with disabilities who bring knives into the school building.

Wechsler Adult Intelligence Scales (WAIS)

An individually administered **instrument** intended for adults that also can be administered to youths ages 16 or 17; consists of 2 scales—**verbal scale** and **performance scale**—composed of 11 subtests.

The 6 verbal scale subtests are (a) information, (b) digit span, (c) vocabulary, (d) arithmetic, (e) similarities and (f) comprehension. The 5 performance scale subtests are (a) picture completion, (b) picture arrangement, (c) block design, (d) object assembly and (e) digit symbol.

Wechsler Intelligence Scales for Children-III (WISC-III)

An individually administered **instrument** given by a **school psychologist** or other clinical examiner as part of a clinical, psychoeducational or neuropsychological test **battery**; measures the **intelligence** of children in the age range from 6 to 16 years and consists of 12 subtests in 2 scales: **verbal scale** and **performance scale.** See also **Wechsler Verbal-Performance Scale discrepancies.**

Wechsler Preschool and Primary Scales of Intelligence (WPPSI)

An individually administered **instrument** given by a **school psychologist** or other clinical examiner to children between the ages of 4 to 6 1/2 years; consists of 2 scales—**verbal scale** and **performance scale**—consisting of 11 subtests: (a) information, (b) vocabulary, (c) arithmetic, (d) similarities, (e) comprehension, (f) picture completion, (g) mazes, (h) block design, (i) sentences, (j) animal house and (k) geometric design; can be used in the assessment of children who have or may have specific language disabilities, brain damage or developmental immaturity.

Wechsler Verbal-Performance Scale Discrepancies

Suggestive, although not dispositive of, neurological disabilities; if **verbal scale IQ** is 12 or more points less than **performance scale IQ,** language disability is possible; if the reverse, perceptual disability is possible.

A common misconception is that the presence of significant verbal-performance scale discrepancies can be the basis of a diagnosis of a **specific learning disability (SLD)** under the IDEA (34 C.F.R. § 300.541). However, because both scales measure ability, as opposed to achievement, this discrepancy cannot be used to establish the requisite "**severe discrepancy between achievement and intellectual ability.**"

Wernicke's aphasia Pattern of speech impairment due to an acquired brain lesion, with impaired comprehension of speech and production of fluent, grammatical speech; characterized by speech which is notable for impoverished vocabulary, abnormally pronounced words and **neologisms.**

whole language method
Method of reading instruction in which children learn to read by reading for content, with learning of the alphabetic code and **phonemes** deemphasized; program elements include opportunities to write and exposure to good literature. See also **balanced reading approach; phonics.**

The debate between advocates of whole language and phonics rages on, particularly with regard to reading instruction for students with reading difficulties. As assessed by the Council for Exceptional Children: "[T]he body of research [by the **United States Department of Education** and the National Institute of Child Health and Human Development (NICHHD)] suggests that the relatively recent swing away from phonics instruction to a singular whole language approach is making it more difficult to lift children with learning disabilities out of the downward learning spiral and, in fact, may impede the progress of many students in learning to read with ease." (*Reading, The First Chapter in Education,* 1996.)

whole word method
Method of reading instruction in which children learn to read by responding to whole words, rather than individual letters or sounds. As opposed to **phonics.**

Wide Range Achievement Tests-Revised (WRAT-R) Brief individually administered test of achievement in word recognition, spelling and arithmetic for children and youth ages 5 years and up; used for **screening.**

Williams syndrome Rare genetic disorder causing **mild mental retardation** accompa-

nied frequently by **autistic behaviors** such as perseveration [**perseveration behaviors**], **language delay** and hypersensitivity to sound, as well as possible heart and kidney malfunction.

within the State In connection with a state's responsibility under the IDEA to make **free appropriate public education (FAPE)** available to all **children with disabilities** within the state, interpreted by the **Office of Special Education Programs (OSEP)** as responsibility for children with disabilities whose **parent** or **guardian** resides within the state and children with disabilities who are wards of the state. *Letter to McAllister,* 21 IDELR 81 (OSEP 1994).

without charge In connection with **special education** funding, the requirement set out in IDEA regulations at 34 C.F.R. § 300.301 that programming and services be provided **at no cost** to **parents,** but also be the primary responsibility of other governmental programs or **private sources of support,** with IDEA funds applied only

when there are no other state, local, federal or private sources of support. See also **free.**

Woodcock-Johnson Psychoeducational Battery A battery of 27 standardized tests measuring **cognitive ability,** scholastic aptitude or interest and achievement level.

The cognitive ability section has 12 subtests arranged to form 11 clusters of 2 or more subtests (some subtests are in more than 1 cluster); the achievement section contains 10 subtests in 5 clusters. The aptitudes or interest section contains 5 subtests in 2 clusters; designed for children ages 3 years through adulthood, although not all subtests are administered at every age level.

Woodcock-Johnson Psychoeducational Battery, achievement subtests 10 subtests grouped into 5 clusters (some subtests are in more than 1 cluster) to measure: letter-word identification, **word attack skills,** passage comprehension, calculation, applied problems, dictation, proofing, science, social studies and humanities.

Woodcock-Johnson Psychoeducational Battery, cognitive ability sub-

11 clusters (some subtests are in more than 1 cluster) to measure various aspects of **cognition,** reasoning and **memory:** picture vocabulary, spatial relations, memory for sentences, visual-auditory learning, blending, quantitative concepts, visual matching, antonyms-synonyms, analysis-synthesis, numbers reversed, concept formation and analogies.

Woodcock Reading Mastery Test Individually administered test used to measure reading growth, detect reading problems, and evaluate and place students.

word attack skills Ability to use **word identification strategies** to analyze unfamiliar words and arrive at pronunciation and possibly meaning without using clues from context; commonly identified deficit in children with **learning disabilities,** such as **dyslexia.**

word identification strategies Word attack techniques that include **phonics,** structural analysis and getting clues from context. See also **word attack skills.**

work activity center See **sheltered workshop.**

wrap around services In connection with mental health services for children and adolescents, a team-based approach to designing, implementing and monitoring **interventions** for students with emotional and behavioral disabilities across all settings in which both the child and his or her family receive a range of community support services to allow the child to benefit from more traditional mental health services, such as **family therapy.**

Use of wrap around strategies has been incorporated into the educational planning process in some schools as a result of **United States Department of Education** demonstration projects and is thought to hold promise. While there appears to be no authoritative court decisions, the limited body of published judicial and administrative decisions suggests that wrap around services may be a **related service** under the IDEA. See, e.g., *Stockton v. Barbour County Board of Education,* 22 IDELR 543 (N.D. W. Va. 1995), in which the district offered a program of services that included wrap around services as an appropriate alternative to **residential placement** for a student with a **serious emotional disturbance.**

325

writing Complex cognitive activity best accomplished by mastery of 3 distinct tasks: prewriting, drafting and revising.

writing remediation Essentially similar for disabled and nondisabled students, consisting of instructional techniques to improve competence in prewriting, drafting and revising, also includes functional writing skills.

youth with disabilities
When used in the IDEA, defined, as a term of art, as "any
child with a disability . . . who—
is twelve years of age or older;
or is enrolled in the seventh or
higher grade in school."

Z

zero inference The principle grounding educational programming for children with severe cognitive disabilities; suspension of the assumption typically made in **regular education** that a child has the basic communication and personal skills, **social skills** and **adaptive behavior** skills to learn in a nonnatural setting and use **generalization** to apply what he or she has learned to other situations and in other settings.

zero reject principle The principle that is the premise of the IDEA: All **children with disabilities,** regardless of severity, are entitled to receive a **free appropriate public education (FAPE).**

The zero reject principle was first fully addressed by the courts in the First Circuit Court of Appeals' 1989 decision in *Timothy W. v. Rochester,*

New Hampshire School District, 15 EHLR 441:393 (1st Cir. 1989). In that case, the court reversed a lower court finding that the child, Timothy, was unable to benefit from **special education.** In its opinion, the court described Timothy as multidisabled and profoundly retarded, having, among other things, spastic **quadriplegia, cerebral palsy,** seizure disorder (**epilepsy**) and **cortical blindness.** Nevertheless, the court found from the evidence that Timothy was aware of his surroundings, recognized and responded to familiar voices and noises, and attempted purposeful communication. Thus, he was entitled to a program of special education designed to enhance, to the extent possible, his receptive abilities and ability to communicate.

The court left open the question of whether a child who is so disabled as to be unaware of his or her circumstances, e.g., a child in a coma, is eligible for **special education** and **related services.** While there has been no published case addressing this precise issue, an **administrative hearing** officer did find that a student in a **persistent vegetative state** (distinguished from a coma by medical professionals) was entitled to educational services. *Weston Public School*, 1987-88 EHLR 509:154 (SEA MA 1987).

APPENDIX A

List of Acronyms

AAC	augmentative and alternative communication
AAMR	American Association on Mental Retardation
ABA	applied behavioral analysis
ABIC	Adaptive Behavior Inventory for Children
ADA	Americans with Disabilities Act
ADD	attention deficit disorder
A-D/HD	attention-deficit/hyperactivity disorder
ADHD	attention deficit hyperactivity disorder
ADL	activities of daily living
AIT	auditory integration training
APE	adaptive physical education
ASL	American Sign Language
BD	behavior disordered
BLAT	Blind Learning Aptitude Test
BTBC-R	Boehm Test of Basic Concepts-Revised
CAI	computer-assisted instruction
CARS	Childhood Autism Rating Scale
CFIDS	Chronic Fatigue and Immune Dysfunction Syndrome
CFS	Chronic Fatigue Syndrome
CIC	clean intermittent catheterization
CMMS	Columbia Mental Maturity Scale
CNS	central nervous system

A-1

CP	cerebral palsy
CPR	cardiopulmonary resuscitation
CRT	criterion-referenced test
DASI	Developmental Activities Screening Inventory
DBRS	Disruptive Behavior Rating Scale
DDST-R	Denver Developmental Screening Test-Revised
DNR	Do Not Resuscitate order
DPT	diagnostic-prescriptive teaching
DRO	differential reinforcement of other behaviors
DSM-IV	Diagnostic and Statistical Manual of Mental Disorders (4th ed.)
DTVMI	Developmental Test of Visual-Motor Integration
EAHCA	Education of All Handicapped Children Act
ED (or DOE)	United States Department of Education
EDGAR	Education Department General Administrative Regulations
EHA	Education of the Handicapped Act
EMR	educable mentally retarded
EPSDT	Early and Periodic Screening, Diagnosis, and Treatment
ERIC	Educational Resources and Information Center
ERIC/CASS	ERIC Clearinghouse on Counseling and Student Services
ERIC/EC	ERIC Clearinghouse on Disabilities and Gifted Education
ESD	extended school day programming
ESEA	Elementary and Secondary Education Act of 1965
ESL	English as a second language
ESY	extended school year programming
FAE	fetal alcohol effects
FAS	fetal alcohol syndrome

FERPA	Family Educational Rights and Privacy Act
FPCO	Family Policy Compliance Office
FTE	full-time equivalent
GED	General Educational Development Test
GEPA	General Education Provisions Act
HCO	hearing carry over services
HCPA	Handicapped Children's Protection Act
H-NTLA	Hiskey-Nebraska Test of Learning Aptitude
IDEA	Individuals with Disabilities Education Act
IEE	independent educational evaluation
IEP	individualized education program
IEU	intermediate educational unit
IFSP	individualized family service plan
IHP	individual habilitation plan
ISO	International Standards Organization
ISS	in-school suspension
IWRP	Individualized Written Rehabilitation Program
K-ABC	Kaufman Assessment Battery for Children
K-TEA	Kaufman Test of Educational Achievement
LACT	Lindamood Auditory Conceptualization Test
LD	learning disability
LEA	local educational agency
LEP	limited-English proficient
LNNB-C	Luria-Nebraska Neuropsychological Battery, Children's Revision
LOF	Letter of Findings
LRE	least restrictive environment
MA	mental age
MCA	McCarthy Scales of Children's Abilities
MCS	multiple chemical sensitivity
MD	muscular dystrophy
MDT	multidisciplinary team
MMPI	Minnesota Multiphasic Personality Inventory
NG tube	nasogastric tube

NIDRR	National Institute on Disability and Rehabilitation Research
NRT	norm-referenced test
OCD	obsessive-compulsive disorder
OCR	Office for Civil Rights
ODD	oppositional defiant disorder
OERI	Office of Educational Research and Improvement
OESE	Office of Elementary and Secondary Education
OHI	other health impairment
OSEP	Office of Special Education Programs
OSERS	Office of Special Education and Rehabilitative Services
OT	occupational therapy
OTA	Office of Technology Assessment
PECS	Picture Exchange Communication System
PIAT	Peabody Individual Achievement Test
PKU	phenylketonuria
PPVT-R	Peabody Picture Vocabulary Test-Revised
PTI	Pictoral Test of Intelligence
RATC	Roberts Apperception Test for Children
RSA	Rehabilitation Services Administration
SAMI	Sequential Assessment of Mathematics Inventories
SDMT	Stanford Diagnostic Mathematics Test
SDRT	Stanford Diagnostic Reading Test
SED	serious emotional disturbance
SEE	Signing Exact English
SEM	standard error of measurement
SIB	Scales of Independent Behavior
SIBIS	Self-Injurious Behavior Inhibiting System
SIT	sensory integration therapy
SIT	Slosson Intelligence Test
SLD	specific learning disability

TACL-R	Test of Auditory Comprehension of Language-Revised
TAT	teacher assistance team
TBI	traumatic brain injury
TDD	telecommunications device for the deaf
TEACCH	Treatment and Education of Autistic and Related Communications Handicapped Children program
TMR	trainable mental retarded
TOWL	Test of Written Language
TPN	total parenteral nutrition
TRO	temporary restraining order
TRS	telecommunications relay services
TT	text telephone
VABS	Vineland Adaptive Behavior Scales
VCO	voice carry over services
VOCA	voice output communication aid
WAIS	Wechsler Adult Intelligence Scales
WISC-III	Wechsler Intelligence Scales for Children-III
WPPSI	Wechsler Preschool and Primary Scales of Intelligence
WRAT	Wide Range Achievement Tests

APPENDIX B

United States Department of Education

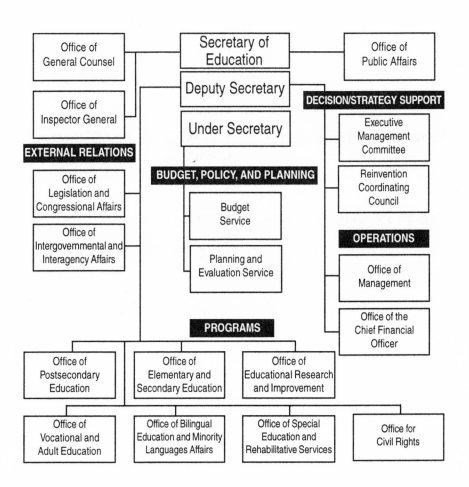

Department of Education Regional Offices

Each of the 10 regions covering the United States and the territories and possessions is headed by a Secretary's Regional Representative. The following gives the territorial responsibilities of each region.

Region I (Boston) Serves Connecticut, Maine, Massachusetts, New Hampshire, Rhode Island and Vermont

Region II (New York) Serves New Jersey, New York, Puerto Rico and Virgin Islands

Region III (Philadelphia) Serves Delaware, District of Columbia, Maryland, Pennsylvania, Virginia and West Virginia

Region IV (Atlanta) Serves Alabama, Florida, Georgia, Kentucky, Mississippi, North Carolina, South Carolina and Tennessee

Region V (Chicago) Serves Illinois, Indiana, Michigan, Minnesota, Ohio and Wisconsin

Region VI (Dallas) Serves Arkansas, Louisiana, New Mexico, Oklahoma and Texas

Region VII (Kansas City) Serves Iowa, Kansas, Missouri and Nebraska

Region VIII (Denver)	Serves Colorado, Montana, North Dakota, South Dakota, Utah and Wyoming
Region IX (San Francisco)	Serves Arizona, California, Hawaii, Nevada, American Samoa, Guam and Trust Territories of the Pacific Islands
Region X (Seattle)	Serves Alaska, Idaho, Oregon and Washington.

Office for Civil Rights Enforcement Offices

Most of OCR's critical activities take place in its enforcement offices. There are 4 enforcement divisions, consisting of 12 enforcement offices. OCR's core organizational unit is the Case Resolution Team. Groups of attorneys, investigators and support staff in OCR's 12 enforcement offices work on the same team to resolve, promptly and appropriately, cases of illegal discrimination. The following list includes the 12 OCR enforcement offices.

Division A

Office for Civil Rights, Boston Enforcement Office	Serves Connecticut, Maine, Massachusetts, New Hampshire, Rhode Island and Vermont
Office for Civil Rights, New York Enforcement Office	Serves New Jersey, New York, Puerto Rico and Virgin Islands

Office for Civil Rights, Philadelphia Enforcement Office	Serves Delaware, District of Columbia, Maryland, Pennsylvania, Virginia and West Virginia

Division B

Office for Civil Rights, Atlanta Enforcement Office	Serves Alabama, Florida, Georgia, North Carolina, South Carolina and Tennessee
Office for Civil Rights, Dallas Enforcement Office	Serves Arkansas, Louisiana, Mississippi, Oklahoma and Texas
Office for Civil Rights, District of Columbia Enforcement Office	Serves District of Columbia, North Carolina and Virginia

Division C

Office for Civil Rights, Chicago Enforcement Office	Serves Illinois, Indiana, Michigan, Minnesota and Wisconsin
Office for Civil Rights, Cleveland Enforcement Office	Serves Ohio
Office for Civil Rights, Kansas City Enforcement Office	Serves Iowa, Kansas, Kentucky, Missouri and Nebraska

Division D

Office for Civil Rights, Denver Enforcement Office	Serves Arizona, Colorado, Montana, New Mexico, North Dakota, South Dakota, Utah and Wyoming

Office for Civil Rights, San Francisco Enforcement Office	Serves California
Office for Civil Rights, Seattle Enforcement Office	Serves Alaska, Hawaii, Idaho, Nevada, Oregon, Washington, American Samoa, Guam and Trust Territories of the Pacific Islands

APPENDIX C

Federal Circuit Courts of Appeals

First Circuit	Maine, Massachusetts, New Hampshire, Rhode Island, Puerto Rico
Second Circuit	Connecticut, New York, Vermont
Third Circuit	Delaware, New Jersey, Pennsylvania, Virgin Islands
Fourth Circuit	Maryland, North Carolina, South Carolina, Virginia, West Virginia
Fifth Circuit	Louisiana, Mississippi, Texas
Sixth Circuit	Kentucky, Michigan, Ohio, Tennessee
Seventh Circuit	Illinois, Indiana, Wisconsin
Eighth Circuit	Arkansas, Iowa, Minnesota, Missouri, Nebraska, North Dakota, South Dakota
Ninth Circuit	Alaska, Arizona, California, Hawaii, Idaho, Montana, Nevada, Oregon, Washington, Guam, Northern Mariana Islands
Tenth Circuit	Colorado, Kansas, New Mexico, Oklahoma, Utah, Wyoming
Eleventh Circuit	Alabama, Florida, Georgia
D.C. Circuit	District of Columbia